Trends in Developing Economies 1993 Extracts

VOLUME 2. Emerging Capital Markets

The World Bank
Washington, D.C.

Copyright © 1993 by the International Bank
for Reconstruction and Development/The World Bank
1818 H. Street, N.W., Washington, D.C. 20433, U.S.A.

All rights reserved
Manufactured in the United States of America
First printing September 1993

This publication has been compiled by the staff of the Socio-Economic Data Division of the World Bank's International Economics Department. The World Bank does not accept responsibility for the accuracy or completeness of this publication. Any judgments expressed are those of World Bank staff or consultants and do not necessarily reflect the views of the Board of Executive Directors or the governments they represent.

The material in this publication is copyrighted. Requests for permission to reproduce portions of it should be sent to the Office of the Publisher at the address in the copyright notice above. The World Bank encourages dissemination of its work and will normally give permission promptly and, when reproduction is for noncommercial purposes, without asking a fee. Permission to photocopy portions for classroom use is granted through the Copyright Clearance Center, 27 Congress Street, Salem, Massachusetts 01970, U.S.A.

The complete backlist of publications from the World Bank is shown in the annual *Index of Publications*, which contains an alphabetical title list and indexes of subjects, authors, and countries and regions. The latest edition is available free of charge from the Distribution Unit, Office of the Publisher, The World Bank, 1818 H Street, N.W., Washington, D.C. 20433, U.S.A., or from Publications, The World Bank, 66 avenue d'Iéna, 75116 Paris, France.

ISBN 0-8213-2566-3

Foreword

This specialized volume of extracts from Trends in Developing Economies (TIDE) presents brief analytical descriptions and data on socio-economic performance and trends in 17 developing countries that have substantial and growing equity markets. The stock markets in these economies have grown rapidly since the early 1980s and market capitalization experienced a ninefold expansion in 1983–1992. Foreign investment in emerging capital markets has also expanded rapidly since 1989; two of these countries, Mexico and the Republic of Korea, are now among the 15 largest equity markets in the world.

This volume of TIDE is designed as a ready reference for the economic analyst, investor, researcher, or businessperson who is particularly interested in emerging capital markets and who wants access to a brief and up-to-date description of recent socio-economic trends in these countries.

The text, tables, and graphs are the same as in the main TIDE book, which includes 119 developing countries. The tables on each country provide information on key ratios, GDP accounts, social conditions, and international transactions. By making this information widely available, the World Bank hopes to contribute to increased understanding of the economies with emerging capital markets and their economic potential. Further information on developments in equity markets in these economies is provided in the *Emerging Stock Markets Factbook*, available from the Capital Markets Department of the International Finance Corporation of the World Bank Group.

D. C. Rao
Director
International Economics Department

Contents

Introduction vii
Overview ix

Argentina	1	Mexico	48
Brazil	8	Nigeria	56
Chile	12	Pakistan	62
Colombia	17	Philippines	67
India	23	Thailand	72
Indonesia	29	Turkey	77
Jordan	33	Venezuela	81
Republic of Korea	38	Zimbabwe	85
Malaysia	43		

Technical notes 90
Symbols and abbreviations 95
Classification of economies 96

Introduction

The special edition of extracts from *Trends in Developing Countries* (TIDE) provides brief reports on 17 countries as of May 1993. The text, tables, and graphs are derived from the main TIDE book, which includes 119 developing countries. TIDE complements the World Bank's comprehensive country studies and annual reviews, such as *World Development Report*, which look at global and regional economic trends and their implications for the developing economies.

TIDE draws upon information from national sources and adds commentary on recent economic developments. Nevertheless, readers should pay more than usual attention to admonitions about the provisional character of data and commentary reported here. In many instances, the data for the most recent years are World Bank staff estimates that are preliminary and subject to revision; they may not conform to data published by national authorities.

The text is descriptive. It is mainly concerned with current events and the recent past in each country, but also places events in context by bringing out the distinguishing characteristics of a country's economy, its problems and prospects, and the principal elements of its development strategy. While the choice of topics may vary from one country text to another, recurrent themes are government initiatives in progress or under consideration, economic and social factors affecting development, and external finance and debt issues.

Each country text is followed by newly designed tables of socio-economic indicators, accompanied by graphs. The graphs help to visualize relationships between economic indicators and to facilitate their comparisons between countries. An effort has been made to ensure consistency between the text and the table, but this has not always been achieved. Differences may reflect the use of data of different vintages or variations in definitions and concepts. The tables contain the latest available information, although it is not always comparable across countries and time periods. The Socio-Economic Data Division of the World Bank's International Economics Department welcomes comments and corrections to the data. An electronic data and text retrieval system of the main TIDE book will be available in 1994.

The reports were written in May 1993, and edited by Joost Polak.

Abbreviations and acronyms with wide application are noted at the end of the book, after the technical notes. Readers interested in more detailed descriptions of the economic indicators should refer to other World Bank publications, notably *World Development Reports*, *World Tables*, and *World Debt Tables*. The statistical tables and notes in these publications are available on diskette, using the ☆STARS☆ retrieval system. Readers interested in the comprehensive country studies should write to the Distribution Unit, Office of the Publisher, 1818 H Street, N.W., Washington, D.C. 20433, U.S.A. for a copy of the World Bank's *Index of Publications*.

Overview

Emerging equity markets have grown rapidly since the early 1980s. Market capitalization grew from $83 billion at the end of 1983 to $774 billion at the end of 1992, a ninefold expansion, and emerging stock markets' share in world equity market capitalization climbed from 2.5 to 7 percent. Trading volumes rose even faster, increasing 24 times over the period 1983–92. Tremendous growth in stock markets in Mexico and the Republic of Korea has propelled these markets into the ranks of the 15 largest equity markets in the world.

The rapid growth of emerging stock markets has been accompanied (in recent years) by generally strong performance of these markets. The IFC's emerging market composite price index shows an annualized mean return (in dollar terms) over the five years ending December 1992 of 14.76 percent, compared to returns of 12.12 percent for the US S&P 500 index and 1.68 percent for the EAFE (Europe, Australia and the Far East) index of selected developed markets. Although emerging markets are fairly volatile (the annualized standard deviation for the five years ending December 1992 was 23.04 percent), these markets are weakly, and in some instances negatively, correlated with stock markets in industrial countries, and thus provide substantial potential risk reduction benefits to international investors.

A significant shift in developing country policies in recent years has helped fuel developing country stock market growth. Along with liberalizing trade, realigning exchange rates, adopting market-oriented policies, and consolidating public finances, developing countries have begun to liberalize investment regulations. Several

Selected Stock Markets, 1993

	Market capitalization (US$ millions) June 1993	Monthly value traded (US$ millions) June 1993	IFCG[a] Price indexes (US$, end 1984=100) June 1993	IFCG[a] Price Indexes 12 month % change June 1993	Annualized mean return (US$ 5 years, ending June 1993)
Argentina	26,968	725	996.2	-26.27	85.92
Brazil	76,023	4,434	163.3	57.01	42.48
Chile	34,725	196	1,839.3	-13.31	32.40
Colombia	5,280	102	946.4	-11.14	34.32
India	59,016	1,122	274.2	-31.44	14.16
Indonesia	17,100	693	78.4	8.71	-2.04
Jordan	5,203	252	164.1	44.48	8.64
Republic of Korea	118,829	26,763	437.1	35.53	4.56
Malaysia	118,829	10,472	218.3	24.52	14.64
Mexico	129,983	3,353	1,740.5	6.68	36.84
Nigeria	1,199	1	32.3	-0.30	7.20
Pakistan	7,078	123	276.8	-20.40	19.08
Philippines	16,611	266	1,821.2	-9.30	15.84
Thailand	62,162	5,108	626.2	27.23	18.96
Turkey	22,880	1,651	322.2	43.04	27.72
Venezuela	7,125	278	421.0	-32.32	33.48
Zimbabwe	667	1	199.4	-32.40	-11.52

Source: IFC Emerging Markets Database
a. International Finance Corporation Global index (IFCG) represents the market as a whole, showing trends in performance from the perspective of local investor. Weighted by market capitalization using a formula based on the chained Paasche method.

emerging stock markets have eased restrictions on repatriation of income and capital and raised ceilings on foreign participation (for example, Korea opened its market to foreign investors in January 1992, and India permitted foreign portfolio investors to invest directly in local equities in September 1992). In addition emerging countries are moving to relax rules governing participation by domestic institutional investors—pension funds and mutual funds—in the local equity market (for example, in early 1993 Chile raised the cciling on domestic pension fund investment in any 'closely' held company from 1 to 3 percent). Another important policy trend in developing countries has been the privatization of state-owned enterprises, which has helped to increase market size (capitalization and trading), broaden the investor base, and restructure corporations along more efficient lines. In addition, far-reaching financial sector reforms in these countries have encouraged growth of new financial intermediaries and deepened financial markets.

Emerging stock markets have also moved to adopt wide-ranging institutional reforms to increase efficiency and reduce transactions costs. Such reforms include strengthening disclosure and accounting standards (which are often below international standards), establishing central clearing and settlement systems, enhancing regulatory structures in these markets, tightening insider trading rules, and improving securities and investor protection laws (Mexico, for example, is proposing domestic securities market reforms along the lines of the United States).

Foreign investment in emerging stock markets has grown explosively since 1989. Gross equity flows, which have responded to both the local developments (noted above) and global factors (namely, declining U.S. interest rates, and recession and weak economic growth in the United States), rose from under $3.5 billion in 1989 to over $10.3 billion in 1992. Much of this increase was accounted for by Latin American equity markets, where gross equity flows grew over tenfold in 1989–92. Whereas most of the initial increase in flows represented flight capital, the presence of international institutional investors in emerging stock markets has increased.

Argentina

Argentina has experienced slow economic growth since the 1940s. By the mid-1970s long-term growth declined noticeably, and in the last half of the 1980s the country suffered its longest period of stagnation in the century. Savings and investment rates fell precipitously from the mid-1970s until 1989. Argentines, responding to the unstable macroeconomic environment, increasingly saved and invested abroad. Labor productivity fell and poverty worsened.

This economic performance was traceable to chronic public sector deficits and endemic inflation. Public sector deficits in the late 1970s ranged from 10 to 14 percent of GDP, and in the early 1980s surpassed 15 percent of GDP. After the return to constitutional democracy in 1983, public demands to control inflation were translated into four successive stabilization programs. All failed to eradicate inflation, and each ended in a more virulent inflation than the one preceding it. The main reason for these failures was the inability of the stabilization programs to redress rapidly and permanently the public sector structural deficit.

Structural deficits emerged from the post-war organization of the economy. Economic policy from the 1940s was used to propagate rules and transfers favoring the interests of private groups with access to power. By the early 1980s public expenditures approached 40 percent of GDP. Unionized labor benefitted from high wages, guaranteed employment, and rigid rules governing hiring and dismissals. Industry benefitted from highly protected markets, tax exemptions through special promotion regimes, subsidized credit—or effective grants, as many loans were not collected—subsidized inputs from public enterprises, and high prices on sales to public enterprises. Housing contractors and middle-class home buyers benefitted from enormous public transfers through earmarked taxes and effective grants through the Housing Bank. Tobacco growers, sugar growers, the merchant marine, and other small interest groups enjoyed special tax breaks. Consumers enjoyed below-cost tariffs from public enterprise and lax collection practices.

Provincial governments could avail themselves of costless credit from the provincial banks, which the central bank reimbursed. The military enjoyed expanding budgets, especially over 1976–82, as well as management perquisites in state companies they controlled. By 1989 subsidies through the budget, tax exemptions, agricultural regulations, public enterprise tariffs, and central bank rediscounts were estimated to amount to roughly 8 percent of GDP—the equivalent of some $8 billion.

The growth of the state and concomitant rents and subsidies, along with the capital flight provoked by an inconsistent exchange rate policy, were financed during the late 1970s largely by external borrowing through the expanding Eurodollar market at low or even negative real international interest rates. This permitted the government to run large deficits and sustain a revalued exchange rate with relatively low levels of inflation in the second half of the 1970s. An abrupt end to voluntary foreign commercial credit in the early 1980s and the sudden rise in real international interest rates provoked a financial collapse and placed additional pressure on public finances. The situation was complicated by the South Atlantic War.

The loss of external finance and lack of adjustment meant the treasury had to resort to increased inflationary finance through monetary creation. The private sector, in an effort to avoid the resulting inflation tax, gradually withdrew its resources from the financial system and reduced its real holdings of currency; this, together with the negative effects of inflation on real tax collections, made Argentina's economy progressively more unstable in the 1980s. Even though the deficit fell from near 20 percent of GDP in the early 1980s to an average of about 10 percent over 1987–89, the base for the inflation tax shrank even faster—efforts to reduce the deficit were not fast or permanent enough to convince the private sector that savings in domestic currency would not be eroded by inflation. Inflation became high and unpredictable, and the main impediment to the recovery of private savings and investment. The decade ended with two episodes of hyperinflation in 1989.

Post-1989 Structural Reforms

The present administration took office in July 1989 during a traumatic hyperinflation—July inflation alone was 200 percent. This culminated a decade-long crisis in public finance. The new team inherited weak public institutions accustomed to deficit spending and with an institutionalized reliance on the inflation tax. In addition, claims on state revenues were far greater than its capacity to mobilize resources—in short, the Argentine state was insolvent.

The government undertook stabilization programs in 1989 and 1990. Neither succeeded, principally because of the intractability of the fiscal deficit. The first terminated in a new hyperinflation at the end of 1989 and in early 1990. The second lasted from March 1990 to December 1990 and ended in a new inflationary outburst but, unlike the previous breakdowns, the economy did not spin into hyperinflation.

Instead, a new fiscal package in February 1991 was sufficient to close the remaining fiscal gap. This was followed by the April 1, 1991 Law of Convertibility fixing the local currency to the dollar and effectively proscribing money creation other than to buy net foreign reserves. The convertibility program disciplines monetary policy and limits the power of the government to finance its deficit through inflation. The law markedly reduced the foreign exchange rate risk to investors and the inflation risk to business and labor—as long as the fiscal fundamentals are in place to support it.

The February 1991 program was able to close the gap in large measure because the government's sustained structural reform efforts had progressively improved the foundations of public finance. The government had undertaken difficult to reverse reforms in the legal framework, institutions, and policies. These included institutional reforms of the federal government, public enterprises, and federal-provincial fiscal relations, and restructuring liabilities with domestic and foreign creditors to adjust them to serviceable levels. Other reforms have helped elicit efficient private investment, notably trade, deregulation, and financial sector reform.

Federal Government

The government undertook a major effort to improve revenues through the implementation of a much-broadened and uniform value added tax first to goods in February 1990, and later extended to services in November 1990. The government also improved the efficiency of the tax administration in 1989, establishing a control system for the largest taxpayers that took effect in February 1991. The tax penalty law, adopted by Congress in 1990, provided much needed sanctions for tax non-compliance. The tax package of February 1991 improved the quality of revenue mobilization substantially because it eliminated export taxes, reduced progressively during 1990 and early 1991, deducted higher taxes on financial transactions from the income/asset tax, and removed several minor taxes. In December 1992 subsidies to industrial promotion were substantially cut by replacing self-monitored tax deductions with a tax bond program. These efforts cumulatively produced dramatic rises in tax collections from the third quarter of 1991 on. The increase in value added tax collection allowed the government to eliminate inefficient taxes, such as the fuel tax and the stamp tax, in November 1992, and several specific sales taxes in May 1993.

Federal employment decreased from 671,000 to 284,000, including 103,000 layoffs and 284,000 teachers and health workers transferred to provincial payrolls. This effort was based on a ministerial reorganization that focused federal activities on core objectives, and improvements in the civil service system through an improved salary structure and efficiency measures. The government was able to increase average salaries and partially restore salary differentials.

The government took several measures to strengthen budgeting procedures and expenditure controls. By 1993 it had eliminated 105 of the 151 earmarked accounts extant in 1990, and reduced the coverage of earmarked taxes. The September 1992 Law of Public Financial Management will permit comprehensive budgeting, effective internal expenditure control, and provide for new external auditing.

The government has embarked on several reforms to separate the central bank from the nonfinancial public sector and establish it as an effective independent monetary authority. The elimination of the central bank's domestic short-term interest-bearing obligations by means of their conversion into external treasury bonds in January 1990 in effect was a first step toward recapitalizing the central bank. The Law of Convertibility established a money-creation rule that effectively limits monetary policy and central bank inflationary financing of public sector deficits. Since early 1991 the central bank has published financial statements that reveal its balance sheet; since April 1991 it has published its reserve position weekly so the public can monitor implementation of the Law of Convertibility.

In September 1992 a new law strengthened the central bank's autonomy, and further restricted its ability to extend credit to the government and the banking system. This measure reinforces the convertibility law, and paves the way for an independent, disciplined, monetary authority. In addition, the central bank intends to complete the process of removing functions ancillary to the functions of a monetary authority by transferring legal authority for failed institutions to the courts.

Public Enterprises

The government has carried out one of the most impressive privatization programs in the Western Hemisphere. The objective was to reduce the budgetary burden of the enterprises, make the firms more competitive, and increase the volume and efficiency of new investment. The privatization program began in earnest in 1990 and gained credibility with the sale of national telecommunications company in November 1990. The program removed politics from price setting in the formerly vast segment of the economy covered by the state. The change in the institutional organization of these sectors cut off public subsidies to consumers and labor groups benefitting from high wages and excess staffing, and transfers for investment. The program also improved public finances: about $9 billion in capital receipts helped close fiscal accounts in 1991 and 1992 and external debt was reduced by $12 billion. Major privatizations included television stations, the telephone company, Aerolineas Argentinas, gas distribution and transmission, and the majority of the national oil company. It granted road and railroad concessions to the private sector, privatized long distance cargo lines, and sharply reduced the railway's work force. The government privatized other public enterprises, including defense industries, the nation's largest distributor of electricity, ports and maritime transport, reinsurance, and the entire power sector. Future privatization plans include the national airport system.

Fiscal Relationships with the Provinces

The government also sought to restructure fiscal relationships with the provinces. The Coparticipation Law of 1988, fixed the share of federal revenues automatically transferred to the provinces at 58 percent. In August 1992 a portion of tax revenues was assigned to the social security system before computing revenue sharing. At the same time, the resources provincial governments could access were limited by progressively terminating central bank lending to provincial banks. The government also reduced extra-coparticipation transfers through the budget. To offset aggregate increases in resources as national tax collection improved, the government also transferred expenditures to provincial administrations, notably secondary education and hospitals, and to the social security system in August 1992.

Debt Restructuring

The final step in dealing with the government's insolvency involved restructuring its debt obligations. The government had financed its deficit through borrowing from the financial system, suspending payment to external creditors, and accumulating arrears with pensioners and suppliers. Restructuring each of these required major initiatives.
Although the government ended new rediscounts to the housing and industrial banks, and liberal rediscounts to provincial banks in 1988, the central bank continued money emission to finance the treasury and its own deficit. In late December 1989, faced with rising central bank deficits and the renewed threat of hyperinflation, the government took the drastic step of converting domestic, short-term (mainly seven-day), interest-bearing obligations of the central bank into $3.5 billion 10-year dollar-denominated treasury bonds. This virtually eliminated the central bank's quasifiscal deficit and the monetary emission necessary to finance it—at the cost of penalizing savers and reducing already low confidence in the financial system.

In April 1988 the government suspended payment on its external debt to commercial creditors. By 1992 it had accumulated $8 billion in arrears as part of a $32 billion medium-term commercial bank debt. Public external debt was $61 billion. The government re-initiated partial payments in June 1990, and established a consistent record of paying about 25 percent of interest due. At the same time, it allowed external debt to be used in exchange for the sale of assets, which reduced the debt stock by $7 billion. The progressive improvement in fiscal fundamentals in 1990/91 allowed the government to begin negotiations with commercial banks on a debt reduction deal. An external debt agreement signed on April 7, 1993, reduced $28 billion in commercial bank debt by approximately 37 percent, and eliminated interest arrears. This debt deal is expected to improve Argentina's creditworthiness. The agreement formalized arrears in a 12-year uncollateralized bond at LIBOR plus 13/16 with a 3-year grace period, after a $700 million downpayment. Existing debt was exchanged for collateralized par bonds with a fixed interest rate, or collateralized discount bonds at 65 percent of face value paying LIBOR. The new collateralized bonds will have a 12-month rolling interest guarantee.

For most of the last decade, the government has paid only about half the legally mandated pensions owed social security recipients. Arrearages were not recorded in the fiscal accounts, but are estimated to be as high as $7 to 10 billion. To stop the accumulation of arrears, the government modified coparticipation in tax revenues in favor of the social security system in August 1992. Since then, the social security system has run a small operating surplus. The government also accumulated arrears in 1990 with suppliers through formal suspension of payment on goods and services already provided, and the health funds have arrears with their service providers that will also result in new debt. Finally, the government, as part of its income tax reform, suspended poorly designed loss carry forward deductions for the corporate income tax, and agreed to issue compensatory bonds.

To settle these claims, Congress authorized the government to issue consolidation bonds. The service of this debt will be capitalized until 1997, but payments on the order of $3 billion will be required in the last years of the decade. The federal government's share of the proceeds of the privatization of the state oil company is earmarked for repurchasing some of the consolidation bonds.

Social Security Reform

The government has moved towards replacing a failed public pension system. In mid-1992 it submitted a law introducing a combined state/private system: the state would supply a uniform basic pension financed on a pay as you go basis while the private sector would supply pension funds. Membership in both schemes would be mandatory. The lower house of the Argentine Congress passed the law—with significant modifications—in May 1993. The government expects the legislative process to be completed before the end of the year, allowing a new system to be established in mid-1994.

Trade, Deregulation and Financial Reforms

In 1991 the government accelerated and largely completed a trade liberalization program that began in late 1986, but had suffered temporary reversals in 1989. Virtually all export taxes and quantitative restrictions—except for automobiles—were eliminated. The maximum ad valorem tariff was reduced from 115 to 35 percent.

The deterioration in the trade balance in 1992, a consequence of massive capital inflows motivated government to use commercial policy to achieve effective devaluation within the fixed exchange rate regime. Exporter rebates were raised from 8 to 13 percent. On the import side, the tariff band was narrowed to 0 to 20 percent. The government also increased a flat tariff surcharge, called a statistical tax, from 3 percent to 10 percent on a temporary basis. This led to an effective depreciation of about 5 percent. In May 1993 the government eliminated both tariffs and the statistical tax on capital goods imports, but in July it provided protection to some paper and textile products through temporary import quotas and tariff surcharges.

A major domestic deregulation decree in October 1991 ended a series of market-impeding rules, dissolved several regulatory bodies, and unified pension and health insurance payments to reduce evasion. Subsequent decrees have deregulated pharmaceutical imports and ports. The industrial promotion program and subsidies to Tierra del Fuego were markedly reduced in November 1992.

The publicly-owned housing and development banks, long subject to political influence and dependent on government financial support, are undergoing major restructuring. Branches of the National Development Bank and the National Housing Bank have been closed since March 1990 and their staffs have been reduced by almost 75 percent. The government is liquidating the development bank and closing the housing bank's retail functions. It has established a second tier bank to be managed, and ultimately owned, by the private sector to mobilize financing for its investment needs.

In response to a short-lived run on the peso in mid-November 1992 the authorities strengthened their commitments to the fixed exchange rate regime by permitting reserve requirements to be met either in foreign or domestic currency, and equalizing reserve requirements on foreign and domestic currency-denominated checking accounts in domestic transactions. In February 1993 these measures were complemented by lowering reserve requirements and further deregulating commercial bank lending to the private sector. Term deposits under 30 days were eliminated to increase the average maturity of deposits in the domestic financial system and reduce the risks of a run on the banks. Finally, since April 1993, bank compliance with reserve requirements is based on a four-week moving average, which should reduce the volatility of short-term interest rates.

Over the last six months Argentina has taken measures to reduce interest rates and stimulate investment. In October 1992 it imposed a 2 percent per month ceiling on loans made by public banks, a measure also aimed at stimulating restructuring of these banks. In March 1993 it began auctioning subsidy credits to banks, with the winner of the subsidy being the bank that offers to charge the lowest rates to final medium- and small-scale industrial borrowers. In May 1993 the authorities announced the extension of the Banco de Nacion's credit lines—the largest official bank—and a reduction in its lending rates from 1.8 percent to 1.6 percent per month. They also declared that the bank's credit policy will be oriented toward export-oriented activities as well as agriculture, industry, mining, and tourism.

Recent Macroeconomic Developments

In 1992 the authorities continued to adjust the economy, extending the recent good economic performance. GDP grew by 8.7 percent, and industrial production grew in the 12 percent range for the second year in a row. Employment rose by about 10 percent and investment expanded briskly in 1992, rising from 12.5 percent to 14.5 percent of GDP. The increased investment was financed by external savings, with gross national savings declining moderately to 9.3 percent of GDP. Public savings rose by about 2 percentage points of GDP, while private savings fell.

Fiscal performance has improved notably in the last two years. The overall balance moved into surplus in

1992 for the first time in decades with an operational primary surplus of 2.0 percent of GDP. Tax revenues increased from 13.5 percent of GDP in 1989 to nearly 24 percent between in 1992. In the same period, public expenditures fell as a percent of GDP. Capital spending and non-privatization receipts both declined slightly. The fiscal surplus also was improved by the drop in dollar interest rate, which cut accrued interest obligations by 1.3 percent of GDP. However, interest obligations still exceeded the operational primary surplus slightly in 1992.

Inflation continues to decelerate. The annualized inflation rate in the last quarter of 1992 was about 9 percent, compared to over 20 percent a year earlier. Nonetheless, inflation still exceeds international rates, which is necessary to sustain the fixed exchange rate regime.

During 1992 capital inflows, jointly with the economic expansion, contributed to an 84 percent increase in imports; exports rose by 1 percent. As a result, the current account deficit for 1992 reached 5.2 percent of GDP, up from 2 percent a year ago. Capital inflows of $12.0 billion, mostly private, more than offset the current account deficit, allowing a $3.4 billion accumulation of reserves.

After signs of slowdown in economic activity during January and February 1993, industrial production recovered in March and April, with the first quarter of 1993 marking the eleventh consecutive month of economic expansion. Capital inflows recovered in the first quarter of 1993, further strengthening the level of international reserves. The monthly inflation rate between January and March 1993 averaged 0.7 percent, about the same as the last quarter of 1992.

Medium-Term Prospects

The government projects real growth averaging 6.5 percent over 1992-95. Over this period its fiscal program for aims at generating a primary surplus sufficient to finance interest obligations, thus eliminating the need for the inflation tax. This involves efforts to raise the primary balance from about $3.3 billion in 1991 to about $4.1 billion in 1995. The success of this program will largely depend on medium-term reforms to improve the structural underpinnings of public finance, such as social security legislation, labor reforms, and the evolution of the fiscal relationships with the provinces, given the increasing decentralization of power and responsibilities from the center to provincial governments.

This scenario is attainable if the government continues to improve its fiscal position, and if private markets generate a smooth transition to a sustainable balance of payments and growth path.

There are significant risks to this program. The probability of adverse events affecting the convertible peso declines, however, as the government progresses on reforms that improve the fundamentals of public finance. Past reforms in the public sector anchor stabilization and are unlikely to be reversed during any financial turbulence. Also, reserves are the highest in a decade and cover the monetary base (although not the deposit base), which would deter a speculative attack on the peso. Even if problems give rise to pressure to alter the policy framework, in all likelihood any emerging policy regime would of necessity focus on maintaining fiscal balance and policies conducive to private investment.

Over the last few years Argentina has enacted serious and difficult structural reforms with considerable public support. The lack of alternatives to fiscal discipline and price stability, and memories of the hyperinflation of 1989/90, have made stability politically popular. These facts are powerful ballast that is likely to keep the ship of structural adjustment headed in the same direction, even in a financial storm.

Argentina

| Population mid-1991 (millions) | 32.7 | | | | Income group: **Upper-middle** |
| GNP per capita 1991 (US$) | 2,790 | | | | Indebtedness level: **Severe** |

KEY RATIOS

	1980	1985	1990	1991	1992
Gross domestic investment/GDP	25.3	17.5	14.0	14.6	16.7
Exports of goods and nfs/GDP	5.1	11.7	10.4	7.7	6.6
Gross domestic savings/GDP	23.8	23.5	19.7	16.2	15.2
Gross national savings/GDP	23.0	..	15.4	13.2	13.3
Current account balance/GDP	..	..	1.2	-1.5	-3.5
Interest payments/GDP	1.7	5.0	1.4	1.7	1.2
Total debt/GDP	35.3	57.4	44.0	33.5	21.3
Total debt/exports	242.4	493.2	412.7	418.5	314.6

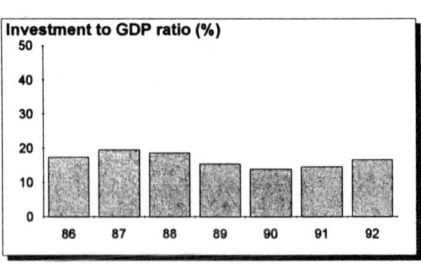

GDP: PRODUCTION
(% GDP)

	1980	1985	1990	1991	1992
Agriculture	6.4	7.6	8.1	6.7	6.0
Industry	41.2	39.0	36.0	32.7	30.7
Manufacturing	29.5	29.5	26.8	24.4	21.9
Services	52.4	53.4	55.9	60.6	63.3

(Growth rates)

	1980-85	1985-90	1990	1991	1992
Agriculture	1.9	1.1	11.4	3.9	0.1
Industry	-2.6	-0.9	0.0	11.2	9.2
Manufacturing	-1.5	-0.8	2.0	11.9	7.3
Services	-0.7	-0.2	-1.5	8.2	9.6
GDP	-1.2	-0.3	0.2	8.9	8.6

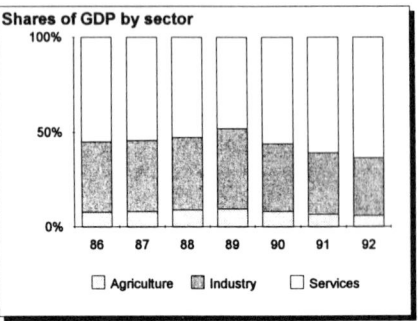

GDP: EXPENDITURE
(% GDP)

	1980	1985	1990	1991	1992
Private consumption	..	..	..	..	..
General government consumption	..	..	..	..	..
Gross domestic investment	25.3	17.5	14.0	14.6	16.7
Exports of goods and nfs	5.1	11.7	10.4	7.7	6.6
Imports of goods and nfs	6.5	6.2	4.6	6.1	8.1

(Growth rates)

	1980-85	1985-90	1990	1991	1992
Private consumption	..	..	..	..	..
General government consumption	..	..	..	..	..
Gross domestic investment	-10.5	-3.2	-9.9	25.1	30.9
Exports of goods and nfs	3.7	5.8	18.9	-8.3	0.6
Imports of goods and nfs	-16.7	-2.8	0.6	64.9	63.1
Gross national product	-2.1	-0.4	5.8	10.4	10.0
Gross national income	-2.3	-0.5	5.2	10.5	10.4

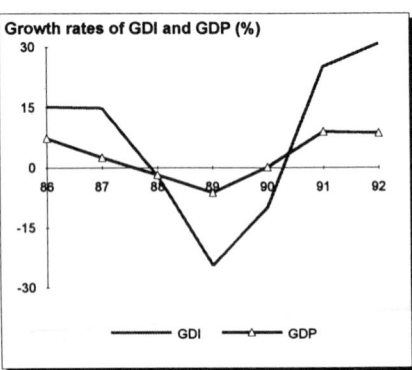

PRICES and GOVERNMENT FINANCE

	1980	1985	1990	1991	1992
Domestic prices					
(% change)					
Consumer prices	75.0	672.2	2,314.0	171.7	24.9
Wholesale prices	100.0	662.8	1,606.9	110.5	6.0
Implicit GDP deflator	93.9	624.8	2,021.1	141.1	15.4
Government finance					
(% GDP)					
Current budget balance	..	..	-1.5	-0.6	0.6
Overall surplus/deficit	..	..	-2.5	-0.6	0.6

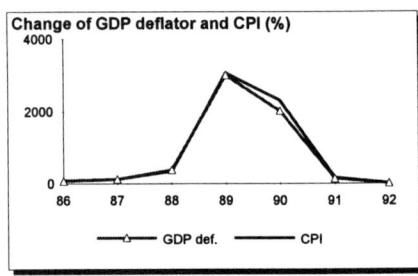

Argentina

POVERTY and SOCIAL (annual growth rates)	1980-85	1985-91
Population	1.4	1.3
Labor force	1.1	1.2

most recent estimate (mre)

Headcount index (% of population)	..
Energy consumption per capita (kg oil equivalent)	1,801.4
Infant mortality (per thousand live births)	25.0
Access to safe water (% of population)	..
Child malnutrition (% of children under 5)	..
Illiteracy (% of population age 15+)	4.7
Secondary enrollment (% of school-age population)	74.0

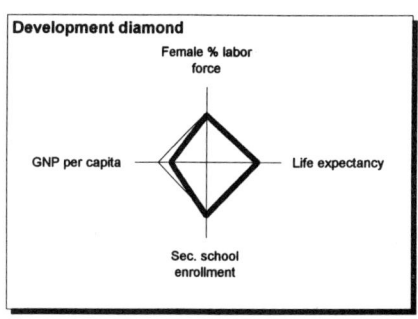

Development diamond

TRADE
(millions US$)

	1980	1985	1990	1991	1992
Total exports (fob)	..	..	12,252	12,107	12,230
n.a.	..	..	..	..	..
n.a.	..	..	..	..	..
Manufactures	..	..	7,089	7,019	7,258
Total imports (cif)	..	..	4,100	8,100	14,870
Food	..	..	233	680	887
Fuel and energy	..	..	203	354	370
Capital goods	..	..	540	2,428	6,103
Export price index (1987=100)	..	..	113	114	117
Import price index (1987=100)	..	..	112	113	118
Terms of trade (1987=100)	..	..	101	101	99
Openness of economy	..	..	12	11	12

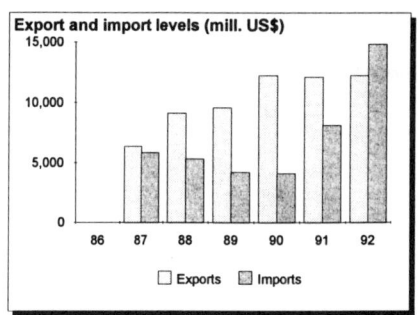

BALANCE of PAYMENTS
(millions US$)

	1980	1985	1990	1991	1992
Exports of goods and nfs	9,893	10,039	14,727	14,843	15,062
Imports of good and nfs	13,081	5,285	6,954	11,843	18,756
Resource balance	-3,188	4,754	7,773	3,000	-3,694
Net factor income	-1,609	-5,706	-6,203	-5,862	-4,257
Net current transfers	23	..	71	0	-32
Current account balance					
Before official transfers	..	..	1,641	-2,833	-7,983
After official transfers	..	..	1,641	-2,833	-7,983
Long-term capital inflow	4,255	4,790	1,021	5,683	6,153
Total other items (net)	-2,186	-2,590	331	-56	5,843
Changes in net reserves	2,598	-1,029	-2,993	-2,794	-3,992
Memo:					
Reserves excluding gold (mill. US$)	6,719	3,273	4,592	6,615	10,403
Reserves including gold (mill. US$)	9,297	4,703	6,222	8,073	11,860
Official exchange rate (local/US$)	0.0	0.0	0.5	1.0	1.0

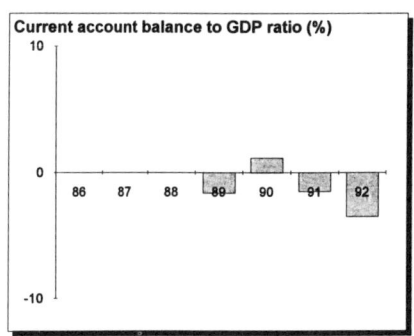

EXTERNAL DEBT

	1980	1985	1990	1991	1992
Export ratios					
Long-term debt/exports	149.7	405.7	324.7	310.0	247.5
IMF credit/exports	0.0	22.4	20.5	16.3	14.7
Short-term debt/exports	92.7	65.2	67.4	92.2	52.4
Total debt service/exports	37.3	58.9	39.6	46.8	53.3
GDP ratios					
Long-term debt/GDP	21.8	47.2	34.6	24.8	16.8
IMF credit/GDP	0.0	2.6	2.2	1.3	1.0
Short-term debt/GDP	13.5	7.6	7.2	7.4	3.5
Long-term debt ratios					
Private nonguaranteed/long-term	39.3	10.9	3.7	3.8	4.7
Public and publicly guaranteed					
Private creditors/long-term	49.3	77.6	73.3	70.0	64.1
Official creditors/long-term	11.3	11.5	23.0	26.2	31.2

7

Brazil

Brazil was seen as a miracle economy in the late 1960s as double digit annual growth rates were recorded and the structure of its economy underwent rapid change. Over 1965–80 GDP growth averaged 9 percent, one of the highest rates in the world. Growth tapered off after the first oil shock of 1973 but was still very respectable until the beginning of the 1980s.

The 1980s presented a very different picture, as Brazil failed to pursue a consistent and viable adjustment policy. Per capita output barely increased during the decade. After 1982 the net flow of capital from abroad dried up and investment and savings fell sharply, with the decline concentrated in government savings. Attempts at fiscal adjustment were sporadic and insufficient. The public sector relied heavily on the inflation tax and the economy moved from an average monthly inflation rate of 3 percent in the late 1970s to rates above 20 percent in the early 1990s.

Brazil also suffered from comprehensive government intervention in the economy. This was reflected in trade restrictions, import licensing and exchange control, fiscal subsidies, and government ownership of many manufacturing, services, and financial institutions. By the 1980s the efficiency and resource-allocation costs of this policy were apparent.

Major policy changes were initiated in 1990. Brazil liberalized trade, eliminated import restrictions on computers and related technical equipment, and began privatization and financial sector reforms. In late 1992 President Ferdinand Collor resigned in the midst of impeachment proceedings and was succeeded by Vice President Itamar Franco.

Macroeconomic Performance

In March 1990 the government introduced a bold stabilization program involving temporary confiscation of about 70 percent of the assets of the financial system, and an array of policies for restructuring the economy by reducing the government's role and intervention. The stabilization program, however, had only temporary success.

In 1990 the government obtained a consolidated operational budget surplus of 1.4 percent of GDP. This was largely due to one-time measures such as a tax on financial gains and below-market interest rates on frozen government bonds. The surplus narrowed in 1991, and the deficit, estimated at 1.7 percent of GDP, reappeared in 1992. The primary balance has been in surplus since 1990; it was 2.1 percent of GDP in 1990 and 3.2 in 1991 but fell to 1.8 percent in 1992.

Since 1991 the government has not interfered with contractual financial arrangements or imposed price controls. It has succeeded in preventing hyperinflation and sustained flight from domestic assets, even in a period marked by political crisis, but inflation has proven stubbornly high as government policies that leaned too heavily on tight monetary policy without strong fiscal adjustment led to extremely high real interest rates that dampened economic activity.

The new Franco government has outlined its general policies and the Congress has approved several additional tax measures for 1993. However, Brazil still lacks a comprehensive and credible macroeconomic program because of frequent changes in the federal government's economic team and the absence of consensus among the executive, the Congress and the states on the extent and distribution of economic and financial adjustments.

External Debt

Since 1990 successive governments have tried to restore external confidence in the Brazilian economy through negotiated agreements with government creditors. An agreement was reached with foreign commercial banks in April 1991 on 1989/90 arrears. An agreement was reached with Paris Club creditors in February 1992 and followed by bilateral ratifications. Finally, in December 1992, Brazil and the advisory committee representing foreign commercial banks announced the term sheet for a debt and debt service reduction agreement for $44 billion of foreign commercial debt. Brazil and the bank advisory committee recently reached a preliminary agreement on the composition of debt instruments. Once creditor banks have accepted this agreement the principal impediment to closing the deal will be securing financing for necessary enhancements—estimated at $3.2 billion. The deadline for the exchange of old and new instruments is end-July 1993, extendable to end-

November 1993. Brazil raised debt service payments to 50 percent of interest due after the term sheet was signed.

Structural Reforms

In tandem with the March 1990 attempt at stabilization the government introduced significant structural reforms in trade liberalization, deregulation and privatization. The adoption of a new constitution in 1988 also had a major impact on economic management, as it reversed the trend towards a highly centralized state favored by the military to one of decentralized activities, particularly at the municipal level.

Import prohibitions on close to 1,800 goods and most quota restrictions were abolished. Import control through foreign exchange allocation was eliminated. Most preferential regimes for imports were eliminated. A market reservation law preventing imports of most high technology goods including computers and accessories ended in October 1992. Significantly, foreign companies no longer need Brazilian partners to set up plants in the country.

Direct export subsidies and export regulations were mostly eliminated. Tariff reductions were announced in 1990. In February 1992, this program was speeded up and by October 1992, the (unweighted) average tariff was down to 17.1 percent (the modal tariff rate was 20 percent). The maximum tariff, currently 45 percent, will be reduced to 35 percent by July 1, 1993, while the average will decline to 14.1 percent. Under the MERCOSUR accord establishing a common market between Brazil, Argentina, Uruguay, and Paraguay import duties on non-MERCOSUR trade will be harmonized by January 1, 1995. By the same date, tariffs on goods traded within the MERCOSUR zone will be phased out entirely. The import licensing fee was reduced from 1.8 percent of the value of imports, to a flat fee equivalent to $100.

Brazil is concerned about the anti-dumping actions and quantitative restrictions that many of its exports such as steel, textiles, footwear and automotive parts face in developed country markets. However, Brazil's trade pattern is diversified by geographic partners and export categories. Approximately 31 percent of exports are to the European Community, 23 percent to the United States, 8 percent to Japan, and 12 percent to other Latin American countries. Less than a third consists of basic products. This pattern helps protect Brazil from external shocks and restrictions.

Brazil favors multilateralism and actively participates in the GATT negotiations. It sees its membership in MERCOSUR as compatible with multilateralism, but is concerned that the proposed North American Free Trade Agreement could impinge on major exports such as shoes, orange juice, textiles, ethanol, and steel products to the United States and Canadian markets. The stability of MERCOSUR also depends on harmonizing exchange rate and macroeconomic policies among the members, and especially the two largest partners, Brazil and Argentina.

A deregulation program eliminated domestic production and distribution quotas, licensing, prior approval of investment plans, and other economic restrictions. It also simplified business and financial transactions. In general, entry into industries is now much easier, and many regulations have been removed on distributing and pricing wheat, fuels, coal, steel, and transportation. The port deregulation law permits privatization of certain port services and freer contracting of labor.

Privatization

In October 1991, after prolonged legal battles, the administration launched a privatization program largely covering manufacturing enterprises in steel, petrochemicals, and fertilizers. By end-1992, 18 enterprises had been privatized, for a total sale price of $3.9 billion. The program was suspended briefly for review after the change in administration, but has been restarted and auctions were carried out in March and April 1993. There is scope for extending the program to cover areas such as utilities, petroleum, and banking, where the state presence is large. This would, however, require constitutional and other legal changes.

Decentralization

The 1988 constitution reduced the federal government's share of tax revenues from 50 to 35 percent and raised state and municipal shares to 41 percent and 24 percent. The decentralization of expenditure responsibilities is less clear cut. This change encourages initiatives, especially at the local government level, but also creates stabilization difficulties because the federal government's share of expenditures has declined less than its share of tax receipts.

Brazil

Population mid-1991 (millions)	151.4	Income group: **Upper-middle**
GNP per capita 1991 (US$)	2,940	Indebtedness level: **Severe**

KEY RATIOS

	1980	1985	1990	1991	1992
Gross domestic investment/GDP	23.3	19.2	21.5	18.9	17.5
Exports of goods and nfs/GDP	9.1	12.2	7.2	8.5	10.0
Gross domestic savings/GDP	21.1	24.4	23.2	20.9	20.8
Gross national savings/GDP	17.9	19.1	20.7	18.7	18.8
Current account balance/GDP	-5.5	-0.2	-0.6	-0.8	1.0
Interest payments/GDP	2.7	3.3	0.5	1.0	2.1
Total debt/GDP	30.2	47.6	24.3	28.7	30.5
Total debt/exports	305.2	362.2	320.6	324.9	308.9

Investment to GDP ratio (%)

GDP: PRODUCTION

(% GDP)	1980	1985	1990	1991	1992
Agriculture	11.0	11.5	10.4	10.8	..
Industry	43.8	45.3	38.5	37.3	..
Manufacturing	33.5	33.7	26.3	25.0	..
Services	45.2	43.1	51.1	51.9	..

(Growth rates)	1980-85	1985-90	1990	1991	1992
Agriculture	3.0	2.3	-3.7	2.6	..
Industry	-0.3	0.7	-7.4	-8.0	..
Manufacturing	-0.6	0.2	-8.7	-9.5	..
Services	1.7	3.0	-2.0	7.6	..
GDP	0.9	1.9	-4.6	0.4	-0.9

Shares of GDP by sector

GDP: EXPENDITURE

(% GDP)	1980	1985	1990	1991	1992
Private consumption	69.7	65.8	61.4	64.7	64.7
General government consumption	9.2	9.9	15.5	14.4	14.4
Gross domestic investment	23.3	19.2	21.5	18.9	17.5
Exports of goods and nfs	9.1	12.2	7.2	8.5	10.0
Imports of goods and nfs	11.3	7.1	5.5	6.5	6.6

(Growth rates)	1980-85	1985-90	1990	1991	1992
Private consumption	2.0	0.9	-0.6	2.5	-0.3
General government consumption	-0.1	9.0	-9.8	-1.9	-11.1
Gross domestic investment	-7.7	0.5	-8.1	-4.1	-2.4
Exports of goods and nfs	9.5	6.0	-4.9	6.6	8.9
Imports of goods and nfs	-8.9	6.0	10.1	10.1	-1.1
Gross national product	0.4	2.1	-4.7	0.8	-0.3
Gross national income	0.3	1.9	-5.5	1.1	0.3

Growth rates of GDI and GDP (%)

PRICES and GOVERNMENT FINANCE

	1980	1985	1990	1991	1992
Domestic prices					
(% change)					
Consumer prices	84.2	226.9	2,937.8	440.9	1,008.7
Wholesale prices	104.9	229.1	2,703.8	401.4	987.8
Implicit GDP deflator	87.3	231.7	2,597.0	401.9	991.4
Government finance					
(% GDP)					
Current budget balance	..	..	..	..	..
Overall surplus/deficit	..	..	..	..	..

Change of GDP deflator and CPI (%)

Brazil

POVERTY and SOCIAL (annual growth rates)	1980-85	1985-91
Population	2.2	1.9
Labor force	2.3	2.1

most recent estimate (mre)

Headcount index (% of population)	..
Energy consumption per capita (kg oil equivalent)	914.8
Infant mortality (per thousand live births)	58.0
Access to safe water (% of population)	87.0
Child malnutrition (% of children under 5)	12.7
Illiteracy (% of population age 15+)	18.9
Secondary enrollment (% of school-age population)	39.0

Development diamond

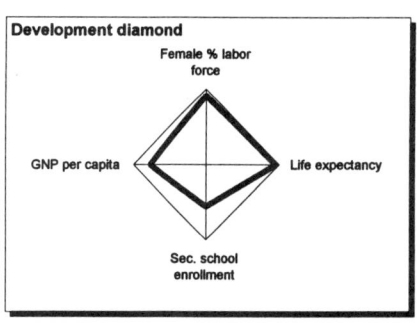

TRADE
(millions US$)

	1980	1985	1990	1991	1992
Total exports (fob)	20,132	25,638	31,391	31,636	36,208
Coffee	2,773	2,607	1,253	1,479	971
Other food	2,244	2,545	2,854	2,026	2,116
Manufactures	8,385	13,356	16,642	16,856	21,569
Total imports (cif)	22,955	13,153	20,661	21,017	20,583
Food	1,793	970	2,057	2,356	2,347
Fuel and energy	10,200	6,176	5,301	4,745	3,689
Capital goods	4,381	2,480	5,932	5,962	6,099
Export price index (1987=100)	107	101	111	110	113
Import price index (1987=100)	120	111	113	107	115
Terms of trade (1987=100)	89	91	98	103	98
Openness of economy	18	17	11	13	14

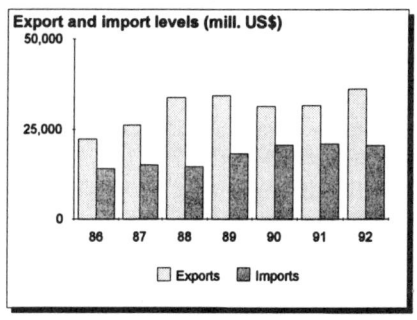

BALANCE of PAYMENTS
(millions US$)

	1980	1985	1990	1991	1992
Exports of goods and nfs	21,857	27,713	33,283	33,107	37,674
Imports of good and nfs	27,788	16,928	23,808	23,825	24,983
Resource balance	-5,931	10,785	9,475	9,282	12,691
Net factor income	-7,044	-11,213	-13,316	-12,353	-8,696
Net current transfers	0	0	834	0	100
Current account balance					
Before official transfers	-12,975	-428	-3,007	-3,071	4,095
After official transfers	-12,933	-412	-3,007	-3,071	4,095
Long-term capital inflow	6,207	1,105	-2,695	-1,089	19,862
Total other items (net)	2,783	-49	6,695	4,358	-9,070
Changes in net reserves	3,706	-259	-1,119	-198	-14,887
Memo:					
Reserves excluding gold (mill. US$)	5,769	10,605	7,441	8,033	22,521
Reserves including gold (mill. US$)	6,875	11,618	9,200	8,749	23,265
Official exchange rate (local/US$)	0.0	0.0	68.3	406.6	4,513.0

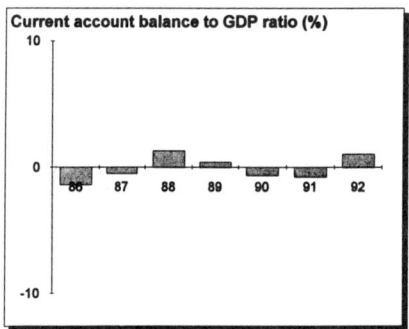

EXTERNAL DEBT

	1980	1985	1990	1991	1992
Export ratios					
Long-term debt/exports	247.0	313.6	249.0	265.3	233.7
IMF credit/exports	0.0	15.8	5.0	3.5	6.2
Short-term debt/exports	58.2	32.8	66.5	56.2	69.0
Total debt service/exports	63.1	38.6	22.1	30.0	38.8
GDP ratios					
Long-term debt/GDP	24.5	41.2	18.9	23.4	23.0
IMF credit/GDP	0.0	2.1	0.4	0.3	0.6
Short-term debt/GDP	5.8	4.3	5.0	5.0	6.8
Long-term debt ratios					
Private nonguaranteed/long-term	28.9	18.7	7.4	8.0	7.9
Public and publicly guaranteed					
Private creditors/long-term	58.8	64.4	62.9	64.8	65.7
Official creditors/long-term	12.3	16.9	29.7	27.2	26.4

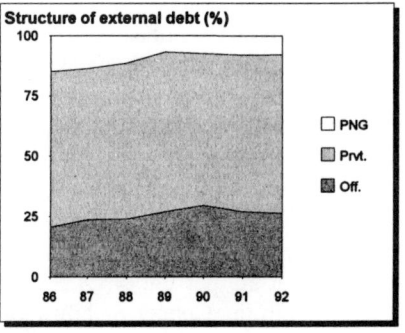

Chile

In March 1990 the first democratically-elected government in more than 16 years assumed power in Chile. Its objective is sustained economic growth with equity and stability. The government is committed to maintaining the private sector as the primary force in economic growth, and to the increased integration of Chile into the international economy, with emphasis on export growth, enhanced international investment, and renewed voluntary access to international capital markets. For 1991/92, growth averaged 8.2 percent, inflation fell to 13 percent, and international reserves rose by about $3.7 billion, reflecting strong export growth and capital inflows. Presidential elections are scheduled for December 1993.

Recent Developments

The present government, with the ministry of finance playing a leading role, has insisted on fiscal responsibility. Consistent with that goal, Congress passed a tax reform bill in 1990 that generated additional annual revenues of over 2 percent of GDP, principally to be used to finance expanded social programs. Main elements of the tax reform included increases in the value added tax and corporate and individual income taxes. New labor legislation, strengthening the bargaining power of previously weakened labor unions, also was approved by Congress.

In 1991 the economy expanded by 6 percent, aided by a strong export growth and accommodative monetary policy. Real investment remained at near-historic high levels. Inflation declined to 18.7 percent, the fiscal accounts were in surplus, and the current account of the balance of payments, for the first time in many years, registered a surplus. Public sector expenditures grew faster than the economy, benefitting primarily the social sectors. This was financed through higher levels of government revenue from the 1990 tax reform. The overall surplus of the non-financial public sector is estimated at 2.3 percent of GDP, including 0.7 percent channeled to the Copper Stabilization Fund.

The 1991 economic expansion reflected a 13.4 percent real growth in non-copper exports. This export growth is attributed to the entry into operation of large investment projects, and occurred despite the peso's real effective revaluation of 10 percent between 1988 and 1991.

In 1992 Chile experienced its ninth consecutive year of growth since the 1981–83 recession, with GNP rising by an all-time high of 10.4 percent. Inflation fell to 12.7 percent. As a result of the strong expansion, unemployment in December reached 4.4 percent of the labor force, bringing the annual rate to an average 4.9 percent.

Reflecting the dynamism of the economy, investment spearheaded the economic expansion of 1992, with fixed capital formation showing a real growth rate of 20.2 percent; overall investment reached 21.3 percent of nominal GDP. Investment growth was marked by a 32 percent expansion in machinery and equipment, and 12.1 percent in construction. Overall consumption grew in 1992 by 10.7 percent, with private consumption expanding by 11.6 percent, and public consumption by 5.0 percent. Despite another 9 percent peso revaluation, exports of goods and services expanded 12.3 percent, becoming the second largest contributor to the 1992 economic expansion after investment. Imports of goods and services grew by 22.1 percent.

Economic expansion was broadly based, with double digit growth in industry, construction, commerce and transport-communications. Laggards were mining (1.1 percent) and agriculture (3.1 percent). The mining sector suffered from a change in the composition of copper production from refined to concentrate form, and declines of 11.4 and 25.3 percent in iron and coal production. Poor results in the traditional agricultural sector contributed to slow expansion in agriculture.

Balance of Payments

In 1991 the current account registered a dramatic improvement, with a surplus of $143 million — compared to a $824 million deficit in 1990. This was a result of larger surpluses in the trade and non-financial services accounts. An 18.6 percent increase in the value of non-copper exports more than compensated for a decline in copper exports, resulting in an 8 percent increase in the value of commodity exports. Commodity imports increased at the moderate nominal rate of 4.5 percent, reflecting a 12 percent decline in capital goods imports. In the fourth quarter of 1991, however, capital goods imports increased substantially and they remained high in early 1992.

The 1991 capital account also showed a surplus, of $1.1 billion. However, in contrast to the larger $3.2 billion surplus in 1990, inflows consisted of medium- and long-term credits, while net short-term credits were actually negative. As a result of positive current and capital account movements, the overall balance of payments account showed a surplus of $1.2 billion. Net international reserves rose to $7.0 billion, the equivalent of over 10 months of merchandise imports.

The balance of payments surplus for 1992 was $2.4 billion, double that of 1991. International reserves reached $9.2 billion, approximately 12 months of merchandise imports. Capital inflows of $2.9 billion contributed to that outcome. Despite repeated increases in reserve requirements since mid-1991, attractive interest rate differentials attracted substantial short-term capital inflows of $1.7 billion. Net foreign direct investment also increased to $540 million. These statistics, however, understate the significant increase in gross foreign direct investment by $480 million, since it includes an increase of $426 million in Chilean investments abroad, principally in Argentina. Medium- and long-term capital flows were little changed from 1991.

Strong capital inflows contributed to another 9 percent peso appreciation in 1992, and the increase in imports. Goods imports expanded by 25.6 percent, contributing to the reversal of the $143 million current account surplus in 1991 to a deficit of $583 million, equivalent to 1.5 percent of GDP, in 1992. In spite of the peso appreciation, the growth of exports of goods and non-factor services remained strong. In 1992 copper exports grew 8.4 percent and non-copper exports grew 13.6 percent. The decline in international interest rates and in the stock of foreign debt contributed to a reduction in the interest payments from $1,586 million in 1991 to $1,492 million. However, the financial service account remained in deficit of $1,860 million due to increased profit remittances.

The continuation of strong capital inflows prompted the central bank to revalue the peso by 5 percent in January 1992. It also widened the band within which the peso can fluctuate from 5 to 10 percent, and imposed a 20 percent (increased to 30 percent in August 1992) reserve requirement on foreign currency deposits, to match the reserve requirement imposed some six months earlier on foreign credits. Subsequently the central bank instituted a "dirty float" policy to smooth-out exchange rate fluctuations within the pre-established band. These measures significantly increased the government's control over monetary policy.

In mid-year, the central bank announced that the peso would no longer be linked exclusively to the dollar, but to a basket of currencies weighted 50 percent to the dollar, 30 percent to the mark, and 20 percent to the yen. These weights roughly correspond to international trade weights. The mid-point of the band will continue to be adjusted daily by the difference between domestic and international inflation, and the central bank will continue its policy of selective interventions.

External Debt

Chile has made significant strides in reducing external indebtedness. Debt-equity conversions have reduced Chile's external debt by $11.3 billion since their inception in 1985 through January 1993. In September 1990 the Chilean government reached an agreement with creditor commercial banks that included rescheduling the total $1.8 billion in amortization from previous multi-year rescheduling agreements falling due before 1995. Chile's annual payments of interest reverted to the previous semi-annual schedule, and major banks purchased $320 million of Chilean five-year bonds at LIBOR plus 1.5 percent in 1991. The agreement also provided flexibility in cash buybacks and debt exchanges by individual banks.

At end-1992, total debt outstanding was $19.6 billion, equivalent to 50 percent of GDP, or 1.9 times the level of merchandise exports. Debt reduction operations have contributed to a reduction in the ratio of external debt to GDP from 113 percent in 1987 to 52 percent in 1992. The significant improvement in debt indicators, plus the reduction in world interest rates, have led to an increase in the secondary market price of Chilean external debt, from 53 cents to the dollar in 1987 to over 90 cents to the dollar in late 1992.

In mid-August 1992 Standard and Poor's issued a full "investment grade" BBB rating to the Republic of Chile's senior long-term foreign currency debt. Chile thus became the first Latin American country to regain an investment grade rating, another milestone in the Latin American debt crisis. Subsequently, early in 1993, Moody's awarded an implicit "investment grade" rating to Chile, further opening the door for the issue of Chilean paper in the U.S. institutional investor market.

Public Finances

Improved public finances have made an important contribution to Chile's economic recovery. The overall nonfinancial public sector deficit declined from 2.4 percent of GDP in 1985 to a surplus equivalent to 4 percent of GDP in 1990, and 3.2 percent in 1992. Rising copper prices contributed to this outcome, but commitment to conservative fiscal policies played a crucial role in eliminating the deficit.

In 1990 the newly elected government reversed the tax reduction trend to finance social sector programs, raising the value added tax from 16 to 18 percent, changing the collection of corporate income tax to an actual rather than distributed profits basis, and increasing income taxes.

In 1991 the government increased its social expenditures, which were largely financed by the tax increases. Nonetheless, the non-financial public sector surplus reached 2.3 percent of GDP, of which 0.7 percent went to the Copper Stabilization Fund. The overall non-financial public sector surplus was probably equal to the projected operational deficit of the central bank, balancing public sector finances.

Public finances remained strong in 1992, exceeding budgetary projections. The non-financial public sector exhibited a surplus equivalent to 3.2 percent of GDP, with savings of 7.8 percent of GDP. Revenues benefitted from strong growth, and expenditures from lower interest payments on external debt. However, a lower operational surplus of public enterprises offset some of these gains, principally due to the copper parastatal's reduced surplus. With a central bank operational cash deficit of 1.2 percent of GDP, the overall public sector generated a surplus of 1.7 percent of GDP—compared to 1.2 percent of GDP in 1991—contributing to the financing of private investment.

Savings and Investment

Chile's private savings and investment have traditionally been low compared to other countries of similar income levels, but rose over the 1980s. Overall private national savings rose from 2.2 percent in 1984 following a major economic crisis to 14.5 percent in 1992. Savings increased due to a number of factors, including the 1981 pension system reform, the tax reform, the reformed housing subsidy program, which necessitated up-front private savings, and the stable policy environment. Public savings, spurred by improved tax administration, public enterprise performance, and wage containment, rose as a share of GDP from 0.8 percent in 1984 to 7.8 percent in 1992 (including the Copper Stabilization Fund).

Total gross investment has also been low traditionally, averaging only 15.3 percent of GDP over the last 30 years and never exceeding an average of 17 percent in any five-year period. However, in the last four years there has been a notable increase, with investment averaging more than 20 percent, a figure reached only twice previously — in 1980 and 1981 — in the last three decades. Since 1988 foreign investment and project finance have provided an important stimulus to overall investment. Continuation of this rate of investment should permit overall economic growth of about 6 percent a year.

Social Development and Poverty

Social development in Chile has been impressive. Indeed its classification among the lower middle-income economies, with a GDP per capita income in 1992 of $2,786, belies its significant progress over the past several decades in improving social welfare. Key social indicators, including average life expectancy at birth, infant mortality rate, the prevalence of malnutrition, educational attainment, and overall adult literacy rate, are more similar to those of higher-income economies than to the developing world. Underlying Chile's solid social development performance is a long history of sustained, substantive investments in the social sectors by successive governments.

The new government has taken decisive action to accelerate social development. It has increased public social spending, financed from revenues generated by the recent tax reform, and instituted a series of measures to improve the quality of social service delivery, strengthen the decentralization process, increase collaboration between public and private health care providers, and revise social subsidies to enhance educational opportunities for low-income children. Despite this performance, poverty remains a significant problem.

Medium-Term Prospects

Having successfully implemented major economic policy adjustments in response to the dislocations of the early 1980s, Chile's medium-term economic growth remains primarily dependent on the government's ability to fulfill its own social development agenda within the context of a conservative fiscal stance. The evolution of terms of trade, international interest rates and world economic growth will also play a crucial role in Chile's medium-term economic performance, given the openness of the economy.

To attain, over the near future, the government's objective of a sustained annual average GDP growth rate of over 5 percent and to service its debt, Chilean exports will have to grow at an annual real rate of approximately 9 percent; and national savings and real investment will have to average, respectively, over 15 percent and 19 percent of GDP. This scenario, which is consistent with current expectations for the Chilean economy and the external sector, would require annual private capital inflows (anticipated primarily in the form of project financing) equivalent to approximately 3.5 percent of GDP. Current capital flows exceed this figure. The willingness of private investors and creditors to increase their exposure in Chile thus will remain a key determinant of the government's ability to reach its medium-term goals.

Chile

Population mid-1991 (millions)	13.4
GNP per capita 1991 (US$)	2,160

Income group: **Lower-middle**
Indebtedness level: **Moderate**

KEY RATIOS

	1980	1985	1990	1991	1992
Gross domestic investment/GDP	21.0	13.7	20.2	18.8	21.3
Exports of goods and nfs/GDP	22.8	29.1	36.5	35.8	33.4
Gross domestic savings/GDP	16.8	16.5	23.1	23.7	23.4
Gross national savings/GDP	13.3	5.2	16.8	18.0	..
Current account balance/GDP	-7.3	-8.4	-3.5	-0.4	-2.4
Interest payments/GDP	3.3	10.2	4.9	8.0	3.8
Total debt/GDP	43.8	127.4	68.8	57.2	51.7
Total debt/exports	192.5	436.6	182.1	153.5	151.3

GDP: PRODUCTION

(% GDP)	1980	1985	1990	1991	1992
Agriculture	7.2	..	..	..	..
Industry	37.3	..	..	..	..
Manufacturing	21.4	..	..	..	..
Services	55.5	..	..	..	..

(Growth rates)	1980-85	1985-90	1990	1991	1992
Agriculture	2.1	4.9	3.3	1.8	3.6
Industry	-0.5	6.0	0.5	5.2	8.0
Manufacturing	-1.9	6.9	0.1	5.5	12.2
Services	-1.5	7.2	3.1	7.3	11.6
GDP	-1.2	6.4	2.1	6.0	10.4

GDP: EXPENDITURE

(% GDP)	1980	1985	1990	1991	1992
Private consumption	70.7	69.3	67.2	66.7	67.5
General government consumption	12.5	14.2	9.7	9.6	9.1
Gross domestic investment	21.0	13.7	20.2	18.8	21.3
Exports of goods and nfs	22.8	29.1	36.5	35.8	33.4
Imports of goods and nfs	27.0	26.3	33.7	31.0	31.3

(Growth rates)	1980-85	1985-90	1990	1991	1992
Private consumption	-3.6	6.7	0.3	5.1	11.6
General government consumption	-0.6	0.8	1.6	3.6	5.0
Gross domestic investment	-14.5	15.3	-2.4	2.0	27.0
Exports of goods and nfs	2.3	9.2	7.2	12.9	12.3
Imports of goods and nfs	-10.6	13.1	0.6	8.5	22.1
Gross national product	-3.1	7.4	3.6	7.7	10.8
Gross national income	-4.6	8.7	0.2	9.0	10.9

PRICES and GOVERNMENT FINANCE

	1980	1985	1990	1991	1992
Domestic prices (% change)					
Consumer prices	35.1	30.7	26.0	21.8	15.4
Wholesale prices	39.5	43.4	21.8	21.5	11.7
Implicit GDP deflator	29.1	32.8	22.4	21.7	13.8
Government finance (% GDP)					
Current budget balance	8.4	-3.4	5.3	4.6	5.3
Overall surplus/deficit	..	..	3.6	2.3	2.3

Chile

POVERTY and SOCIAL *(annual growth rates)*	1980-85	1985-91
Population	1.7	1.7
Labor force	2.5	2.1

most recent estimate (mre)

Headcount index (% of population)	..
Energy consumption per capita (kg oil equivalent)	886.9
Infant mortality (per thousand live births)	17.0
Access to safe water (% of population)	87.0
Child malnutrition (% of children under 5)	10.3
Illiteracy (% of population age 15+)	6.6
Secondary enrollment (% of school-age population)	74.0

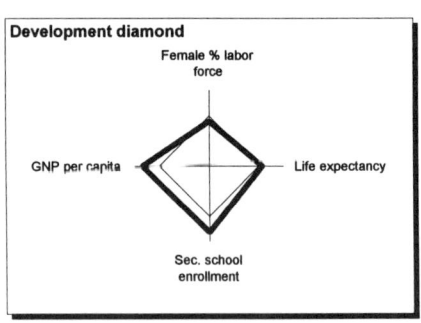

TRADE

(millions US$)	1980	1985	1990	1991	1992
Total exports (fob)	4,706	3,804	8,310	8,929	9,986
Copper	2,125	1,789	3,795	3,617	3,886
Meat	340	515	979	1,221	1,230
Manufactures	1,751	1,168	2,741	3,316	4,033
Total imports (cif)	5,469	2,955	7,678	8,094	10,129
Food	711	222	..	..	..
Fuel and energy	..	..	1,129	1,034	1,114
Capital goods	1,134	588	2,322	2,041	2,786
Export price index (1987=100)	137	86	129	126	..
Import price index (1987=100)	104	85	121	120	..
Terms of trade (1987=100)	132	101	107	105	..
Openness of economy	37	42	58	54	53

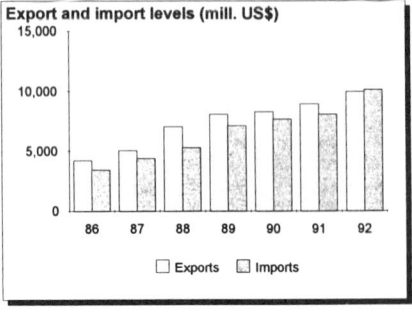

BALANCE of PAYMENTS

(millions US$)	1980	1985	1990	1991	1992
Exports of goods and nfs	5,968	4,468	10,152	11,190	12,539
Imports of good and nfs	7,023	3,921	9,364	9,577	11,694
Resource balance	-1,055	547	788	1,612	846
Net factor income	-1,029	-1,936	-1,811	-1,809	-1,860
Net current transfers	0	47	54	59	111
Current account balance					
Before official transfers	-2,020	-1,342	-969	-138	-903
After official transfers	-1,971	-1,328	-824	143	-583
Long-term capital inflow	2,242	900	2,025	1,170	1,176
Total other items (net)	974	330	1,167	-29	1,776
Changes in net reserves	-1,321	98	-2,368	-1,283	-2,369
Memo:					
Reserves excluding gold (mill. US$)	3,123	2,450	6,068	7,041	9,168
Reserves including gold (mill. US$)	4,128	2,950	6,784	7,700	9,790
Official exchange rate (local/US$)	39.0	161.1	305.1	349.4	362.6

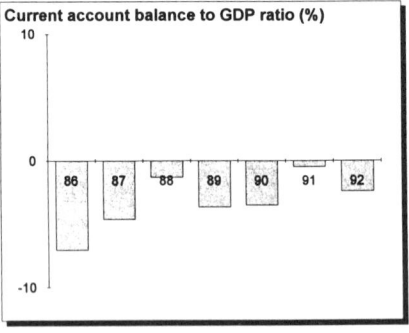

EXTERNAL DEBT

	1980	1985	1990	1991	1992
Export ratios					
Long-term debt/exports	149.8	377.5	139.2	126.5	119.6
IMF credit/exports	2.0	23.3	11.0	8.2	5.8
Short-term debt/exports	40.8	35.7	31.9	18.9	25.9
Total debt service/exports	43.1	48.6	26.0	33.9	23.8
GDP ratios					
Long-term debt/GDP	34.1	110.2	52.6	47.1	40.8
IMF credit/GDP	0.4	6.8	4.2	3.1	2.0
Short-term debt/GDP	9.3	10.4	12.1	7.0	8.9
Long-term debt ratios					
Private nonguaranteed/long-term	49.9	26.8	29.2	32.0	31.1
Public and publicly guaranteed					
Private creditors/long-term	35.5	61.2	35.4	32.2	32.1
Official creditors/long-term	14.6	11.9	35.4	35.8	36.7

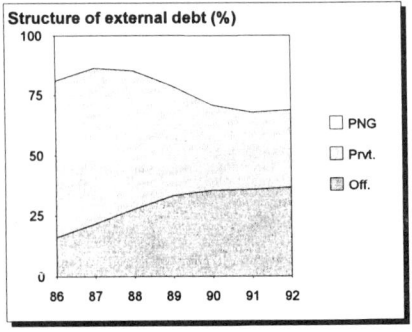

Colombia

Colombia's population, estimated at 32.8 million in mid-1991, occupies an area of just over a million square kilometers. Two-thirds of the population now lives in urban areas. Solid growth of about 4.5 percent a year for the past four decades, combined with a drop in the population growth rate to 1.7 percent, have facilitated substantial improvement in social conditions. Life expectancy at birth stands at 69 years, compared with 59 years in 1965. Primary school enrollment was close to 90 percent in 1990, as was the literacy rate. Nonetheless, poverty remains a critical problem. It is estimated that in 1992 almost 6 million Colombians—19 percent of the population—had incomes below a commonly accepted subsistence level, with three out of four of these poor living in rural areas. Some 12 percent of children under age 5 are malnourished and about a third of the population lacks access to safe water. Sharp regional disparities in the quality of life contribute to social disintegration in large areas of the country.

Natural resources are plentiful. These include agricultural land, water for irrigation, energy resources—oil, natural gas, and coal—nickel, gold, and emeralds. Colombia has a significant locational advantage because it is close to North America with coasts on the Pacific and Atlantic Oceans. Mountainous terrain, however, makes internal transportation costly and slows physical and social integration. Rich physical resources, a literate and dependable work force, a robust private sector, competent macroeconomic management, and political stability are major factors explaining Colombia's good record of economic development and social improvements over the last 30 years.

Colombia's competent macroeconomic management, based on the government's continuous commitment to correcting internal and external imbalances, is best evidenced by its growth record in the 1980s. Colombia maintained an average annual growth rate of 3.4 percent while adjusting to a world-wide recession and coffee and oil price swings. Between 1980 and 1985 Colombia's economy grew at an average 2.2 percent, followed by a successful macroeconomic adjustment that raised the average growth rate to 4.5 percent between 1985 and 1990. Positive economic growth was achieved every year during the decade.

Colombia's relatively smooth economic growth masked some important structural deficiencies. A closer look at economic performance indicators suggests a lack of dynamism in the economy since the mid-1970s. The contribution of manufacturing to GDP remained relatively constant, growth in non-traditional exports was not diversified, and the manufacturing sector remained oriented toward the domestic market. The low and frequently negative productivity growth observed in most sectors suggests that economic growth depended on increasing capital inputs rather than efficiency gains.

The government recognized that macroeconomic measures alone could not raise productivity and output growth in the long term and undertook an economic modernization program in early 1990 to improve resource allocation and use. The program contained structural reforms and accompanying macroeconomic policies designed to raise economic growth to 5 percent a year, bring inflation below 20 percent, and reduce the incidence of poverty. Its centerpiece was a trade reform program, which envisaged the gradual elimination of quantitative restrictions on manufactured imports and scheduled reductions in the levels and dispersion of tariffs to reach an average tariff rate of 15 percent in 1994. Taking advantage of a strong balance of payments in 1990/91, a new administration advanced the timetable for implementation. Quantitative restrictions on industrial imports—which formerly covered 80 percent of domestic production—were lifted in November 1990. In August 1991 the government advanced the 1994 tariff targets so that trade reform was put in place in 18 months, rather than the 5 years originally envisaged. Average nominal protection—excluding agricultural products covered under a price band system, and automobiles—was lowered from 28 percent to 15 percent and average effective protection from 44 percent to 25 percent. The government also went beyond the original scope of the program by extending trade liberalization to agriculture and negotiating free trade agreements with several countries. The state monopoly on imports of key agricultural products was eliminated and replaced with a variable tariff scheme. Although progress in completing a regional trade agreement under the Andean Pact has been slow, Colombia and Venezuela agreed to free their bilateral trade and adopted common external tariffs on February 1992. Later in August, Colombia signed similar agreements with Ecuador and Bolivia. Negotiations are now under way for an agreement among Mexico, Venezuela, and Colombia, and separate talks are being held with Chile.

Colombia has experienced impressive change during the last few years. On the political front this has been marked by a new constitution and a renewed commitment to decentralizing public administration. On the economic front the government has abandoned the inward-oriented development model of the past and has begun to redefine the role of the state in the economy. Besides trade liberalization, the government has actively pursued and broadened the scope of structural reform in Colombia.

To improve resource mobility and facilitate the supply response to the new trade regime, reforms in the financial sector authorized ownership of financial institutions by foreign investors and free entry into all segments of the market, subject only to prudential requirements. Access to foreign exchange was improved, and the government liberalized direct foreign investment. The labor regime was modified, although perhaps not forcefully enough, to reduce labor rigidities and facilitate industry restructuring. Reforms in the public sector improved the efficiency and focus of public expenditures. Public monopolies were eliminated in sectors critical to trade flows, including railways, ports, shipping, and agricultural marketing. Most of the government's non-oil industrial holdings were divested, as were three of the five banks nationalized during the banking crisis of 1982–85, and further divestment is underway.

Colombia's intention to reorient the role of the state in a liberalized economy is spelled out in its 1990–94 development plan, which emphasizes the social sectors, infrastructure, and environmental protection. The pace and breadth of change indicate a turning point in the development process in Colombia.

Recent Economic Performance

The macroeconomic policies accompanying the economic modernization program were designed to support structural reform while reducing inflation. In 1989/90, in anticipation of the trade liberalization effort and in response to the collapse of the world coffee market, the government undertook an aggressive exchange rate policy by allowing the real exchange rate to depreciate 22 percent. Non-traditional exports grew 24 percent in 1990, while imports failed to respond quickly to trade liberalization; the result was a current account surplus in 1990 equivalent to 1.4 percent of GDP. The expansion of exports contributed significantly to 4 percent GDP growth. This was accompanied, however, by accelerated inflation, which reached a 15-year peak of 32 percent in December 1990.

In 1991 the authorities tightened fiscal and credit policies to reduce inflation. The deficit of the non-financial public sector was reduced from 0.6 percent of GDP in 1990 to 0.2 percent in 1991, and domestic interest rates rose sharply. But this rise—combined with falling world interest rates and slower depreciation of the peso—widened the differential between the returns on peso and dollar assets, encouraging strong capital inflows partly fed by drug money. The capital inflows undermined the tight monetary policy, strengthened the balance of payments and resulted in an 9 percent real appreciation of the peso during 1991. By accelerating trade liberalization, the government aimed to reduce the growing external imbalance, but success was limited as imports were slow to respond. The balance of payments surplus reached $1.9 billion, with gross international reserves increasing to over 9 months of imports of goods and services. The 12-month inflation rate fell only to 27 percent by year-end. Real GDP growth was relatively weak at 2.1 percent in 1991.

The government's macroeconomic program for 1992 envisaged 3 percent growth in real GDP percent and aimed at reducing inflation to 22 percent by end-1992. The program was to further tighten fiscal policy through tax reform, aiming at a 0.3 percent of GDP surplus for the nonfinancial public sector, while modifying monetary policy to bring about a decline in interest rates, capital inflows, and real appreciation of the exchange rate. Economic performance during 1992 did not substantially deviate from these macroeconomic targets despite a dilution of the tax reform package in Congress, which reduced expected revenues from the package by half, a crisis in the power sector that led to severe rationing of electricity, and intensified violence by guerrillas and drug traffickers, which amplified the degree of uncertainty in the economy and increased fiscal pressures from the security effort.

Early in 1992 monetary policy accommodated a sizeable drop in domestic interest rates; a pronounced slowdown in the combined net placement of open-market instruments helped lower average deposit rates from 37 percent at end-1991 to 22 percent in June 1992. As a result, the surge in capital inflows observed in 1991 and the first half of 1992 subsided, as did the pace of reserve accumulation by the central bank. For the year as a whole the real appreciation of the peso was 2 percent. Imports grew sharply, while exports remained stable, and the current account surplus fell to about 2 percent of GDP. This surplus, coupled with the strength of capital inflows observed in the early part of 1992, led to an increase in international reserves of about $1.3 billion.

The economy grew by about 3.5 percent in 1992, aided by a recovery of private investment in response to the sharp drop in interest rates, and despite the difficulties encountered during the year. The expansion of GDP was fueled by a construction boom, which grew 11.5 percent after a sizeable decline over 1989-91, and strong growth in manufacturing and commerce. The performance of these sectors more than offset a decline in agriculture, brought on by lower world prices for exports such as cotton and coffee, a severe drought, and increased violence in some regions.

Gains on the inflation front, however, were modest: the consumer price index rose 25 percent. To some extent, this can be related to wage adjustments—minimum wages and wages for the public sector were raised 27 percent, the level of the previous year's inflation—and to the government's deviation from its fiscal targets. In addition to the drop in expected tax revenues for 1992, public finances were adversely affected by the sharp decline in international coffee prices, the weakening of public electricity companies owing to shortfalls in revenues and unanticipated expenditures related to the crisis in the power sector, and added security expenditures. For the year as a whole the deficit for the nonfinancial public sector is estimated at 0.4 percent of GDP.

Medium-Term Outlook

Activity continued to be buoyant in the first quarter of 1993, with manufacturing growing fast, particularly the automotive, furniture, and domestic appliances subsectors. A real GDP growth rate of 4.5 percent is projected in 1993, as agriculture output recovers modestly and manufacturing and construction remain buoyant. Consumer price inflation dropped to 23 percent as of end-April 1993 and is expected to finish the year close to the government's target of 22 percent. Imports continue to surge due to strong economic growth, the continued appreciation of the peso, and the full effect of trade liberalization, while exports have remained rather flat due in part to lower coffee prices. It is expected that the current account for 1993 will move into a deficit on the order of 2 percent of GDP. The capital account should remain in surplus, with direct foreign investment over $700 million, leading to an increase in international reserves of more than $500 million for the year. The outlook for the fiscal deficit is subject to several uncertainties, including a lower than projected increase in tax revenues, continued depressed coffee prices, increased military outlays, and pressures for fiscal incentives for agriculture. The expected increase in public expenditures includes severance payments to reduce the civil service by 32,000 employees, and expanded investments in the new Cusiana oil fields. On balance, the deficit of the nonfinancial public sector is likely to increase to over 1 percent of GDP in 1993.

In the medium term Colombia is expected to consolidate the gains of the structural reform of the past two years and accelerate the pace of economic growth. Improved resource allocation and availability of foreign exchange stemming from capital inflows and higher oil revenues offer Colombia the means to reach a higher growth path than in the past. By 1994/95, the Cusiana fields—with reserves estimated at least 2 billion barrels—will begin to produce large amounts of oil and gas, ensuring ample exports and domestic energy supplies for years to come. By maintaining prudent macroeconomic policies and the pace of structural reforms, the government should be able to achieve its goal of 5 percent-plus growth and under 20 percent inflation.

External Debt

Colombia's external debt levels are low by Latin American standards. Total external debt outstanding and disbursed at the end of 1991 was $17.5 billion, or about 41 percent of GDP, and 169 percent of exports of goods and services. Those relatively low debt ratios are the result of prudent economic and debt management. Colombia's debt strategy since 1985 has been aimed at a phased return to voluntary lending by avoiding debt restructuring and seeking semi-voluntary refinancing facilities. Four integrated loan facility operations were arranged between 1985 and 1991, and Colombia has been able to maintain commercial bank exposure at nearly nominal levels since 1986. The availability of foreign exchange provides the government the opportunity to pursue an even more active debt management strategy to prepay debt and to directly access the international capital markets.

Since late 1991 the Colombian authorities have been seeking to identify and structure financially attractive operations for debt prepayment. The strategy, aimed only at sovereign debt, has as its main objective reducing the cost of outstanding public debt and, when possible, extending maturities. During 1992 the government raised $500 million in dollar-denominated bonds, using the proceeds for debt prepayment. In April 1993 the Republic of Colombia launched its first Eurobond issue, marking its return to the international capital markets and opening the door for further Colombian debt to be issued. The $125 million five-year bullet was issued at a spread of 215 basis points over treasuries and was regarded an unqualified success by market participants. The issue should serve as a benchmark to assess Colombian risk as new issuers approach the markets in the future.

The government's medium-term debt strategy aims to diversify the public sector's sources of financing by substituting external with internal debt, and to diversify its sources of internal debt by developing local capital markets. Efforts will be made to improve the profile of public debt, seeking lower interest rates and longer maturities, and integrate the debt strategy with other elements of macroeconomic management. Decentralized public agencies will be encouraged to contract external debt directly rather than through the central government. It is likely that the government will revise its borrowing strategy from multilateral creditors, seeking a high-quality but not necessarily high-volume portfolio.

With the stock of debt to private creditors constant in nominal terms and strong growth in petroleum, coal, and non-traditional exports, Colombia should make rapid progress in reducing its debt further and improving its debt-servicing capacity. The debt-service to export ratio is projected to decline from its peak of 38 percent in 1992 to less than 20 percent by the year 2000. By the same token, the ratios of debt outstanding and disbursed to GDP and to exports of goods and services should be cut in half between 1992 and 2000.

Colombia

Population mid-1991 (millions)	32.8
GNP per capita 1991 (US$)	1,260

Income group: **Lower-middle**
Indebtedness level: **Moderate**

KEY RATIOS

	1980	1985	1990	1991	1992
Gross domestic investment/GDP	19.1	19.0	18.2	15.3	17.9
Exports of goods and nfs/GDP	16.2	13.8	20.4	21.1	21.2
Gross domestic savings/GDP	19.7	20.3	23.9	23.3	24.8
Gross national savings/GDP	19.5	17.5	21.3	23.0	23.2
Current account balance/GDP	0.3	-4.6	1.3	5.6	1.8
Interest payments/GDP	0.9	2.5	3.3	3.1	3.2
Total debt/GDP	20.8	40.8	42.8	41.7	39.5
Total debt/exports	110.0	287.5	182.1	168.4	172.0

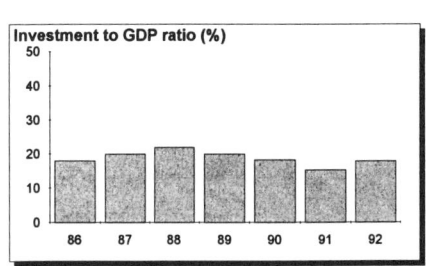

GDP: PRODUCTION

(% GDP)	1980	1985	1990	1991	1992
Agriculture	19.4	17.0	16.1	17.4	..
Industry	31.6	34.6	36.5	34.9	..
Manufacturing	23.3	21.7	20.3	19.7	..
Services	49.0	48.4	47.4	47.7	..

(Growth rates)	1980-85	1985-90	1990	1991	1992
Agriculture	1.4	4.4	5.8	5.5	-1.1
Industry	3.0	5.1	2.2	1.0	4.7
Manufacturing	1.3	4.5	4.2	0.8	4.9
Services	2.0	4.0	4.8	2.8	3.6
GDP	2.2	4.4	4.1	2.7	3.1

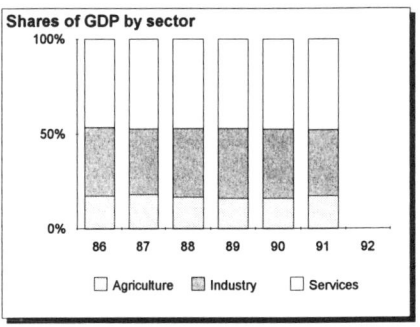

GDP: EXPENDITURE

(% GDP)	1980	1985	1990	1991	1992
Private consumption	70.2	69.0	65.4	66.1	64.8
General government consumption	10.1	10.7	10.7	10.6	10.4
Gross domestic investment	19.1	19.0	18.2	15.3	17.9
Exports of goods and nfs	16.2	13.8	20.4	21.1	21.2
Imports of goods and nfs	15.6	12.5	14.8	13.0	14.4

(Growth rates)	1980-85	1985-90	1990	1991	1992
Private consumption	2.1	3.7	4.1	0.1	2.2
General government consumption	3.0	5.5	3.1	2.3	12.4
Gross domestic investment	-0.4	2.5	-2.7	0.6	21.0
Exports of goods and nfs	1.8	8.5	16.7	4.3	4.2
Imports of goods and nfs	-1.9	4.2	10.8	-10.8	35.6
Gross national product	1.3	4.5	3.9	3.0	4.1
Gross national income	1.1	4.0	3.9	3.0	8.0

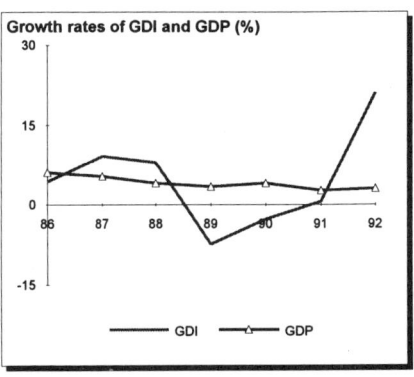

PRICES and GOVERNMENT FINANCE

	1980	1985	1990	1991	1992
Domestic prices					
(% change)					
Consumer prices	26.5	24.0	29.1	30.4	27.0
Wholesale prices	24.2	25.0	26.6	27.6	20.1
Implicit GDP deflator	27.6	24.7	28.5	27.0	29.1
Government finance					
(% GDP)					
Current budget balance	..	4.3	6.8	6.8	6.5
Overall surplus/deficit	..	-4.6	-0.6	-0.2	-0.4

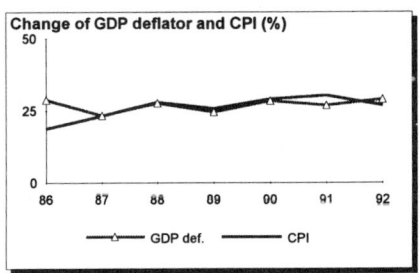

Colombia

POVERTY and SOCIAL
(annual growth rates)

	1980-85	1985-91
Population	2.1	1.8
Labor force	2.8	2.5

most recent estimate (mre)

Headcount index (% of population)	..
Energy consumption per capita (kg oil equivalent)	811.0
Infant mortality (per thousand live births)	23.0
Access to safe water (% of population)	..
Child malnutrition (% of children under 5)	10.0
Illiteracy (% of population age 15+)	13.3
Secondary enrollment (% of school-age population)	52.0

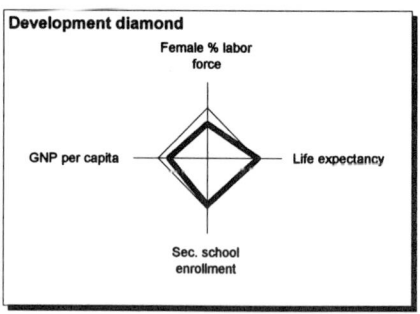

Development diamond

TRADE
(millions US$)

	1980	1985	1990	1991	1992
Total exports (fob)	..	..	7,079	7,507	7,345
Coffee	2,208	1,702	1,399	1,324	1,259
Gold	310	365	374	409	363
Manufactures	..	..	1,720	2,327	2,350
Total imports (cif)	4,283	3,673	5,108	4,548	6,116
Food	..	..	..	..	..
Fuel and energy	530	466	316	237	273
Capital goods	1,456	1,165	1,881	1,455	2,061
Export price index (1987=100)	..	..	101	106	..
Import price index (1987=100)	..	..	106	115	..
Terms of trade (1987=100)	..	..	95	92	..
Openness of economy	..	..	30	29	29

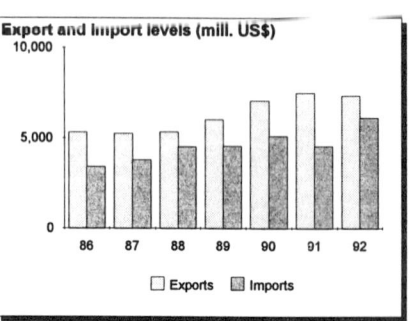

BALANCE of PAYMENTS
(millions US$)

	1980	1985	1990	1991	1992
Exports of goods and nfs	5,747	4,642	8,687	9,115	9,348
Imports of goods and nfs	5,597	4,989	7,089	6,633	8,354
Resource balance	150	-347	1,598	2,482	994
Net factor income	-211	-1,710	-2,080	-1,832	-1,802
Net current transfers	165	455	1,027	1,697	1,656
Current account balance					
Before official transfers	103	-1,602	544	2,347	848
After official transfers	104	-1,596	544	2,347	848
Long-term capital inflow	808	2,338	191	161	339
Total other items (net)	385	-477	-100	-589	161
Changes in net reserves	-1,297	-265	-634	-1,919	-1,347
Memo:					
Reserves excluding gold (mill. US$)	4,831	1,595	4,212	6,029	..
Reserves including gold (mill. US$)	6,474	2,197	4,453	6,335	7,389
Official exchange rate (local/US$)	47.3	142.3	502.3	633.0	759.3

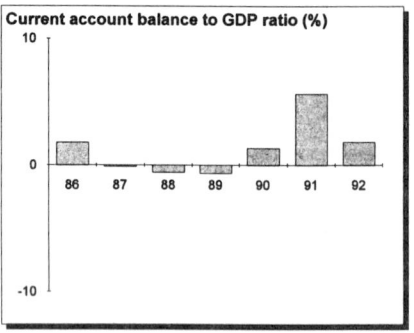

EXTERNAL DEBT

	1980	1985	1990	1991	1992
Export ratios					
Long-term debt/exports	73.0	224.9	166.9	151.4	156.7
IMF credit/exports	0.0	0.0	0.0	0.0	0.0
Short-term debt/exports	37.0	62.6	15.2	17.0	15.3
Total debt service/exports	15.1	40.0	38.6	35.3	35.1
GDP ratios					
Long-term debt/GDP	13.8	31.9	39.2	37.5	36.0
IMF credit/GDP	0.0	0.0	0.0	0.0	0.0
Short-term debt/GDP	7.0	8.9	3.6	4.2	3.5
Long-term debt ratios					
Private nonguaranteed/long-term	11.2	14.1	7.1	7.1	5.1
Public and publicly guaranteed					
Private creditors/long-term	36.8	38.4	38.9	38.6	42.6
Official creditors/long-term	52.0	47.6	54.0	54.3	52.3

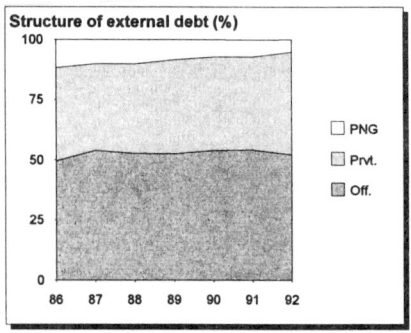

India

With 850 million inhabitants, India's population is the world's second largest. With a per capita income of $330, it is also one of the world's poorest. From independence until very recently, India pursued a planned approach to development combining prudent macroeconomic management, an active state role in key sectors such as banking, basic industries, utilities, and infrastructure, and extensive regulation of the economy. This regulation went beyond the usual inward-looking industrialization policies that most developing countries pursued after World War II. The government regulated the most basic business decisions for all firms above a certain size—borrowing, investment, capacity utilization, pricing and distribution. Despite being highly regulated, the private sector continued to be important, is present in most sectors of the economy, and generates about two-thirds of India's GDP.

Thus, while using them to serve the goals of a planned growth process, India has developed all the basic institutions of a modern capitalist society, including a strong entrepreneurial class.

This development strategy produced mixed results. It transformed a stagnant economy into one growing at persistently positive rates—on average, GDP per capita grew at 1.4 percent per year through the 1970s—eradicated famines, reduced the incidence of poverty from over 50 percent in the 1960s to less than 30 percent in the late 1980s, and developed a diversified industrial base and a relatively large and sophisticated financial sector: Bombay's stock exchange is the developing world's third largest after Korea's and Malaysia's. Conservative macroeconomic management kept inflation low, and fiscal and balance-of-payments imbalances seldom persisted. India has never defaulted on its external debt.

These successes were achieved in a very complex society divided along ethnic, linguistic, and religious lines, and under democratically elected governments: over the four decades since independence, India has established and operated democratic systems and processes that have ensured a remarkable degree of political freedom and stability.

India's strategy also has had serious shortcomings. Its growth rates have been much lower than could have been expected in a country saving and investing over one-fifth of its GDP. At over 2 percent a year, population growth has remained high, and health and education indicators, while showing some progress, have remained among the world's lowest—particularly for women. India continues to have one of the highest levels of poverty in the developing world, and accounts for about a third of the world's absolute poor.

Recent Economic Developments

In the past decade there has been a growing recognition among India's policy makers that the development policies pursued since independence have reduced economic growth below its potential and that a more market-oriented approach to economic management would generate higher growth and greater resources for social programs, and reduce the incidence of poverty. In the 1980s important policy changes started to liberalize trade, industrial and financial policies, while subsidies, tax concessions, and currency depreciation improved export incentives. These measures helped GDP growth to accelerate to over 5 percent a year during the 1980s and reduced poverty more rapidly, but India's most fundamental structural problems were addressed only very partially. Tariffs continued to be extremely high and quantitative restrictions remained pervasive. While controls on capacity utilization and borrowing were lifted, the investment licensing regime continued to make investment decisions conditional on cumbersome government approvals, and resulted in foreign investment levels well below those achieved in other large developing economies—$200 to $400 million a year, as opposed to $700 to $1,000 million in Indonesia, $1 to $2 billion in Thailand and Brazil, and $2 to $3 billion in China.

State-owned banks continued to dominate the banking system and to serve mainly as instruments for financing economic activities selected by the government. In the early 1990s regulations required 63.5 percent of deposits to be invested in the Reserve Bank of India or in government debt instruments, and directed credit to priority sectors still accounts for 40 percent of commercial bank credit. With few exceptions, the inefficiency of public enterprises—which generate 17 percent of GDP—continued to be a serious issue.

In the late 1980s these problems were compounded by political uncertainty—there were two general elections and four changes of government between end-1989 and July 1991—that slowed reform and prevented the government from addressing serious macroeconomic imbalances. The central government fiscal deficit reached 8.4 percent of GDP in fiscal 1991 and, if uncorrected, would have exceeded 10 percent of GDP the next year. From single digits throughout the 1980s, inflation rose to 10.2 percent on a point-to-point basis in November 1990, and remained in double digits for almost two years. The current account deficit of the balance of payments rose to almost 3 percent of GDP, India's external debt grew to $70 billion, and the debt service ratio increased to 29 percent.

Combined with political uncertainty and the consequent lack of an effective adjustment strategy, the August 1990 developments in the Persian Gulf put additional pressure on the balance of payments, and eroded the confidence of foreign lenders. This triggered accelerated capital outflows and led commercial banks to reduce their exposure in India. The Indian government responded by compressing imports drastically, and mobilizing part of India's gold stock. Multilaterals and bilateral lenders, particularly Japan, provided significant assistance in the first half of 1991. These efforts notwithstanding, foreign exchange reserves declined to about $1 billion—two weeks of imports—in June, putting India on the verge of defaulting on its external debt.

Changing Course

The government that came to power in June 1991 overcame the balance of payments crisis and initiated a forceful stabilization of the economy coupled with a major transformation of India's development strategy. Several major policy papers, including the Eighth Plan for 1992-97, have articulated the new government's main objectives: reducing macroeconomic imbalances, transforming India into an internationally competitive economy open to trade and foreign investment, encouraging the development of the private sector, and re-focusing government activities on developing infrastructure and human resources and alleviating poverty.

Progress in stabilizing the economy and reforming policies has been significant. The new government rapidly resolved the macroeconomic crisis it inherited, reducing fiscal and balance of payments imbalances. By August 1992 reserves recovered to over $6 billion, about three months of imports, and inflation fell to below 10 percent; it has since fallen to less that 7 percent. Primarily through non-interest expenditure cuts concentrated on subsidies, defense, and capital spending, the central government fiscal deficit was reduced from 8.4 percent of GDP in fiscal 1991 to 6.2 percent of GDP in fiscal 1992 and 5.7 percent of GDP in fiscal 1993.

The fiscal deficit figure exceeded a target of 5 percent of GDP, mostly because of December 1992 to February 1993 unrest in Bombay and other parts of the country that disrupted economic activities and significantly reduced tax collections. Despite this moderate slowdown in fiscal adjustment the primary deficit has been reduced from 4.4 percent of GDP in fiscal 1991 to 1 percent of GDP in fiscal 1993. While the focus of fiscal adjustment has been on the central government, states and public enterprises have also been forced to adjust their spending as the central government curtailed loans and transfers. Including the states and public enterprises, the consolidated public sector deficit is estimated to have declined from 13 percent of GDP in fiscal 1991 to 9 percent of GDP in fiscal 1993. Mostly through further expenditure reduction, the fiscal 1994 budget aims at reducing the fiscal deficit to 4.7 percent of GDP, equivalent to a small primary surplus.

The deficit on the current account of the balance of payments, helped by a 22 percent devaluation in dollar terms in July 1991—and further devaluation in the context of the spring 1992 establishment of a free market for foreign exchange—and contractionary demand management, declined from $7.7 billion (2.6 percent of GDP) in fiscal 1991 to $5 billion in fiscal 1992 (2.1 percent of GDP) in spite of a significant import liberalization.

The reduction in fiscal and balance of payments imbalances was achieved without major disruptions in growth, which fell from 5.2 percent in fiscal 1991 to about 1.2 percent in fiscal 1992, and rebounded to 4 percent the next year.

Structural Reforms

In July 1991 India announced its intention to reform policies governing international trade, private investment in industry—and labor and capital mobility—the financial sector, taxation, and public enterprises. Shortly after the July 1991 budget high-level committees and working groups were appointed to reassess policies in these areas and formulate proposals for change in the short and medium terms. Significant progress has been made in reforming trade and industrial policies; progress in the other structural reform areas has been more gradual and more modest.

A first set of trade reforms over July-December 1991 eliminated a costly subsidy scheme for exports, and reduced import licensing restrictions. Sweeping additional measures were taken in March/April 1992 to eliminate virtually all licensing restrictions on imports of capital goods and intermediates and introduce the Liberalized Exchange Rate Management System establishing a foreign exchange market. This was effectively a dual exchange rate system under which foreign exchange at the official exchange rate of Rs25.8 to the dollar was provided for imports authorized by the Ministry of Finance, mostly for petroleum products and fertilizers. Foreign exchange for all other imports was sold in a newly established interbank market for foreign exchange, at the market rate. Forty percent of current account receipts from exports and invisible transactions were required to be surrendered at the official exchange rate. The remaining 60 percent could be sold at the free market rate. All capital transactions, including interest payments on external debt but excluding grants and IMF transactions, were effected at the free market rate. This system was thus equivalent to a float coupled with an export tax—the level of the tax being determined by the difference between the official and market rates—the proceeds of which subsidized designated imports. The government also announced that the exchange rate would be unified over two to three years.

The government reunified the exchange rate more quickly than expected. The exchange system proved highly successful. While the removal of import licensing restrictions and foreign exchange controls led to an increase in imports, this increase did not create unmanageable pressures on the balance of payments, or weaken the rupee. Since it was introduced, the rupee has been relatively stable in the Rs30 to Rs32 to the dollar range. These results led the government to unify the exchange rate ahead of schedule, on February 27, 1993 when the fiscal 1994 budget was presented to Parliament. Since then, the rupee has remained stable—and the central bank has had to intervene to prevent its appreciation. For exporters, the reunification of the exchange rate is tantamount to a 7 percent devaluation. It has no impact on importers, as they already had to meet their foreign exchange requirements through the market.

With the reunification of the exchange rate, India moved to a floating exchange rate system, with all permitted current and capital foreign exchange transactions taking place in the inter-bank market. All surrendering requirements have been abolished. Foreign exchange dealers are free to maintain balances in convertible currencies domestically and abroad, and deal spot and forward in all major currencies. Except for some services, such as purchase of insurance abroad and imports of consumer goods still subject to licensing restrictions, all current account transactions are permitted and do not require government approval. India's capital account remains closed, however, and most capital account transactions continue to require government approval. The government has indicated that, barring exceptional circumstances, it does not intend to intervene in the foreign exchange market to influence the long-term evolution of the exchange rate; its interventions will mostly be for foreign exchange purchases to maintain reserves at the minimum of about three to four months worth of imports.

In addition to liberalizing the foreign exchange market and reducing import licensing restrictions, the government's three budgets—in July 1991, February 1992, and February 1993—have reduced tariffs. The maximum tariff has been reduced from 350 percent in 1990 to 85 percent since March 1993, with significant declines also for tariffs below the maximum. These changes have reduced the import-weighted average tariff from 87 percent in fiscal 1991 to 47 percent, and have significantly reduced dispersion. Although the reforms introduced over the last two years have liberalized India's trade regime significantly, import tariffs continue to be among the highest in the world. The need to reduce the fiscal deficit, and the large revenues generated by taxing imports, have constrained the speed at which tariffs could be reduced.

A new industrial policy announced with the revised July 1991 budget liberalized one of the most controlled investment regimes in the world. The new policy reduced the number of sectors reserved for public investment and the number of sectors in which private investment, domestic or foreign, required prior government approval. It facilitated foreign investment and made it more attractive, and amended the antitrust laws to eliminate the need for prior government approval for expansion, diversification, merger, and acquisition. Several other measures have further deregulated the industrial sector. In January 1993 the Foreign Exchange Regulation Act of 1973 was amended to eliminate discriminatory treatment of enterprises with more than 40 percent foreign equity, and the power and mining sectors have been opened to domestic and foreign private investors.

Since December 1991 the government has liberalized capital and money markets, introduced prudential regulations that meet international standards, and reduced controls on domestic bank expansion. The share of deposits required to be invested in the Reserve Bank of India or government debt instruments has been reduced, barriers to private sector entry into the banking system removed, and interest rates partially deregulated. In the fiscal 1994 budget the government announced that measures would be taken over the course of the year to recapitalize banks to enable them to meet the more stringent capital adequacy standards set by the new prudential regulations.

The government has been pursuing a three-pronged strategy on public enterprises. Reducing budgetary support and eliminating barriers to entry and monopoly privileges in sectors traditionally dominated by parastatals, and tariff reductions, have created a competitive environment for most public enterprises in mining and manufacturing. Mechanisms have been created to facilitate closing parastatals that cannot withstand domestic or external competition. The government can now restructure or close down chronically loss-making enterprises and a National Renewal Fund has been established to mitigate the social cost of retrenchment. Major restructuring exercises, some involving the retrenchment of several thousand workers, have been initiated. The government has reduced its equity holding in parastatals—by Rs30 billion in fiscal 1992, and a further Rs19 billion the next year.

The tax reform committee recommended major changes in most of India's taxes. These changes aim at transforming India's tax system from one with high, and highly differentiated, tax rates falling on a narrow base, into one with tax rates at moderate levels falling on a broad base. The committee recommended that the government's dependence on high tariff and excise rates — customs revenues account for 45 percent of central government tax revenues, and revenues from excises 30 percent — be reduced by introducing a value added tax. It also recommended a major simplification of personal and corporate income taxes to reduce marginal rates and broaden their bases. Most of the recommended changes in the personal income tax have been implemented and significant progress has been made towards reaching the tariff schedule recommended by the committee. Over the next few years, the government is expected to take further steps to reduce tariffs, and reduce taxes on corporate income and peak excise rates. It has asked the National Institute of Public Finance and Policy to design a value-added tax and the first steps towards its implementation are expected to be taken next year.

Social Sector Policies

The government has placed improving the living standards of the poor and accelerating development of India's human resources among its most important policy priorities. Early reforms in the social sectors are expected to focus on restructuring poverty alleviation programs to increase their cost-effectiveness and enable them to meet the special challenges created by the adjustment program. In the more medium term, the government is seeking to increase the efficiency, cost-effectiveness and coverage of public health and primary education and ensure that these programs reach the poor.

Medium-Term Prospects

Growth declined in the first year of the adjustment program, falling from 5.2 percent in fiscal 1991 to 1.2 percent in fiscal 1992 as a result of poor agricultural and manufacturing performance. Agricultural output declined by 1.4 percent as an irregular monsoon reduced food grain production and manufacturing output declined by 2.4 percent as a result of output declines of 13 percent in the capital goods and consumer durables industries. Contractionary demand management policies that depressed public and private investment were the main reason for the decline in capital goods, while consumer goods were affected by the import squeeze, which reduced the availability of imported inputs, and the July 1991 devaluation, which increased their cost. Growth recovered in fiscal 1993, however, and is estimated to have reached nearly 4 percent as agricultural recovery offset sluggish manufacturing growth of 3.5 percent. Assuming favorable monsoons, better growth performance is expected in fiscal 1994.

External Debt

Despite increasing reserves over the last two years, managing India's balance of payments remains a difficult and challenging task. Over the next four years India will need to repay about one-third of its $76 billion external debt as of March 1993: some $23 billion. Financing the current account deficit and debt repayments will require about $8 billion of gross inflows in fiscal 1994, and about $10 billion a year in the subsequent three years. While over three-fourths of these external financing needs could be met through disbursements on existing and expected commitments from bilateral, multilateral sources and private creditors, the need for exceptional balance of payments financing will remain substantial.

India

Population mid-1991 (millions): **866.5**
GNP per capita 1991 (US$): **330**

Income group: **Low**
Indebtedness level: **Moderate**

KEY RATIOS

	1980	1985	1990	1991	1992
Gross domestic investment/GDP	20.9	24.0	26.5	24.1	23.2
Exports of goods and nfs/GDP	6.5	6.0	7.9	9.4	9.8
Gross domestic savings/GDP	17.4	20.9	24.5	23.7	21.7
Gross national savings/GDP	19.2	21.2	23.8	23.2	21.0
Current account balance/GDP	-1.7	-2.8	-2.6	-0.8	-2.1
Interest payments/GDP	0.3	0.6	1.1	1.1	1.6
Total debt/GDP	12.0	19.1	23.4	28.8	34.2
Total debt/exports	136.2	264.0	269.8	274.9	319.5

GDP: PRODUCTION
(% GDP)

	1980	1985	1990	1991	1992
Agriculture	38.1	33.0	31.8	32.2	32.0
Industry	25.9	28.1	28.8	27.9	27.9
Manufacturing	17.7	17.9	18.6	17.8	17.8
Services	36.0	38.8	39.5	39.9	40.0

(Growth rates)

	1980-85	1985-90	1990	1991	1992
Agriculture	3.2	4.8	4.8	-1.4	3.5
Industry	6.3	7.4	6.9	0.0	4.2
Manufacturing	7.0	7.7	7.5	-2.3	4.2
Services	5.8	6.5	4.2	4.3	4.2
GDP	5.2	6.2	5.6	1.2	4.5

GDP: EXPENDITURE
(% GDP)

	1980	1985	1990	1991	1992
Private consumption	73.0	68.0	64.0	64.9	67.0
General government consumption	9.6	11.1	11.6	11.4	11.3
Gross domestic investment	20.9	24.0	26.5	24.1	23.2
Exports of goods and nfs	6.5	6.0	7.9	9.4	9.8
Imports of goods and nfs	10.1	9.1	9.9	9.8	11.3

(Growth rates)

	1980-85	1985-90	1990	1991	1992
Private consumption	5.4	5.1	-0.4	5.9	7.0
General government consumption	7.3	6.3	2.4	0.1	3.3
Gross domestic investment	3.9	7.8	18.9	-14.9	0.1
Exports of goods and nfs	3.7	8.5	15.1	8.5	5.2
Imports of goods and nfs	5.0	3.9	-3.7	-8.0	13.9
Gross national product	5.0	6.2	5.6	0.8	4.9
Gross national income	5.1	6.1	4.7	0.9	4.7

PRICES and GOVERNMENT FINANCE

	1980	1985	1990	1991	1992
Domestic prices (% change)					
Consumer prices	11.4	5.6	9.0	13.9	11.8
Wholesale prices	20.0	4.6	9.0	13.5	11.9
Implicit GDP deflator	11.5	7.5	10.7	13.3	10.1
Government finance (% GDP)					
Current budget balance	..	2.2	-0.1	0.5	0.7
Overall surplus/deficit	..	..	..	..	..

India

POVERTY and SOCIAL
(annual growth rates)

	1980-85	1985-91
Population	2.2	2.1
Labor force	2.0	1.9

most recent estimate (mre)

Headcount index (% of population)	25.4
Energy consumption per capita (kg oil equivalent)	230.7
Infant mortality (per thousand live births)	90.0
Access to safe water (% of population)	73.0
Child malnutrition (% of children under 5)	49.3
Illiteracy (% of population age 15+)	51.8
Secondary enrollment (% of school-age population)	44.0

Development diamond
- Female % labor force
- GNP per capita
- Life expectancy
- Sec. school enrollment

TRADE
(millions US$)

	1980	1985	1990	1991	1992
Total exports (fob)	..	9,463	18,491	18,135	18,400
Tea	..	511	596	494	554
Iron	..	473	584	585	590
Manufactures	..	5,639	13,781	13,773	15,136
Total imports (cif)	..	17,298	25,241	19,726	22,347
Food	..	1,321	690	426	1,311
Fuel and energy	..	4,054	6,028	5,365	6,100
Capital goods	..	3,503	5,833	4,233	4,007
Export price index (1987=100)	..	94	109	100	95
Import price index (1987=100)	..	90	116	104	104
Terms of trade (1987=100)	..	104	94	96	91
Openness of economy	..	12	15	15	17

BALANCE of PAYMENTS
(millions US$)

	1980	1985	1990	1991	1992
Exports of goods and nfs	11,265	12,773	23,425	23,337	23,616
Imports of goods and nfs	17,378	19,422	29,390	24,252	27,233
Resource balance	-6,113	-6,649	-5,965	-915	-3,617
Net factor income	356	-1,552	-3,744	-3,786	-3,614
Net current transfers	2,860	2,207	2,021	2,685	2,200
Current account balance					
Before official transfers	-2,897	-5,994	-7,688	-2,016	-5,031
After official transfers	-2,254	-5,635	-7,212	-1,565	-4,531
Long-term capital inflow	1,982	4,273	3,662	3,473	5,099
Total other items (net)	-1,088	2,174	565	696	-813
Changes in net reserves	1,360	-812	2,985	-2,604	245
Memo:					
Reserves excluding gold (mill. US$)	6,858	6,657	1,521	3,627	5,757
Reserves including gold (mill. US$)	11,924	9,730	5,637	7,616	9,539
Official exchange rate (local/US$)	7.9	12.2	18.0	24.5	29.0

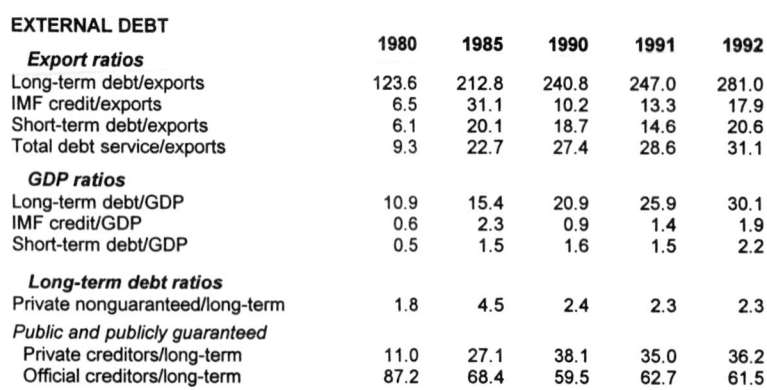

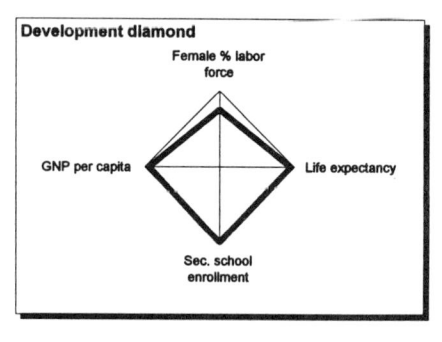

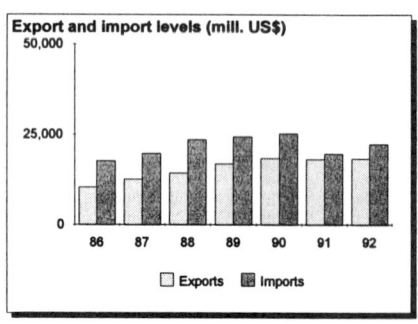

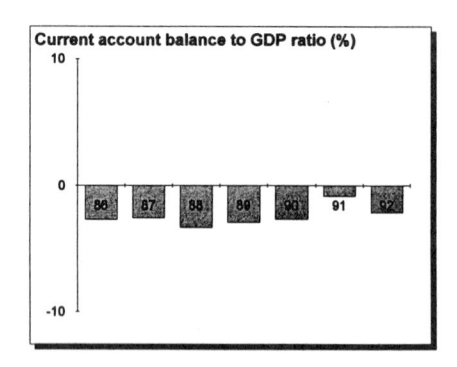

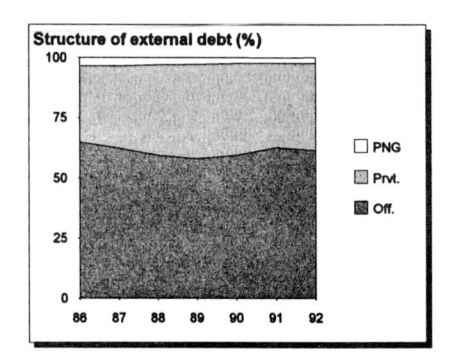

EXTERNAL DEBT

	1980	1985	1990	1991	1992
Export ratios					
Long-term debt/exports	123.6	212.8	240.8	247.0	281.0
IMF credit/exports	6.5	31.1	10.2	13.3	17.9
Short-term debt/exports	6.1	20.1	18.7	14.6	20.6
Total debt service/exports	9.3	22.7	27.4	28.6	31.1
GDP ratios					
Long-term debt/GDP	10.9	15.4	20.9	25.9	30.1
IMF credit/GDP	0.6	2.3	0.9	1.4	1.9
Short-term debt/GDP	0.5	1.5	1.6	1.5	2.2
Long-term debt ratios					
Private nonguaranteed/long-term	1.8	4.5	2.4	2.3	2.3
Public and publicly guaranteed					
Private creditors/long-term	11.0	27.1	38.1	35.0	36.2
Official creditors/long-term	87.2	68.4	59.5	62.7	61.5

Indonesia

The Republic of Indonesia is an archipelago of more than 13,000 islands, with a land area of about 2 million square kilometers. Indonesia's mid-1991 estimated population of 181.3 million, growing at about 1.8 percent a year, make it the world's fourth most populous nation. Indonesia has a diversified resource base, with plentiful primary energy resources, significant mineral deposits, large timber potential, and a well-developed system of agricultural commodity production and exports. A high proportion of these primary resources are in the relatively less populated islands of Sumatra and Kalimantan. Two-thirds of the population lives in Java, which has one of the highest rural population densities in the world. About a quarter of the population lives in urban areas, and urban population growth is over 5 percent a year. The 1991 estimate of GNP per capita was $610. Indonesia has made significant progress in reducing both the absolute number of poor and the incidence of poverty.

Indonesia implemented a comprehensive adjustment program during the 1980s in response to a series of external shocks, including the collapse of oil prices. Oil was then its main source of foreign exchange and budget revenue. Stabilization measures were undertaken to bring spending in line with reduced revenues. Public expenditures were curtailed, monetary growth was restrained, and the exchange rate was devalued sharply. These measures restored stability while protecting economic growth.

Structural reforms were also undertaken. Deregulation since 1985 has lowered trade barriers and eased restrictions on domestic and foreign investment. The share of imports subject to non-tariff restrictions declined from 43 percent in 1986 to around 13 percent, while average nominal tariffs have been halved. Foreign investment is allowed in nearly all sectors and restrictions on land leasing have been significantly eased. Complementary reforms have been undertaken in customs, ports, and shipping operations.

Financial sector reforms have been a prominent component of the structural reform program. Credit ceilings and interest rate controls were removed in 1983. In 1988 measures were taken to make entry easier; this led to the chartering of many new banks. The resulting competition and expansion of banking activity contributed significantly to private investment growth. To promote the soundness of the financial system, the prudential regulation of the banking sector was enhanced, which affected commercial bank portfolios and their uncovered foreign exchange exposure. A further round of reforms in 1990 reduced the role of subsidized directed credits and strengthened the framework for capital market development. In 1991 Bank Indonesia mandated higher risk-adjusted capital requirements that were phased in over 1992 and 1993.

These deregulatory efforts have stimulated private domestic and foreign investment and diversified Indonesia's production and export base. Non-oil exports have risen to about 70 percent of total exports, compared to about 20 percent a decade ago. The private sector accounts for an estimated three-quarters of non-oil economic activity and about two-thirds of fixed investment.

Poverty Reduction

Indonesia has steadily reduced poverty from about 60 percent of the population in 1970 to about 15 percent in 1990. Other indicators of improving living standards for the poor include significant increases in caloric intake, falling infant mortality, universal primary education, and rapidly expanding secondary and tertiary enrollments. Success in reducing poverty is partly attributable to the policies adopted before the external shocks of the 1980s, particularly development of widespread social and economic infrastructure and emphasis on rural development. It is also attributable to government economic adjustment measures that generated broad-based growth in incomes and employment and avoided substantial cutbacks in development expenditures in sectors—such as agriculture and human resource development—that are critical for poverty reduction.

Recent Developments

Signs of an overheating economy emerged in 1990/91 as rapid private sector growth led to a surge in imports and accelerating inflation. Capital goods accounted for two-thirds of the increase in imports, reflecting a rapid increase in private investment. At the same time, there was a slowdown in non-oil export growth. As a result, the current account deficit widened to about 3 percent of GNP in 1990/91, and inflation reached 7.9 percent.

The government took measures to reduce aggregate demand. Monetary policy was tightened by reducing subsidized directed credits, requiring some public enterprises to purchase Bank Indonesia certificates—thus reducing the money supply—and curtailing public sector foreign borrowing. Domestic interest rates rose sharply, and credit growth decelerated from about 70 percent in 1990/91 to about 35 percent in 1991/92. Fiscal measures also helped dampen domestic demand. Continuing improvements in tax administration and selective tax increases contributed to stronger growth in non-oil tax revenues than anticipated. The overall budgetary position showed a small surplus in 1991/92, despite a sharp drop in oil revenues caused by the fall in world oil prices.

With tight domestic monetary policies and expanding domestic demand, particularly private investment, offshore borrowing by the private sector and commercial banks rose significantly in 1990 and in the first half of 1991. In addition, substantial new foreign borrowings were planned to finance a number of large, capital-intensive, public and publicly-related projects. The government established the Commercial Offshore Loan Team in September 1991 to coordinate approaches to international capital markets. In October 1991 the team deferred a number of large projects and established annual ceilings for commercial borrowings for such projects.

These policies achieved substantial adjustment by the end of 1992/93. The current account deficit narrowed to 2.4 percent of GNP from 3.8 percent in 1991/92, while inflation was brought down to 7.5 percent in 1992 from 9.4 percent in 1991. Economic growth was only modestly affected, slowing to 5.8 percent in 1992 from 6.6 percent in 1991. The external sector contributed to the adjustment as non-oil imports grew by 7.7 percent while non-oil exports grew at 26.6 percent, allowing a reduction in the current account deficit despite a $1.1 billion deterioration on the oil accounts. Public and private growth slowed in 1992, further contributing to the adjustment. The industry growth rate slackened to 5.5 percent, but non-oil manufacturing remained buoyant. Agriculture grew by 3.6 percent, picking up smartly from the previous year's drought-plagued poor performance.

The capital account featured a sharp rise in short-term capital inflows linked to the high real interest rates associated with the restrained monetary stance. A decline in net long-term loan disbursements was coupled with a slight increase in foreign direct investment. Overall, the medium- and long-term debt service ratio improved marginally from 31.6 percent of exports to 30.0 percent, while total debt outstanding declined from 59.0 percent of GNP in 1991 to 57.9 percent in 1992.

Medium-Term Prospects

Indonesia has experienced steady growth within a stable macroeconomic framework, despite large external shocks and considerable uncertainty in the world trading environment. Growth has been based on dynamic private sector activity in the non-oil sector. The main challenges for the future are to grow in a manner and at a rate sufficient to absorb the growing labor force effectively and productively. This is necessary to further reduce the incidence of poverty, and ensure longer-term sustainable development.

Over the medium term, the balance of payments position is expected to be eased by the demand-constraining effects of prudent macroeconomic policies and the supply expansion from ongoing investments in new export capacity. During the remainder of the decade, non-oil exports are projected to grow about 9 percent a year in real terms, while growth in non-oil imports is projected to average about 7 percent. This is expected to lead to a steady reduction in the current account deficit to about 2 percent of GNP by 1995.

Economic growth is expected to slow slightly to about 6 percent over the next few years as the contribution from oil stabilizes. This level is consistent with external and internal balances. Over the medium term growth in the non-oil economy can be sustained at around 6.5 to 7.0 percent a year. Ongoing trade and industrial sector reforms should continue to open profitable areas for relatively labor-intensive efficient export industries.

The expected pace and pattern of growth would allow Indonesia to absorb its expanding labor force at higher levels of productivity, and income. The sustained improvement in the fiscal position would also enable the government to provide effective programs that enhance the opportunities, productivity, and quality of life for the poor. Overall, Indonesia is expected to be able to secure an increase in real GDP of almost 70 percent during the 1990s, raise per capita incomes by over 40 percent in real terms, and achieve continued reductions in poverty.

External Debt

With continued sound economic management and given projected trends in the world economy, Indonesia should continue to make good progress in reducing its debt burden and improving its debt servicing capacity. The debt service ratio for medium- and long-term debt is expected to decline from about 30 percent in 1993 to 25 percent in 1995 and below 20 percent by the year 2000. Similar declines are projected in the ratios of debt-to-exports and debt-to-GNP.

Indonesia

Population mid-1991 (millions)	181.3
GNP per capita 1991 (US$)	610

Income group: **Low**
Indebtedness level: **Moderate**

KEY RATIOS

	1980	1985	1990	1991	1992
Gross domestic investment/GDP	24.3	28.0	35.4	35.1	36.3
Exports of goods and nfs/GDP	33.0	22.2	27.5	27.4	27.4
Gross domestic savings/GDP	37.1	29.8	37.1	35.7	40.3
Gross national savings/GDP	33.0	25.8	32.4	31.1	36.0
Current account balance/GDP	3.6	-2.2	-3.0	-3.6	-3.2
Interest payments/GDP	1.5	2.3	3.0	3.0	3.1
Total debt/GDP	26.8	39.3	62.9	63.2	60.7
Total debt/exports	94.2	169.9	225.1	223.2	204.9

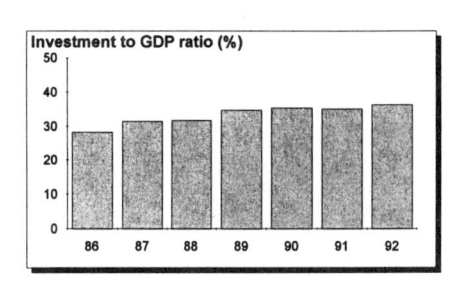

GDP: PRODUCTION

(% GDP)	1980	1985	1990	1991	1992
Agriculture	24.0	23.2	21.4	19.5	18.6
Industry	41.7	35.8	39.3	41.2	40.8
Manufacturing	13.0	16.0	20.3	21.3	20.7
Services	34.3	40.9	39.2	39.3	40.7

(Growth rates)	1980-85	1985-90	1990	1991	1992
Agriculture	3.0	3.1	2.0	1.3	3.6
Industry	4.7	6.4	9.7	9.9	5.5
Manufacturing	13.0	10.1	12.2	9.8	8.7
Services	6.6	7.1	7.3	5.8	7.2
GDP	5.0	5.9	7.0	6.4	5.8

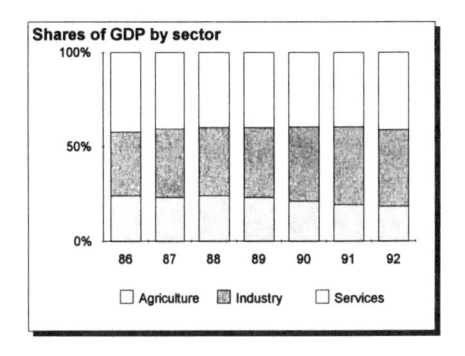

GDP: EXPENDITURE

(% GDP)	1980	1985	1990	1991	1992
Private consumption	52.3	59.0	54.0	55.1	50.8
General government consumption	10.5	11.2	8.9	9.2	8.9
Gross domestic investment	24.3	28.0	35.4	35.1	36.3
Exports of goods and nfs	33.0	22.2	27.5	27.4	27.4
Imports of goods and nfs	20.2	20.4	25.7	26.8	23.4

(Growth rates)	1980-85	1985-90	1990	1991	1992
Private consumption	5.5	4.2	9.3	8.9	3.2
General government consumption	4.7	5.0	3.2	7.2	3.3
Gross domestic investment	10.7	4.5	18.1	-1.2	0.5
Exports of goods and nfs	-4.3	8.8	1.4	19.4	7.9
Imports of goods and nfs	2.7	2.3	20.8	14.2	-5.2
Gross national product	5.3	6.2	6.7	6.5	6.1
Gross national income	4.8	4.8	10.2	4.2	6.2

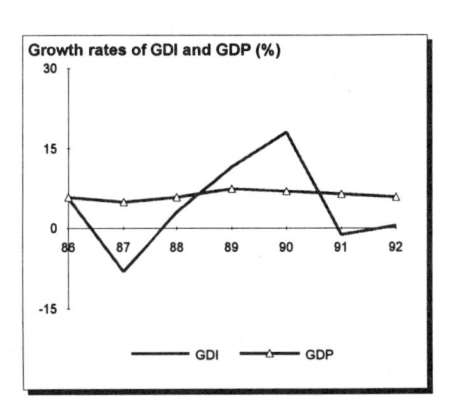

PRICES and GOVERNMENT FINANCE

	1980	1985	1990	1991	1992
Domestic prices (% change)					
Consumer prices	18.0	4.7	7.5	9.2	7.5
Wholesale prices	26.8	5.0	10.0	5.2	5.2
Implicit GDP deflator	31.9	5.1	10.1	8.4	6.2
Government finance (% GDP)					
Current budget balance	..	6.2	8.6	7.1	6.7
Overall surplus/deficit	..	-2.8	1.7	-0.8	-1.3

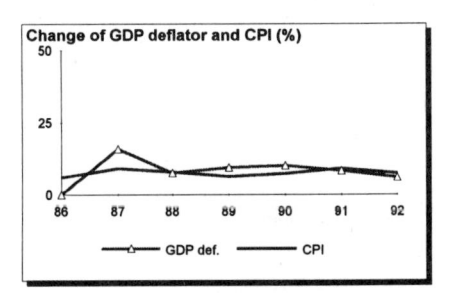

Indonesia

POVERTY and SOCIAL
(annual growth rates)

	1980-85	1985-91
Population	1.9	1.8
Labor force	2.4	..

most recent estimate (mre)

Headcount index (% of population)	16.7
Energy consumption per capita (kg oil equivalent)	272.4
Infant mortality (per thousand live births)	74.0
Access to safe water (% of population)	42.0
Child malnutrition (% of children under 5)	14.0
Illiteracy (% of population age 15+)	23.0
Secondary enrollment (% of school-age population)	45.0

Development diamond: Female % labor force, GNP per capita, Life expectancy, Sec. school enrollment

TRADE a/
(millions US$)

	1980	1985	1990	1991	1992
Total exports (fob)	..	18,823	28,016	29,354	34,910
Fuel	..	12,804	12,636	10,581	10,348
Rubber	..	714	902	932	1,078
Manufactures	..	2,287	9,472	12,171	17,261
Total imports (cif)	..	14,056	25,671	27,819	31,048
Food	..	812	940	979	1,172
Fuel and energy	..	2,870	4,062	3,591	3,812
Capital goods	..	5,394	11,685	13,100	14,487
Export price index (1987=100)	..	117	125	116	126
Import price index (1987=100)	..	85	114	117	122
Terms of trade (1987=100)	..	138	110	99	103
Openness of economy	..	38	50	49	52

BALANCE of PAYMENTS
(millions US$)

	1980	1985	1990	1991	1992
Exports of goods and nfs	22,122	19,371	29,295	32,282	36,334
Imports of goods and nfs	16,101	17,840	27,511	31,120	34,329
Resource balance	6,021	1,531	1,784	1,162	2,005
Net factor income	-3,211	-3,542	-5,190	-5,504	-6,196
Net current transfers	0	0	166	130	173
Current account balance					
Before official transfers	2,805	-1,950	-3,240	-4,212	-4,019
After official transfers	3,006	-1,923	-2,988	-4,080	-3,669
Long-term capital inflow	2,153	1,880	4,724	5,912	3,584
Total other items (net)	-2,553	553	515	-303	1,442
Changes in net reserves	-2,606	-510	-2,251	-1,529	-1,357
Memo:					
Reserves excluding gold (mill. US$)	5,392	4,974	7,459	9,258	10,449
Reserves including gold (mill. US$)	6,803	5,989	8,657	10,358	11,482
Official exchange rate (local/US$)	627.0	1,110.6	1,842.8	1,950.3	2,029.9

EXTERNAL DEBT

	1980	1985	1990	1991	1992
Export ratios					
Long-term debt/exports	81.7	151.7	185.6	181.8	163.8
IMF credit/exports	0.0	0.2	1.7	0.5	0.0
Short-term debt/exports	12.5	18.0	37.8	40.9	41.1
Total debt service/exports	13.9	28.8	31.1	32.7	32.4
GDP ratios					
Long-term debt/GDP	23.3	35.1	51.9	51.5	48.5
IMF credit/GDP	0.0	0.1	0.5	0.1	0.0
Short-term debt/GDP	3.6	4.2	10.6	11.6	12.2
Long-term debt ratios					
Private nonguaranteed/long-term	17.3	12.6	18.8	19.9	21.1
Public and publicly guaranteed					
Private creditors/long-term	30.1	38.2	21.1	18.0	15.9
Official creditors/long-term	52.6	49.2	60.0	62.1	63.1

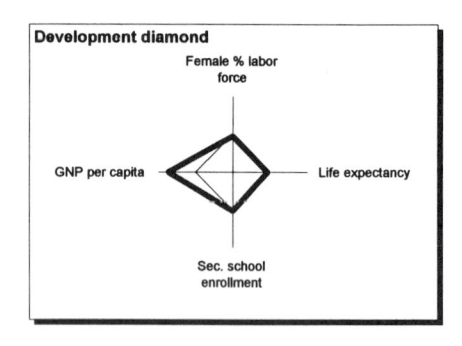

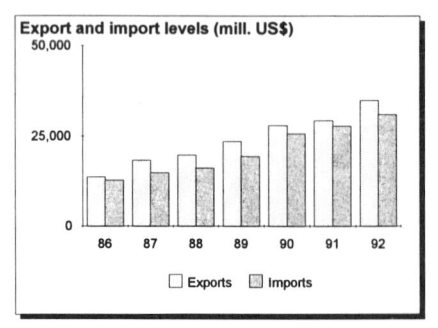

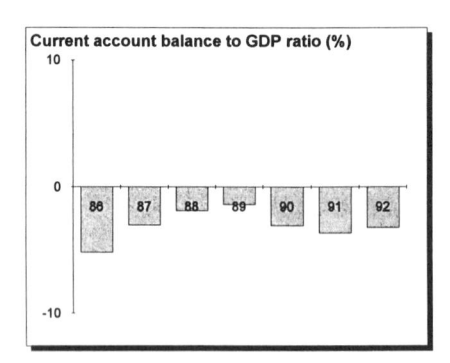

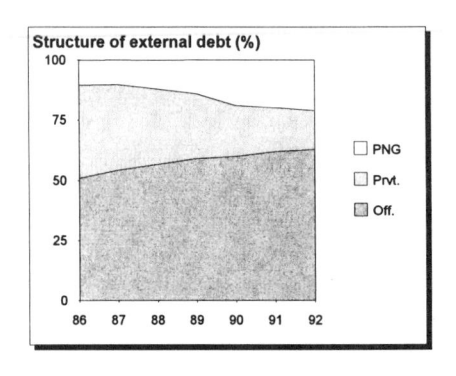

a. Fiscal year (April to March).

Jordan

Jordan's economy is relatively small and its performance and prospects reflect its resource base and its proximity to the high-income, oil-exporting countries. Apart from its well trained human resources, the only natural resources Jordan has are phosphate, potash, and limestone. Less than 5 percent of its agricultural land is arable; water is scarce, and virtually all of its energy needs have to be imported. Jordan has a narrow productive base, with a very large services sector contributing some 65 percent of GDP. Worker remittances and financial assistance from high-income oil exporting regional countries greatly influence Jordan's income levels and economic activity.

Jordan has developed a strong human resource base, and its education attainment, particularly in science and engineering, is among the highest of the lower-middle income countries. Its illiteracy rate of 20 percent is about 27 percentage points lower than the regional average. The public health service in Jordan is highly accessible, and child immunization rates are 5 to 10 percentage points higher than regional averages. Jordan's infant mortality rate, 51 per 1,000 live births is also well below the regional average. Jordan's strong human capital base has enabled it to compensate for its poor resource endowment by exporting its surplus skills to the oil-producing countries in the region.

Jordan enjoyed rapid economic growth during the 1970s and the first half of the 1980s. Since then its economy has been adversely affected by the sharp drop in oil prices and the subsequent slowdown in regional economies. GDP declined by an average of 3 percent a year between 1987 and 1991; this combined with an average growth in population of 3.7 percent—excluding returning emigrants—resulted in a sharp fall in per capita income to an estimated $1,050 in 1991. During this period Jordan incurred large fiscal and balance of payments deficits; the external borrowing needed to finance the deficits led to a heavy external debt burden.

Situated in a politically volatile region, stability in and outside Jordan is always a major factor influencing economic performance. Jordan has managed to maintain both political stability at home while moving forward with political liberalization: comprehensive general elections were held in October 1989 for the first time in more than two decades. The next general elections are scheduled for October 1993.

Recent Economic Performance

Jordan began a series of policy adjustments in 1988 to overcome the economic stagnation and imbalances that developed in the 1980s. Since 1989 it has undertaken a series of fiscal adjustments to reduce the budget deficit, including containing military expenditures, reducing consumer subsidies and tariffs, and reforming taxes to enlarge the revenue base and enhance revenue performance. Jordan devalued its exchange rate significantly in 1989, and has since pursued a flexible exchange rate policy to maintain competitiveness. It lowered maximum tariff rates, with a few exceptions, from 318 to 50 percent, cut back tariff exemptions that once covered nearly half of all imports, and removed quantitative import restrictions. It has deregulated interest rates and adopted measures to strengthen institutional support for private sector development in trade and industry.

The adjustment program was being successfully implemented when the Gulf Crisis intervened in mid-1990. Jordan lost its major export markets and aid from the Gulf countries, and suffered losses in revenue from transit trade and worker remittances. It also had to shoulder the cost of social services for approximately 300,000 returnees. After the crisis, the government resumed its reform program.

Jordan has reached a debt rescheduling agreement with the Paris Club; bilateral agreements with all of the 12 members have been concluded. Substantial progress has been made in negotiations with the London Club. The debt owed to the former Soviet Union was bought back at a substantially reduced price.

Adjustment efforts since 1989 have improved the incentive structure and business confidence. These improvements, combined with unusually large transfers of savings and remittances since the Gulf Crisis ended have led to a surge in economic activity. Economic performance in 1992 was much better than anticipated at the beginning of the year. Data for 1992 indicate that real GDP growth exceeded 11 percent. Spearheaded mainly by a surge in home-building, the construction sector is estimated to have grown in real terms by some 22 percent. After a bad year in 1991 agriculture, mining, and manufacturing have come back strongly. Agriculture and manufacturing are estimated to have grown 10 percent each, and growth in these sectors provided an impetus for recovery in the service sectors.

Jordan's stabilization efforts have also improved its internal and external imbalances. The budget deficit was brought down from 21 percent of GDP in 1989 to just under 18 percent in 1991. The government took several measures to increase revenues and cut expenditures, including canceling a $1 billion contract to buy military aircraft that would have added about 2 percent of GDP to interest payments on external debt. This trend continued into 1992.

Preliminary estimates indicate that GDP growth, good revenue performance and restraints on expenditures, have reduced the deficit to 4 percent of GDP, well below the government's 13.7 percent target. Through the successful implementation of stabilization and demand management measures, inflation, as measured by the GDP deflator, continued to decline from about 21.5 percent in 1989 to around 5.3 percent in 1992.

External Balances

The current account deficit, excluding Gulf Crisis-related grants, improved slightly in 1991, to $712 million, compared to $754 million in 1990. The deficit is estimated to have increased to $745 million in 1992. This deficit, along with scheduled amortization and payment of arrears, raised Jordan's financial requirements to over $1.9 billion, but disbursements of external grants and loans, debt rescheduling, and transfers of worker savings and remittances were more than sufficient to meet the requirements. As a result, external reserves at the Central Bank of Jordan, excluding foreign exchange deposits by residents, increased from $220 million in 1990 to about $750 million by end-1992, equivalent to about three months of imports.

Development Strategy

Jordan's long-term strategy calls for reducing dependence on the economic performance of neighboring countries by diversifying export markets and expanding domestic production and employment. However, favorable developments in the region could present Jordan with renewed opportunities for growth. A resumption of sustained growth in neighboring countries would result in strong demand for Jordanian manufactures and farm produce. Reconstruction in Iraq would find Jordan is poised to become a major supplier/re-exporter of construction materials and services, and provide maintenance services for power plants, commercial aircraft, roads and telecommunications. Normalization of relationships in the region should also result in the resumption of external financial support on concessional terms.

These developments — and particularly their timing — are uncertain, however, and Jordan faces substantial risks to its growth prospects. One risk stems from Jordan's continued need for exceptional financial support at highly concessional terms over the next two to three years, and annual debt rescheduling through 1998. Worker remittances are also difficult to predict, and substantial declines in those remittances could greatly enlarge Jordan's balance of payments gap and cause sharp import compression that would curtail GDP growth. Jordan is also vulnerable to falling phosphate prices.

Jordan is seeking to balance its short-run stabilization objectives with longer-run objectives of restructuring the economy, reducing poverty and population growth, and protect the environment. Its broad strategy is to diversify the economy by implementing an outward-oriented and private-sector-led approach while maintaining macroeconomic balances, creating an enabling business environment, and providing needed physical and social infrastructure.

Jordan must import all its primary energy needs, and the government has recently formulated an energy sector adjustment program to improve sector efficiency through the economic pricing of energy products, energy demand management and conservation programs. It is developing a long-term strategy for energy resource development, including ways to use natural gas and actions needed for environmental protection and energy conservation.

Jordan has taken measures to deregulate agricultural production and trade and to improve farmer support services. Road transporters in Jordan benefit from low trucking tariffs set by the government; in addition, as much as 40 to 60 percent truck overloading is allowed. Very high axle loads and a lack of quality assurance in road construction have led to an exceptional rate of road pavement deterioration, which is exacerbated by insufficient road maintenance funding. The trucking fleet in Jordan is about ten years old, and vehicle replacement is retarded by transport tariffs and high import duties. The decapitalization of road assets and aging trucking fleet are critical developmental constraints, as Jordan is dependent on efficient transport to and from the port of Aqaba for international trade and on income generated from transit traffic. The government has decided to lower the axle load limit to 13 tons over two years and is studying cost recovery, tariff setting and the road overloading/deterioration issues.

Public Enterprises

Several of Jordan's public enterprises have become highly indebted, incur losses and are a major burden on the budget. To begin with, the government plans to concentrate on the most problematic of these enterprises. The Water Authority of Jordan, which is responsible for most domestic and industrial water supply and sewerage systems, has severe financial problems, and requires large tariff increases to cover its operations and maintenance costs and service its debt. The government's objective is to attain full cost recovery over the medium term. The Aqaba Railway Corporation is incurring operational losses despite raising its freight charges in 1991. The dedicated phosphate railway is plagued by old tracks, poor equipment maintenance, weak management, and debt service difficulties.

The financial situation of Royal Jordanian Airlines is also precarious, and the government has decided, in principle, to privatize it.

Poverty Reduction Efforts

Preliminary studies show that poverty has grown over the past four years as per capita incomes and consumption have declined; it is estimated that 9 percent of Jordanians live in households that fall below the abject poverty line, and 20 percent live in households below the poverty line.

Though real wages have fallen in the public and the private sectors sectoral rigidities in the labor market may prevent labor from moving to its most efficient use and generate additional unemployment. Present macroeconomic and sectoral policies may not generate sufficient private sector investment and employment to promote the growth necessary to contain poverty and to prevent it from spreading to the near-poor. Accelerated growth will be encouraged by trade reform, privatization, competition and private sector development, and governmental reform.

Jordan provides health and education services for the poor, and social indicators are good for a country of Jordan's income level. Population increases and reduced expenditures under the adjustment program could reduce the quality of these services unless there is better resource mobilization.

Medium-Term Prospects

The government has set growth and economic stabilization targets for the next five years, including maintaining GDP growth at 5 to 6 percent, reducing the fiscal deficit to 2.5 percent of GDP and achieving a current account surplus of 2 percent of GDP by 1998, and containing inflation at 4 to 5 percent.

The GDP growth target of 5 to 6 percent for over 1993–98 envisages an investment level of 23 percent of GDP in 1993, declining to about 19.5 percent in 1998, and an import elasticity, on average, of about 0.7. The implicit improvement in investment and import efficiency reflects the anticipated impact of policy reforms and the absence of serious capacity bottlenecks. At the same time, an increasing share of investment must be financed by domestic savings, which are projected to increase from dissavings in 1992 to 5 percent of GDP in 1998. The required increase in domestic savings, which would entail declines in per capita consumption in the medium term, will be achieved through several policy changes. A sharp reduction of the budget deficit is expected to play an important role in raising public savings: the deficit reduction from 6 percent of GDP in 1993 to 2 percent in 1998 would raise public savings from nearly zero percent of GDP in 1993 to 6.4 percent in 1998. Jordan's recent lifting of interest ceilings constitutes an important first step toward more effective use of financial market instruments to mobilize domestic resources.

External Debt

Jordan's large external debt stock of over 120 percent of GDP between 1993 and 1995 will also influence its growth prospects and balance of payments position over the medium term. Jordan is using buybacks, annual rescheduling and external borrowing at the most concessionary terms to restructure its external debt, and intends to seek exceptional donor assistance to bridge its balance of payments gaps over the next two to three years.

Jordan

Population mid-1991 (millions) a/	3.7
GNP per capita 1991 (US$)	1,050

Income group: **Lower-middle**
Indebtedness level: **Severe**

KEY RATIOS

	1980	1985	1990	1991	1992
Gross domestic investment/GDP	..	21.7	28.8	24.0	31.6
Exports of goods and nfs/GDP	..	37.2	49.6	43.0	43.0
Gross domestic savings/GDP	..	-17.4	-16.3	-15.8	-17.8
Gross national savings/GDP	..	-2.2	-14.9	-14.7	-6.6
Current account balance/GDP	..	-19.6	-29.0	-21.4	-22.7
Interest payments/GDP	..	4.1	7.6	7.4	8.9
Total debt/GDP	..	82.4	210.4	211.4	169.4
Total debt/exports	79.0	134.3	270.5	283.4	226.6

GDP: PRODUCTION

(% GDP)	1980	1985	1990	1991	1992
Agriculture	..	4.9	7.9	7.2	7.3
Industry	..	26.9	29.4	27.1	27.5
Manufacturing	..	11.9	15.2	14.2	15.3
Services	..	68.2	62.7	65.7	65.2

(Growth rates)	1980-85	1985-90	1990	1991	1992
Agriculture	..	..	..	..	..
Industry	..	..	..	..	..
Manufacturing	..	..	..	..	..
Services	..	..	..	..	..
GDP	..	-1.6	1.7	1.8	11.3

GDP: EXPENDITURE

(% GDP)	1980	1985	1990	1991	1992
Private consumption	..	90.6	91.1	89.2	94.2
General government consumption	..	26.8	25.2	26.6	23.7
Gross domestic investment	..	21.7	28.8	24.0	31.6
Exports of goods and nfs	..	37.2	49.6	43.0	43.0
Imports of goods and nfs	..	76.3	94.7	82.9	92.4

(Growth rates)	1980-85	1985-90	1990	1991	1992
Private consumption	..	..	..	..	..
General government consumption	..	..	..	..	..
Gross domestic investment	..	..	..	..	..
Exports of goods and nfs	..	..	..	..	..
Imports of goods and nfs	..	..	..	..	..
Gross national product	..	-3.5	0.8	3.3	13.6
Gross national income	..	..	..	..	..

PRICES and GOVERNMENT FINANCE

	1980	1985	1990	1991	1992
Domestic prices					
(% change)					
Consumer prices	11.1	3.0	16.2	8.2	4.0
Wholesale prices	..	..	..	..	..
Implicit GDP deflator	..	-1.8	10.2	4.5	5.3
Government finance					
(% GDP)					
Current budget balance	..	-11.6	-12.5	-13.1	1.5
Overall surplus/deficit	..	..	..	..	..

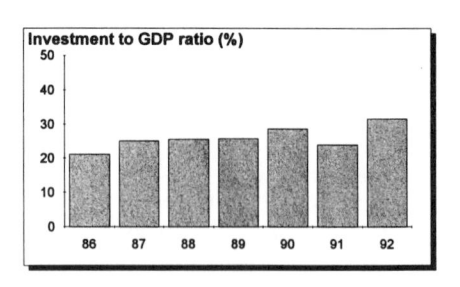

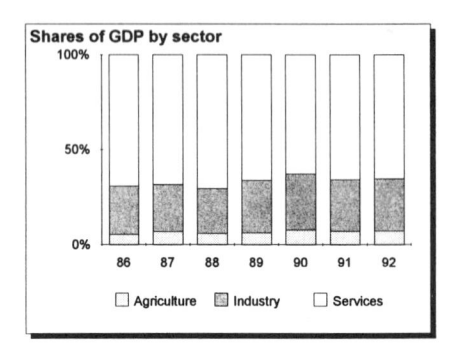

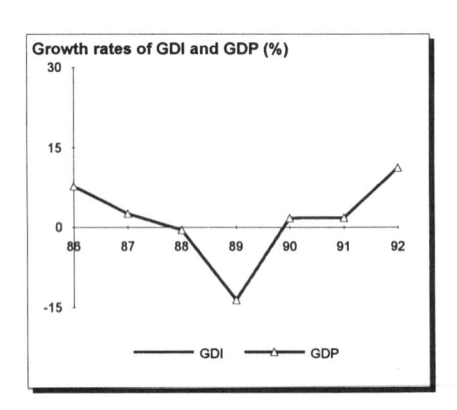

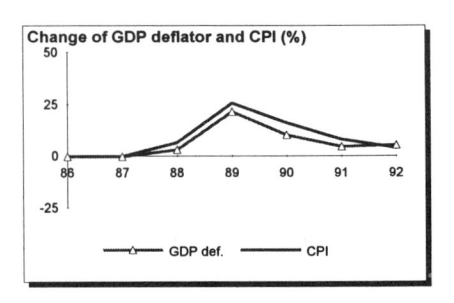

Jordan

POVERTY and SOCIAL
(annual growth rates)

	1980-85	1985-91
Population	3.9	5.0
Labor force	4.3	4.3

most recent estimate (mre)

Headcount index (% of population)	..
Energy consumption per capita (kg oil equivalent)	994.3
Infant mortality (per thousand live births)	29.0
Access to safe water (% of population)	..
Child malnutrition (% of children under 5)	..
Illiteracy (% of population age 15+)	19.9
Secondary enrollment (% of school-age population)	79.0

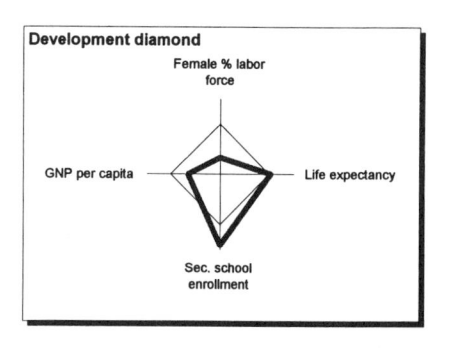

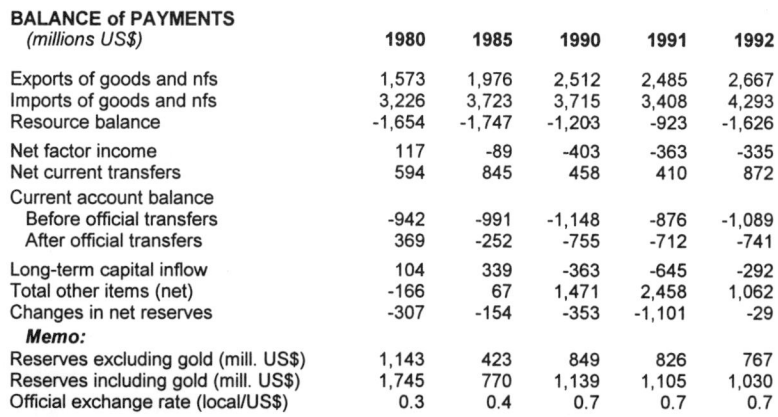

Development diamond

TRADE
(millions US$)

	1980	1985	1990	1991	1992
Total exports (fob)	..	789	1,064	1,132	1,220
Phosphorus	..	168	209	181	180
Other metals	..	79	133	142	127
Manufactures	..	263	394	349	445
Total imports (cif)	..	2,723	2,732	2,571	3,339
Food	..	481	657	662	681
Fuel and energy	..	566	470	430	446
Capital goods	..	1,393	1,519	1,379	2,129
Export price index (1987=100)	..	93	116	119	..
Import price index (1987=100)	..	92	112	108	..
Terms of trade (1987=100)	..	101	104	110	..
Openness of economy	..	70	96	91	95

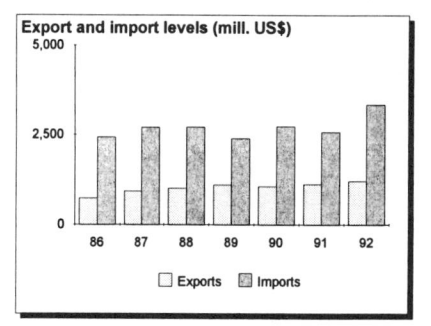

Export and import levels (mill. US$)

BALANCE of PAYMENTS
(millions US$)

	1980	1985	1990	1991	1992
Exports of goods and nfs	1,573	1,976	2,512	2,485	2,667
Imports of goods and nfs	3,226	3,723	3,715	3,408	4,293
Resource balance	-1,654	-1,747	-1,203	-923	-1,626
Net factor income	117	-89	-403	-363	-335
Net current transfers	594	845	458	410	872
Current account balance					
Before official transfers	-942	-991	-1,148	-876	-1,089
After official transfers	369	-252	-755	-712	-741
Long-term capital inflow	104	339	-363	-645	-292
Total other items (net)	-166	67	1,471	2,458	1,062
Changes in net reserves	-307	-154	-353	-1,101	-29
Memo:					
Reserves excluding gold (mill. US$)	1,143	423	849	826	767
Reserves including gold (mill. US$)	1,745	770	1,139	1,105	1,030
Official exchange rate (local/US$)	0.3	0.4	0.7	0.7	0.7

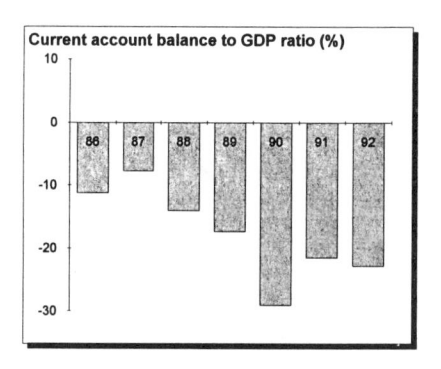

Current account balance to GDP ratio (%)

EXTERNAL DEBT

	1980	1985	1990	1991	1992
Export ratios					
Long-term debt/exports	59.5	109.9	232.0	248.3	207.5
IMF credit/exports	0.0	2.0	3.1	3.1	2.4
Short-term debt/exports	19.5	22.4	35.4	32.0	16.8
Total debt service/exports	8.4	18.2	19.7	20.9	37.7
GDP ratios					
Long-term debt/GDP	..	67.4	180.5	185.2	155.1
IMF credit/GDP	..	1.2	2.4	2.3	1.8
Short-term debt/GDP	..	13.7	27.6	23.9	12.5
Long-term debt ratios					
Private nonguaranteed/long-term	0.0	0.0	0.0	0.0	0.0
Public and publicly guaranteed					
Private creditors/long-term	18.5	34.2	40.6	37.1	46.7
Official creditors/long-term	81.4	65.8	59.4	62.9	53.3

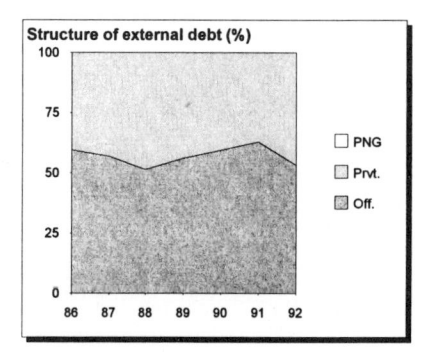

Structure of external debt (%)

a. East Bank.

Republic of Korea

Korea has been among the most successful developing countries in the post-war period. A little more than 30 years ago, it was among the poorest countries, heavily dependent on agriculture and facing perennial balance of payments deficits financed almost entirely through foreign grants. Since 1960, however, real GNP growth averaging about 9 percent has increased per capita incomes almost 15-fold. This performance has been underpinned by annual export growth of about 20 percent in real terms, and Korea has become the world's 11th largest trading nation, with exports that span a wide range of sophisticated industrial products.

Korea's remarkable success can be attributed to several factors. Important elements include its strong outward orientation and its reliance on signals and incentives—such as exchange rates, interest rates and domestic pricing—that have been broadly in line with market-based outcomes. Macroeconomic management has been generally conservative and flexible, with policy makers adjusting rapidly and decisively to external shocks, as was demonstrated after the second oil price shock in the late 1970s. Finally, medium-term structural adjustment issues were tackled forthrightly through a series of pre-announced reform programs in the trade, industry, and energy sectors.

The Korean economy fared well in the 1980s within this framework of efficiency-oriented macroeconomic and structural policies. After averaging almost 9 percent growth during the Fifth Plan (1982–86) and reducing fiscal and current account deficits substantially, a major economic boom followed over 1986–88. Aided chiefly by favorable external factors such as low oil prices, low value of the won, and low interest rates, real GNP grew at over 12 percent a year. Average export growth of over 20 percent during this period led to large and rising current account surpluses—over 8 percent of GNP in 1988—which allowed a substantial improvement in Korea's external debt position.

Recent Developments

Korea's economic situation shifted dramatically in 1989. GNP growth decelerated to 6.8 percent and, after rebounding to about 9.0 percent in 1990 and 1991, declined to 4.8 percent in 1992. The drop in GNP growth was chiefly a result of slow export growth, due in large part to high wage increases in the late 1980s. The current account balance turned to a deficit in 1990, and worsened to about 3 percent of GNP in 1991.

The key difference between these two periods was in the main source of economic growth. Over 1989–91 domestic demand rather than the external sector was the primary source of growth. Exports actually decreased by 3.8 percent in 1989, and even in 1990 and 1991 grew more sluggishly than in the past. In contrast, imports grew at over 15 percent a year. Domestic demand growth was underpinned by growth in private consumption and construction investment. Private consumption grew faster than GNP, at an average rate of 10.1 percent over 1989–91, due mainly to large wage increases—over 20 percent a year in manufacturing—and capital gains from appreciating real estate prices. Construction investment rose at over 19 percent a year as a result of President Roh Tae Woo's 1987 campaign pledge in 1987 to build two million housing units.

By the second half of 1991 it was evident to the Korean authorities that overheated domestic demand was resulting in serious external and domestic imbalances. Inflationary pressures were beginning to re-emerge, with consumer price index inflation in 1991 reaching almost double-digit levels. The current account balance continued to deteriorate, and by 1991 the current account deficit had risen to $8.6 billion. The policy response to these imbalances in late 1991 took the form of administrative measures to curb construction investment, limits on foreign borrowing by commercial banks, and a slight tightening of monetary policy. In 1992 these measures were supplemented with a reduction in the official wage guideline for large companies, and a tightening of fiscal policy.

These policies to restrain domestic demand were intended to reduce inflation and improve the current account deficit while slowing GDP growth to about 7 percent. However, economic activity slowed more than was anticipated. Compared to about 8.4 percent in 1991, real GDP growth in 1992 fell to 4.8 percent, the slowest growth since 1980. Moreover, annualized growth rates fell continuously in 1992, with less than 3 percent growth in the last quarter. This sharp decline in growth reflects particular weakness in fixed investment in construction and equipment, which actually declined in 1992. These measures were successful in stabilizing the economy, however, consumer price inflation slowed in 1992 to less than 5 percent, while weak domestic demand slowed import growth to about 3 percent. Exports remained buoyant in 1992, although growth slowed in the fourth quarter, and the current account deficit fell to $4.6 billion, almost half its 1991 level.

Poverty and the Environment

While absolute poverty has virtually been eliminated in Korea, a perception of relative deprivation among the low- and middle-income groups has grown as democratization has progressed. It is widely believed that the distribution of wealth, if not income, has become more skewed due toward "unearned" capital gains from recent increases in real estate prices and the lack of an efficient tax system to capture the surplus. There is also a perception that the concentration of economic power increased during the 1980s, and that existing legislation to counter monopolistic and restrictive trade practices should be strengthened.

Among the most visible side effects of rapid economic growth in Korea has been a worsening of environmental conditions. Problems of air and water pollution, land degradation, and solid waste generation became more evident during the 1980s. Moreover, with political liberalization, citizen groups and the media increased the pressure on the government to improve environmental management. The scope of environmental legislation was broadened in 1991, and its implementation strengthened with the upgrading of the Ministry of the Environment. The government now has a stronger mandate to address environmental problems.

Medium-Term Prospects

The government's development objectives are outlined in the Seventh Five-Year Economic and Social Development Plan (1992–96), whose goal is to establish the foundation for Korea to become an advanced country by the end of the century. The plan has four basic policy goals: strengthening industrial competitiveness; improving social welfare and equity; promoting liberalization, and encouraging market forces and private sector initiatives.

As the Korean economy matures, the growth rates attained over 1986–91 will be difficult to replicate while maintaining price stability and external balance. Despite the current slowdown, however, GNP growth for the Seventh Plan period is still expected to range between 7 and 8 percent. The new administration of President Young-Sam Kim, the first civilian government in Korea in over 30 years, is also revising the plan. The revised version, to be released by end-1993, is expected to place greater emphasis on equity and economic liberalization. Recent estimates by the Korea's Economic Planning Board anticipate slightly lower growth—7 percent a year—for the revised plan period covering 1993-97. Consumer price inflation is expected to decline to about 3 percent by 1997.

The national savings rate during the Seventh Plan period is expected to remain roughly constant at about 35 percent of GNP. The share of investment to GDP has already fallen from its 1991 peak of almost 39 percent and is anticipated to stabilize at about 35 percent. Export volumes are expected to grow at about 8 to 9 percent during this period as recovery proceeds in OECD economies. Import volume growth would rise to between 5 and 6 percent as more rapid growth resumes in Korea. The merchandise trade balance is anticipated to switch into surplus by the end of the period.

The current account deficit is expected to decline further in 1993. Government estimates show a current account surplus of over 1 percent of GNP by 1997. However, this outcome may not occur if further liberalization of the capital account results, as would be expected, in net capital inflows and higher investment. Hence, a small current account deficit may remain in the medium term. A continuing deficit would not be a significant concern, given Korea's low debt-service burden following the reduction in its stock of external debt in the late 1980s.

It is widely perceived within Korea both in government and in industry, that lags in upgrading technology could be the main operative constraint to attaining industrialized country status. Indeed, the Seventh Plan has identified technology development as the most crucial issue and the government plans to invest 1 trillion won—$1.4 billion—in a science and technology development fund in an effort to boost the ratio of research and development investment to GNP from the current 2 percent to an ambitious 3 to 4 percent by 1996. The government also plans to increase its the science and technology budget from its current share of 3 percent of total government budget to 4 to 5 percent by 1996, raising the government's share in science and technology investment to 30 percent from the current 25 percent. Tax and financial incentives for technology development of the private sector will also be strengthened.

Korea also plans to continues liberalizing its economy. Since the early 1980s Korea has made substantial progress in trade liberalization with the exception of agricultural products and services. Over 1992-94 the government plans to reduce the ratio of restricted items for agricultural imports to 8 percent from about 17 percent. This import liberalization for agricultural products will be difficult because of the historical importance

Korea has placed on food self-sufficiency. Moreover, to the extent that agricultural incomes have not risen as rapidly as in urban areas in the recent past, structural reform of the agricultural sector is seen to conflict with equity goals.

Korea's financial sector has historically been used as an instrument of industrial policy through the use of directed credits and controlled interest rates. However, with the growing complexity of the Korean economy and the need to restructure the industrial sector, continuing reliance on administrative measures such as window guidance in setting interest rates and credit allocation through policy loans imposes significant efficiency costs. The government announced a gradual program for interest rate deregulation in 1991. The first phase was completed in June 1992, and underscored the need for a comprehensive program for financial sector reform. This blueprint for liberalization was finalized by the new administration, and has been announced recently. It proposes a program for financial reform phased over four or five years, including interest rate deregulation, opening of capital markets, use of indirect monetary policy instruments, reduction in directed credit programs, and the stronger prudential supervision of financial institutions.

The main uncertainty in the medium-term outlook for the Korean economy arises from the prospects for reunification of the Korean peninsula. The favorable international political situation and the realization of mutual benefits from closer economic relations led to the opening of the indirect trade in 1988. Exchanges accelerated in 1991 with the two Koreas joining the United Nations in September and signing an accord on reconciliation, nonaggression, exchanges, and cooperation in December. Since then, disagreements over international inspections of nuclear facilities in the Democratic People's Republic of Korea have stalled normalization, and rapid reunification appears unlikely. Irrespective of its timing, reunification would impose high economic and social costs in the short and medium terms, as is illustrated by the German experience.

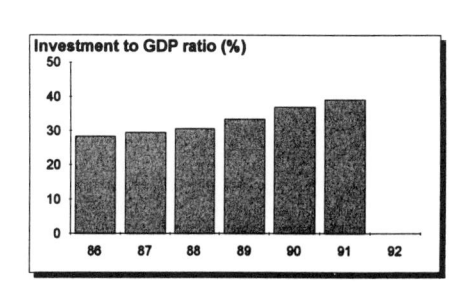

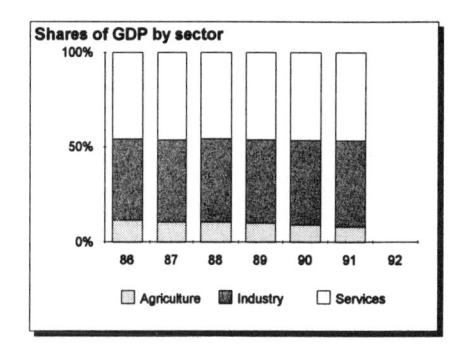

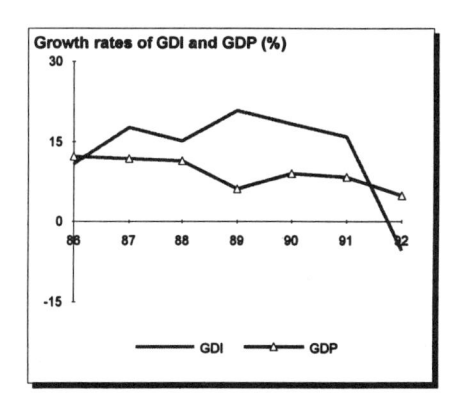

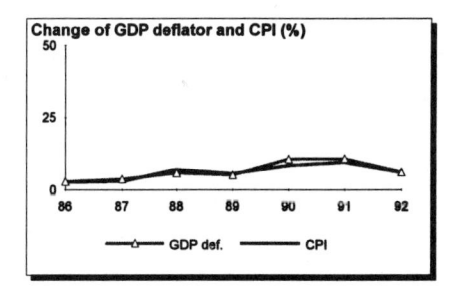

Republic of Korea

Population mid-1991 (millions)	43.3
GNP per capita 1991 (US$)	6,630

Income group: **Upper-middle**
Indebtedness level: **Below average**

KEY RATIOS

	1980	1985	1990	1991	1992
Gross domestic investment/GDP	31.7	29.3	36.9	39.1	..
Exports of goods and nfs/GDP	34.0	34.6	31.0	29.3	..
Gross domestic savings/GDP	24.3	30.5	36.4	36.5	..
Gross national savings/GDP	21.5	27.7	35.8	35.8	..
Current account balance/GDP	-8.6	-1.0	-0.9	-3.0	-1.6
Interest payments/GDP	2.6	3.0	0.7	0.6	0.5
Total debt/GDP	47.1	50.7	14.3	14.3	10.8
Total debt/exports	130.6	142.4	45.2	47.6	35.1

GDP: PRODUCTION

(% GDP)	1980	1985	1990	1991	1992
Agriculture	14.9	12.8	9.0	8.1	..
Industry	41.3	41.9	44.7	45.4	..
Manufacturing	29.7	30.3	28.9	27.5	..
Services	43.7	45.3	46.3	46.5	..

(Growth rates)	1980-85	1985-90	1990	1991	1992
Agriculture	5.7	0.0	-5.1	-0.8	5.4
Industry	10.9	11.6	11.8	8.9	3.2
Manufacturing	11.2	11.6	9.1	8.5	4.8
Services	7.4	10.0	9.3	9.5	6.3
GDP	8.5	9.6	9.0	8.4	4.8

GDP: EXPENDITURE

(% GDP)	1980	1985	1990	1991	1992
Private consumption	64.2	59.4	53.0	52.7	..
General government consumption	11.5	10.1	10.6	10.8	..
Gross domestic investment	31.7	29.3	36.9	39.1	..
Exports of goods and nfs	34.0	34.6	31.0	29.3	..
Imports of goods and nfs	41.5	33.3	31.5	31.9	..

(Growth rates)	1980-85	1985-90	1990	1991	1992
Private consumption	7.1	9.0	10.2	8.6	6.7
General government consumption	3.0	8.6	8.9	9.2	8.8
Gross domestic investment	9.0	15.6	18.3	16.0	-5.3
Exports of goods and nfs	9.9	10.5	4.2	9.8	9.8
Imports of goods and nfs	5.9	14.9	14.4	17.4	2.9
Gross national product	8.5	10.2	9.2	8.3	4.7
Gross national income	8.7	11.3	8.6	8.4	..

PRICES and GOVERNMENT FINANCE

	1980	1985	1990	1991	1992
Domestic prices (% change)					
Consumer prices	28.7	2.5	8.6	9.6	6.2
Wholesale prices	38.9	0.9	4.2	5.4	2.1
Implicit GDP deflator	26.0	4.1	10.8	10.8	6.3
Government finance (% GDP)					
Current budget balance	5.6	6.0	9.1	7.2	..
Overall surplus/deficit	0.7	0.7	3.3	0.8	..

Republic of Korea

POVERTY and SOCIAL (annual growth rates)	1980-85	1985-91
Population	1.4	1.0
Labor force	2.6	2.1

	most recent estimate (mre)
Headcount index (% of population)	13.3
Energy consumption per capita (kg oil equivalent)	1,897.6
Infant mortality (per thousand live births)	12.8
Access to safe water (% of population)	93.0
Child malnutrition (% of children under 5)	..
Illiteracy (% of population age 15+)	3.7
Secondary enrollment (% of school-age population)	87.0

Development diamond

TRADE

(millions US$)	1980	1985	1990	1991	1992
Total exports (fob)	17,505	30,283	65,016	71,870	..
n.a.	..	..	..	..	..
n.a.	..	..	..	..	..
Manufactures	15,442	28,681	61,728	..	..
Total imports (cif)	22,292	31,136	69,844	81,525	..
Food	2,189	1,795	..	..	..
Fuel and energy	6,638	7,333	..	..	..
Capital goods	5,125	11,081	..	..	..
Export price index (1987=100)	93	89	124	125	..
Import price index (1987=100)	110	99	113	113	..
Terms of trade (1987=100)	85	90	110	111	..
Openness of economy	64	66	55	54	..

Export and import levels (mill. US$)

BALANCE of PAYMENTS

(millions US$)	1980	1985	1990	1991	1992
Exports of goods and nfs	21,921	32,035	74,294	81,742	90,868
Imports of goods and nfs	25,655	30,555	76,278	89,885	..
Resource balance	-3,734	1,480	-1,984	-8,143	..
Net factor income	-2,036	-2,945	-463	-430	..
Net current transfers	0	0	266	20	300
Current account balance					
Before official transfers	-5,371	-910	-2,181	-8,553	-4,605
After official transfers	-5,321	-887	-2,172	-8,726	-4,605
Long-term capital inflow	1,987	2,229	-1,123	5,029	2,464
Total other items (net)	3,645	-1,150	2,087	2,549	5,577
Changes in net reserves	-311	-192	1,208	1,148	-3,436
Memo:					
Reserves excluding gold (mill. US$)	2,925	2,869	14,793	13,701	17,121
Reserves including gold (mill. US$)	3,101	2,972	14,916	13,815	17,228
Official exchange rate (local/US$)	607.4	870.0	707.8	733.4	780.7

Current account balance to GDP ratio (%)

EXTERNAL DEBT

	1980	1985	1990	1991	1992
Export ratios					
Long-term debt/exports	80.8	105.4	31.2	34.4	25.2
IMF credit/exports	3.0	4.6	0.0	0.0	0.0
Short-term debt/exports	46.8	32.4	14.0	13.2	9.9
Total debt service/exports	19.7	27.3	10.7	7.1	6.3
GDP ratios					
Long-term debt/GDP	29.1	37.5	9.9	10.4	7.7
IMF credit/GDP	1.1	1.6	0.0	0.0	0.0
Short-term debt/GDP	16.9	11.5	4.4	4.0	3.0
Long-term debt ratios					
Private nonguaranteed/long-term	12.6	19.0	22.3	24.1	29.3
Public and publicly guaranteed					
Private creditors/long-term	52.7	52.1	39.3	44.7	35.1
Official creditors/long-term	34.7	28.9	38.3	31.2	35.6

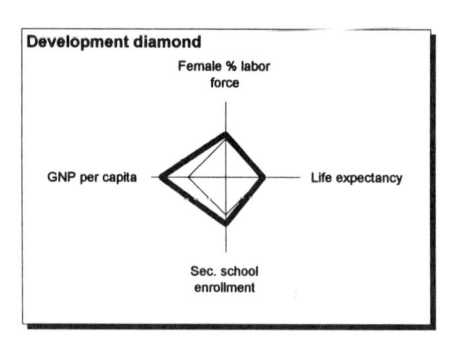

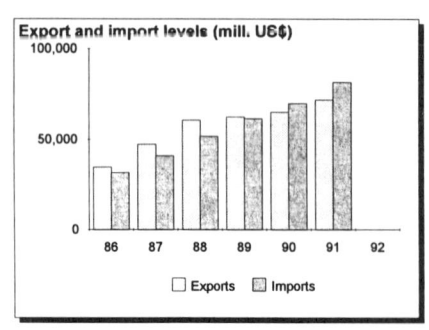

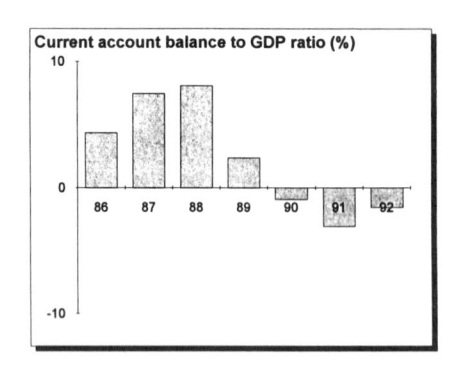

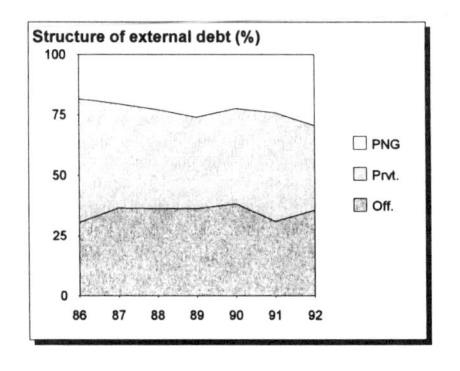

Structure of external debt (%)

Malaysia

Malaysia's successful development experience, evidenced by annual average economic growth of 6.5 percent over the last 25 years and per capita income of about $2,500, makes it a second-generation newly industrialized country. The optimism in Malaysia, reflected in the target of achieving developed country status within the next 30 years, is based on impressive economic growth that puts it on the verge of becoming an upper middle-income country. While this owes much to a favorable combination of factor endowments and markets, much credit is also due to the quality of macroeconomic management, particularly since the mid-1980s, a high rate of domestic savings, sound policies for long-term development, and well-managed public institutions. Achievements in Malay poverty alleviation, educational advancement and improved race relations are significant. These social policy achievements also facilitated Malaysia's remarkably quick adjustment to and recovery from the severe economic recession of 1985/86.

By most economic indicators, Malaysia's economic performance was strong in the 1970s when per capita GDP growth averaged 4.9 percent, compared to the 4 percent annual growth achieved in the 1960s. Several factors contributed to this performance, including Malaysia's wealth of natural resources, especially ample reserves of cultivable land and oil and gas; an outward-oriented growth strategy; favorable developments in the world economy; good economic and financial management; and stable social and political institutions.

Malaysia has given substantial attention to agriculture, resulting in high productivity gains that cushioned the sector against occasionally steep commodity price declines. Manufacturing growth has also been rapid, at about 12 percent a year over the last two decades, initially led by domestically oriented subsectors, but more recently by export-oriented industries. Malaysia has also kept its economy very open. Exports were 80 percent of GDP in 1992, while imports, fueled by high growth and an average nominal tariff rates of 13 percent, were 81 percent of GDP. This increasing export orientation was accompanied by transition from an initial dependence on rubber and tin to a broadly diversified basket including palm oil, logs, petroleum and gas, cocoa, and manufactured goods.

Malaysia is a multiracial society with 58 percent of the population Malay and other indigenous groups, 32 percent Chinese, and the remainder largely of Indian origin. At independence it inherited deep divisions in the distribution of income between ethnic communities. Poverty affected all ethnic groups, but was disproportionately high among Malays; their average per capita incomes were only half those of the Chinese community. In 1971 the government declared a New Economic Policy through 1990 that accorded priority to eradicating poverty and reducing racial imbalances in income, employment, and ownership of assets. By 1990 only 15 percent of households were living below the poverty line in rural areas and 4.5 percent in urban areas, compared with 44.8 percent and 21.8 percent in 1973. There has also been substantial progress toward reducing disparities in income and asset ownership.

With the share of exports to GDP at 80 percent and external demand an important engine of growth and income generation, Malaysia is a small, very open economy that is sensitive to developments in the external environment. In the past, most recently in 1985/86, external terms of trade shocks have led to recession and prolonged unemployment. To avoid such external shocks, Malaysia has successfully diversified its exports. In 1975 primary goods constituted 64 percent of total exports; the share has now gone down to 40 percent, with manufactured goods accounting for the majority. While this has reduced vulnerability to terms of trade shocks associated with collapse in commodity prices, risk from recessions in trading partners has increased.

Recent Developments

Malaysia has enjoyed sustained economic growth in the six years since the recession of 1985/86. The average growth rate of 8.4 percent in this period rests on Malaysia's competitive advantage based on sound macroeconomic management, a pragmatic, market-oriented development strategy, and a disciplined and educated labor force.

Underlying the continued macroeconomic stability, shown by high growth and inflation rates under 5 percent, have been conservative fiscal and monetary policies for managing domestic aggregate demand. Liberalized tax and regulatory treatment has contributed to Malaysia's attraction as a destination for foreign direct investment, which averaged $3.3 billion in each of the last three years and has been the driving engine of the economy. This could have resulted in excess liquidity and potential inflationary pressure, but the central bank effectively addressed this through its open market operations. The exchange rate has also been managed within a narrow band, allowing a slow appreciation of the ringgit in response to the large inflow of portfolio funds taking advantage of the buoyant performance of the Kuala Lumpur Stock Exchange and the interest rate differential between Singapore and Malaysia. The resulting macroeconomic stability has boosted business confidence and resulted in high growth.

Malaysia pragmatic, market-oriented approach is recognized in the post-1990 development strategy, which prescribes a supportive role for the government through investment in skills and infrastructure upgrading, but recognizes government's fiscal limitations. A privatization program is in full gear, with private sector firms invited to participate in mass urban transport, the power and gas industries, water, sewerage, and industrial waste treatment. This system has the potential to expand public infrastructure without increasing financial burdens on the budget. The private sector is also expected to play an increasing role in education, training, and research.

The competitive edge given Malaysia by its disciplined and educated labor force and relatively low unit labor costs will become harder to sustain. The labor market is tightening rapidly with shortages emerging in several important industrial sectors. This has started to exert pressure on wages. There is already a growing need to import contract labor from neighboring countries to relieve this supply bottleneck.

Several indicators suggest that 1993 economic growth will moderate to 7.5 percent compared to the average of 8.4 percent over the last six years. This is associated with changing patterns of trade and investment, but there are signs of economic slowdown as well, such as falling orders in the manufacturing sector, the loss of 5 percent of value on the stock exchange, and a softening of the property market due to excess capacity and recent foreign investment regulations restricting Singaporeans' entry in the real estate sector. This moderation in economic growth, however, is regarded by the authorities as a timely correction of the overheating of recent years, which had started to push inflation above the psychological barrier of 5 percent.

Several very large projects are likely to put renewed pressure on the budget. These include a new international airport at Sepang and a new stadium for the forthcoming Asian games.

The large inflows of foreign direct investment — mainly from Asia — that expanded the manufacturing base and facilitated access to markets abroad are of major importance for the economy. Measured in terms of approvals granted by the Malaysian Industrial Development Authority, foreign direct investment in Malaysia has increased dramatically from M$2.1 billion in 1981 to M$16 billion in 1987, with Taiwan (China), Japan, Korea, United States, and Indonesia being the largest sources. The bulk of investment is in basic metals products, petroleum industries, chemicals and chemical products, electrical and electronic products and non-metallic products.

Malaysia's success in attracting foreign investment is partly due to its location and cultural ties with Singapore and Taiwan (China). But economic and political stability are equally important. Consistently good growth performance, low inflation, a stable exchange rate, the development of an efficient and competitive private sector, and a favorable regulatory framework have reduced the risk of doing business in Malaysia. Business costs are also lowered by a competent labor force and good infrastructure. The last two features are currently the focus of public policy, since the government is keenly aware of the intensive competition for investible funds and the ease with which external circumstances can slow those flows. Several indicators now suggest that the external environment could become tighter in the medium term. Japan, by far Malaysia's largest trading partner and source of foreign investment, is in recession and that is beginning to have an impact. This, combined with increased regional competition, particularly from Indonesia, Thailand, China, and now Viet Nam, resulted in a softening of foreign investment flows in 1992.

In recent years trade and investment links with East Asia have strengthened at the expense of those with Europe and North America. This enabled Malaysia to avoid the fallout from the European and American recessions. The current Japanese recession, however, is a strong reminder that, in a global economic setting, small open economies such as Malaysia, do best by maintaining diversified market access. This realization is likely to result in attempts to improve trade relations with the European Community and North America. There is some concern that the North America Free Trade Agreement might redirect foreign direct investment from the East Asia region to Mexico as investors seek to locate themselves in an entry point into the larger North American market. Partly as a response to this concern, Malaysia has been a forceful protagonist for the creation of an East Asian Economic Caucus and is actively participating in the initial rounds of tariff reductions under the framework of the new Association of Southeast Asian Nations Free Trade Area.

Medium-Term Prospects

Malaysia is in a strong position to pursue its goal of becoming an industrialized economy early in the 21st century. To consolidate and build upon the growth momentum of recent years, Malaysia's prime minister has set a target of achieving industrial country status in three decades. "Vision 20-20", as this target has come to be called, requires annual growth rates of 7 percent over the next 30 years. This would double GNP every ten years, and by 2020 income per capita would increase to nearly four times the 1991 level of $2,500. This is not as ambitious a target as it might seem as it translates into Malaysia achieving, in 30 years, the present real income level of Singapore. It does, however, pose challenges on several fronts.

Malaysia's long-term planning establishes a clear set of priorities for addressing these challenges. The government's strategic priority has been to establish political consensus around a new set of policies for equity and social restructuring, which will essentially rely on vigorous, market-based growth as the principal means of improving income distribution, but will be accompanied by targeted programs to meet the needs of the hard-core poor. Its second goal is a strategic shift from public to private sector in the economy. This involves pursuing the unfinished economic liberalization agenda, implementing the privatization program and capital market reforms and deriving maximum advantage from direct foreign investment, including strengthening its linkages with domestic industry.

A third goal is natural resource management, where Malaysia recognizes that its long-term economic interests indicate a need for stronger management of mineral, land and water based resources, which in some cases — such as timber — have been exploited at unsustainable rates. Other important long-term issues addressed in the plan include organizing and financing social services, including health and technical and higher education, and reforming the fiscal system to handle expenditure growth in these and other areas.

Thus, the economy's growing strength and prosperity are beginning to define broad policy priorities for the future. The most important concern is maintaining international competitiveness since, given the small domestic market, most growth will have to be generated through exports. A need for productivity improvement, with more internationally competitive Malaysian firms making market niches abroad is clearly acknowledged in the government's Second Outline Perspective Plan issued in July 1991 along with the Sixth 5-Year Plan covering 1991-95. Investment to upgrade labor skills to continue to attract foreign investment and move the production base to high-tech, greater value-added products is the second thrust of the new development strategy. The Sixth Plan has allocated M$2.6 billion to higher education and M$580 million to industrial training—increases of 50 and 93 percent over the Fifth Plan.

The importance of maintaining adequate infrastructure is recognized in plan documents as crucial for sustaining rapid growth and preserving Malaysia's attractiveness to foreign investors, and the plan allocates M$10.8 billion to developing transport and telecommunications, 44 percent of the total consolidated public sector development expenditure for the plan period. The government expects much of this investment to be provided through the private sector.

Environment and Poverty

The Sixth Plan also gives new emphasis to conservation and sustainable natural resource development. It specifies that forest areas will be exploited carefully to ensure sustainable growth and safeguard the heritage of future generations. Since uncontrolled exploitation accelerates the depletion rate and undermines the development of vital sectors, the government is formulating a National Conservation Strategy to provide the framework for comprehensive resource planning and management, and has taken strong measures to discourage illegal logging and under-declaration of timber royalties. Programs are being developed for the reforesting 6.1 million hectares of logged-over forest, which represent 17.5 percent of the national land area, and additional forested areas are to be designated as forest reserves, animal sanctuaries and national parks. Malaysia's coastal and marine ecosystems will be further protected to preserve biodiversity, promote tourism and encourage marine research.

Successful poverty alleviation programs complemented by impressive achievements in expanding education and health services reduced the incidence of poverty to under 15 percent in 1990. The hard-core poor are now under 2 percent of the population. Targeted programs will continue to redress core poverty in specific locations and among households where the household head is sick or has died. Most movement out of poverty is expected, however, to come from economic growth and the movement of the poor from low- to higher-paid jobs.

Malaysia

Population mid-1991 (millions)	18.2
GNP per capita 1991 (US$)	2,520

Income group: **Lower-middle**
Indebtedness level: **Below average**

KEY RATIOS

	1980	1985	1990	1991	1992
Gross domestic investment/GDP	30.4	27.6	32.1	36.3	35.2
Exports of goods and nfs/GDP	57.5	54.9	77.3	81.8	79.5
Gross domestic savings/GDP	32.9	32.7	32.6	31.1	33.8
Gross national savings/GDP	29.1	25.5	28.2	26.5	29.8
Current account balance/GDP	-1.3	-2.1	-3.9	-9.5	-5.4
Interest payments/GDP	1.4	4.7	2.7	2.6	2.6
Total debt/GDP	27.0	66.0	42.5	45.5	37.4
Total debt/exports	44.6	115.9	52.3	54.2	..

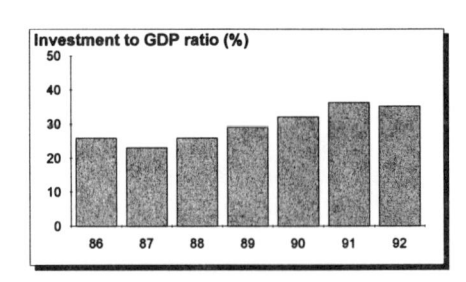

GDP: PRODUCTION
(% GDP)

	1980	1985	1990	1991	1992
Agriculture	21.9	..	..	..	..
Industry	37.8	..	..	..	..
Manufacturing	20.6	..	..	..	..
Services	40.3	..	..	..	..

(Growth rates)

	1980-85	1985-90	1990	1991	1992
Agriculture	2.9	5.0	0.3	0.0	1.2
Industry	6.7	10.0	13.2	11.2	11.0
Manufacturing	6.1	14.1	15.7	13.9	13.0
Services	5.9	5.4	11.0	10.0	6.9
GDP	5.4	6.9	9.7	8.7	8.5

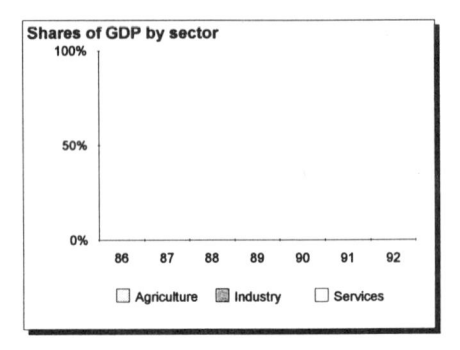

GDP: EXPENDITURE
(% GDP)

	1980	1985	1990	1991	1992
Private consumption	50.5	52.0	53.4	54.7	52.7
General government consumption	16.5	15.3	14.0	14.2	13.5
Gross domestic investment	30.4	27.6	32.1	36.3	35.2
Exports of goods and nfs	57.5	54.9	77.3	81.8	79.5
Imports of goods and nfs	55.0	49.8	76.8	87.0	80.9

(Growth rates)

	1980-85	1985-90	1990	1991	1992
Private consumption	4.0	7.9	13.2	10.1	4.9
General government consumption	3.6	4.2	5.5	12.4	4.1
Gross domestic investment	5.3	10.0	21.5	25.4	6.7
Exports of goods and nfs	8.2	13.8	18.3	15.0	11.9
Imports of goods and nfs	5.9	15.7	25.7	23.7	7.9
Gross national product	4.3	7.5	11.2	8.1	9.0
Gross national income	4.4	7.5	11.1	8.6	9.8

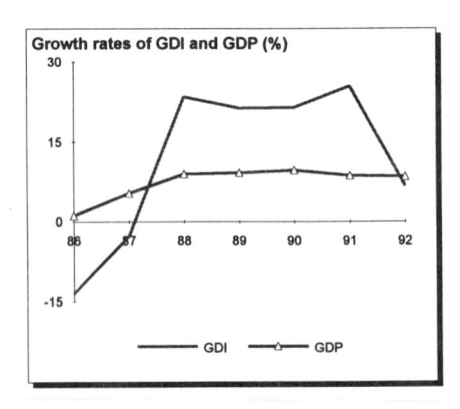

PRICES and GOVERNMENT FINANCE

	1980	1985	1990	1991	1992
Domestic prices					
(% change)					
Consumer prices	6.7	0.4	2.6	4.4	4.8
Wholesale prices	..	-2.1	0.9	..	..
Implicit GDP deflator	6.9	-1.5	2.7	3.2	4.4
Government finance					
(% GDP)					
Current budget balance	3.2	1.4	2.1	2.1	3.0
Overall surplus/deficit	..	..	..	..	..

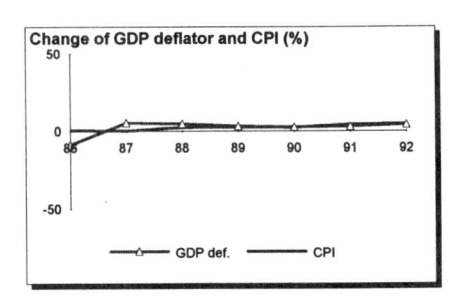

Malaysia

POVERTY and SOCIAL
(annual growth rates)

	1980-85	1985-91
Population	2.6	2.5
Labor force	2.9	2.7

most recent estimate (mre)

Headcount index (% of population)	15.5
Energy consumption per capita (kg oil equivalent)	973.6
Infant mortality (per thousand live births)	15.0
Access to safe water (% of population)	79.0
Child malnutrition (% of children under 5)	23.6
Illiteracy (% of population age 15+)	21.6
Secondary enrollment (% of school-age population)	56.0

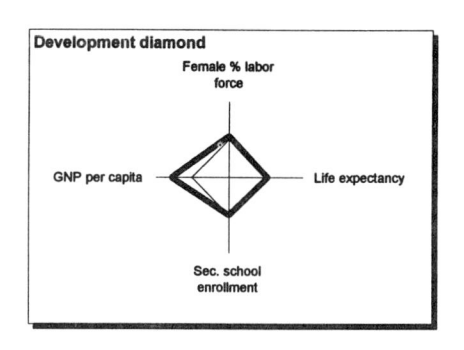

TRADE
(millions US$)

	1980	1985	1990	1991	1992
Total exports (fob)	12,941	15,311	28,956	34,264	38,338
Fuel	3,082	3,503	3,932	3,706	3,542
Rubber	2,121	1,157	1,119	1,079	1,002
Manufactures	3,601	5,023	17,429	20,576	25,875
Total imports (cif)	10,773	12,259	29,251	36,768	39,363
Food	1,225	1,326	1,694	1,869	2,376
Fuel and energy	2,116	1,916	2,366	2,554	2,733
Capital goods	4,183	5,341	14,734	19,764	21,654
Export price index (1987=100)	128	110	104	106	107
Import price index (1987=100)	89	96	111	114	113
Terms of trade (1987=100)	144	115	94	93	95
Openness of economy	97	88	136	151	135

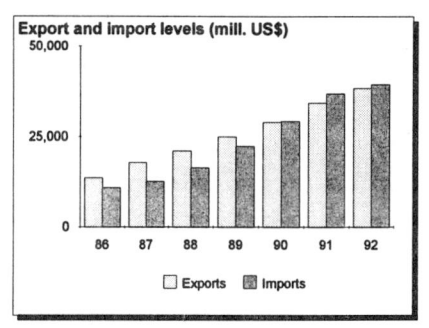

BALANCE of PAYMENTS
(millions US$)

	1980	1985	1990	1991	1992
Exports of goods and nfs	14,098	17,185	32,906	37,726	45,948
Imports of goods and nfs	13,489	15,604	32,718	40,174	46,731
Resource balance	609	1,581	187	-2,448	-783
Net factor income	-873	-2,188	-1,872	-2,038	-2,445
Net current transfers	-43	-46	3	26	137
Current account balance					
Before official transfers	-307	-653	-1,681	-4,460	-3,090
After official transfers	-285	-613	-1,630	-4,361	-2,794
Long-term capital inflow	1,021	1,582	2,011	3,657	6,820
Total other items (net)	-268	182	1,574	-1,378	-271
Changes in net reserves	-464	-1,148	-1,953	2,084	-3,755
Memo:					
Reserves excluding gold (mill. US$)	4,387	4,912	9,754	10,886	..
Reserves including gold (mill. US$)	5,755	5,677	10,659	11,717	..
Official exchange rate (local/US$)	2.2	2.5	2.7	2.8	2.6

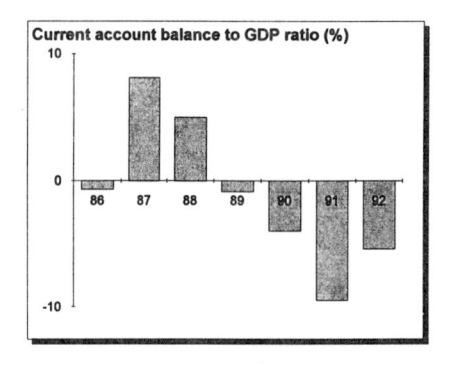

EXTERNAL DEBT

	1980	1985	1990	1991	1992
Export ratios					
Long-term debt/exports	35.4	100.1	46.8	47.4	..
IMF credit/exports	0.0	0.7	0.0	0.0	..
Short-term debt/exports	9.1	15.1	5.5	6.8	..
Total debt service/exports	6.3	30.6	11.2	8.4	..
GDP ratios					
Long-term debt/GDP	21.5	57.0	38.0	39.8	33.1
IMF credit/GDP	0.0	0.4	0.0	0.0	0.0
Short-term debt/GDP	5.5	8.6	4.5	5.7	4.3
Long-term debt ratios					
Private nonguaranteed/long-term	23.8	16.6	9.2	12.3	8.3
Public and publicly guaranteed					
Private creditors/long-term	48.8	65.5	64.9	62.8	67.3
Official creditors/long-term	27.5	17.9	26.0	24.9	24.4

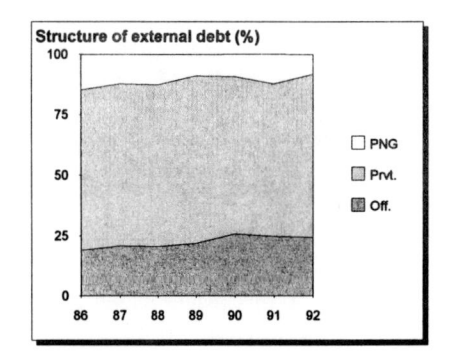

Mexico

In the aftermath of the debt crisis of 1982 Mexico broke with its earlier policies of protection and state regulation and adopted an outward-oriented, private sector-led, development strategy. The new policies have stabilized the macroeconomic situation and led to a modest recovery in growth. Central to the stabilization was a turnaround in the government's fiscal accounts. The primary fiscal balance (excluding interest payments) went from a deficit of 7.3 percent of GDP in 1982 to a surplus of 4.2 percent of GDP in 1983, and maintained surpluses from 6.0 to 7.6 percent of GDP over 1988 to 1991. The overall fiscal balance went from a deficit of 15.6 percent of GDP in 1982 to a surplus of 1.6 percent of GDP in the first half of 1992 (excluding privatization proceeds). Privatization proceeds from 1984 to mid-1992 totalled $21.9 billion, and were almost entirely allocated to public—mainly domestic—debt reduction. Inflation was less than 12 percent in 1992, down from an average of 90 percent over 1982–88.

Growth recovery has, however, been modest. GDP was roughly unchanged between 1982 and 1988, implying an 11.0 percent decline in per capita GDP. GDP growth then averaged 3.7 percent over 1989-91, but with population growth of 1.9 percent a year this left per capita GDP in 1991 6.1 percent below the level of 1982. Certain structural changes portend brighter prospects: the fiscal accounts are much stronger, and Mexico enjoys a more diversified export base as non-oil exports represent 66.8 percent of total exports as compared to only 22.0 percent in 1982.

Foreign debt service burden was cut from about 50 percent of exports over 1982–88 to about 32 percent in 1990/91 after the restructuring (with partial debt reduction) of almost $50 billion of foreign commercial debt under the Brady Plan. And there has been a dramatic reversal of capital flows: after having a negative capital account in 1987/88, between 1991 and the first half of 1992 Mexico received more than $30 billion in capital inflows.

Agreement was reached in August 1992 among the executive branch authorities of Mexico, the United States, and Canada, on a North American Free Trade Agreement. Legislative ratification in these three countries, and its entry into force, would strengthen the foundations of Mexico's trade liberalization reforms and make it even less likely that they would be reversed.

The most backward sector in Mexico's economy has not escaped the modernization drive: in early 1992 the constitution was amended to allow communal land owners to sell or lease their land, removing an obstacle for more efficient land use and long-term development in agriculture.

Despite the successful implementation of sweeping economic reforms, economic growth has slowed since mid-1991. In 1992 GDP grew only 2.6 percent, and the government expects only 2.5 to 3 percent growth in 1993. With population growth of 1.9 percent a year, and labor force growth of 3.1 percent, this growth will permit only a small rise in real per capita incomes. In addition, the trade accounts have worsened markedly, with a current account deficit for 1992 of $22.8 billion, 7.1 percent of GDP. On the positive side, single digit inflation is likely this year. Medium-term prospects are therefore good, provided that short-term difficulties can be surmounted.

Background

Before the debt crisis Mexico enjoyed a prolonged period of high economic growth and price stability. GDP grew at 6.2 percent a year over 1940–80. This growth masked, however, a steady deterioration in productivity growth. By one estimate, total factor productivity growth was a high 4.4 percent a year in the 1940s, only a little over 1 percent a year in the 1950s and 1960s, and essentially zero in the 1970s. Conservative fiscal policies kept inflation in single digits until 1972, but large increases in public expenditures in the early 1970s pushed inflation to double digits and led to the collapse of the exchange rate in 1976. Fiscal accounts continued to deteriorate over the next six years. By 1981 the primary deficit reached 8.0 percent of GDP, compared to 0.4 percent a decade earlier, and inflation was almost 30 percent. The exchange rate became overvalued, imports increased fourfold from 1975 to 1981 and capital flight ensued. Foreign debt exploded from $7 billion in 1972 to $78 billion in 1981.

In 1982 rising world interest rates and falling oil prices gave the final blow to these policies. Foreign creditors refused to extend new credits or roll over Mexico's short-term debt. By August foreign reserves were exhausted, forcing a float of the peso and the temporary suspension of foreign debt service. In September the banks were nationalized. Inflation sky-rocketed to 60 percent, GDP fell by 0.6 percent, and the peso depreciated almost 30 percent.

An IMF-supported stabilization program was launched in 1983. In a single year, the primary fiscal balance turned from a 7.3 percent deficit to a 4.2 percent surplus and the peso depreciated further in real terms, while inflation was running at 100 percent. The results were a sharp improvement in the non-interest current account balance, from a $5.8 billion deficit in 1981 to a $14.6 billion surplus in 1983, and a rebuilding of reserves, but a severe recession with GDP falling by more than 4 percent. The government persevered with these policies through mid-1985, and the economy responded with GDP growing by about 3 percent and inflation falling to 60 percent in 1984/85.

The fragile recovery of 1984 and the first half of 1985 could not withstand two major shocks. The Mexico City earthquake of September 1985 caused major disruptions with damages estimated at 2 percent of GDP. The collapse of oil prices in 1986 provoked a $8.6 billion fall in oil exports and a shortfall in government revenues equivalent to 2 percent of GDP. More fundamentally, however, the focus of the government's program had been on macroeconomic policies, especially fiscal austerity, to stabilize the economy, and not on basic structural reforms to remedy the underlying deficiencies that were the ultimate cause of the crisis.

Economic Adjustment

This changed in 1985/86 as recognition grew that Mexico would have to deal with these structural problems to achieve sustainable growth. A new adjustment program, signalling an important change in direction, was adopted in July 1986. In addition to rigorous fiscal austerity measures, the program sought a greater integration of the Mexican economy with the rest of the world. Exports were aggressively promoted through 35 percent real depreciation of the peso and far-reaching trade liberalization. As part of its commitment to an open economy, Mexico joined the GATT. Although non-oil exports responded by growing more than 40 percent, 1986 was not a good year: GDP fell by almost 4 percent and inflation climbed to nearly 90 percent.

Economic stagnation and triple digit inflation continued into 1987, while the non-interest current account recorded a $11.8 billion surplus. Quarterly wage indexation and frequent exchange rate adjustments to maintain export competitiveness created inflationary pressures. The stock market plunge in October 1987 triggered a run on the peso and a financial crisis. The government responded to this crisis and the continuing high inflation with an Economic Solidarity Pact under which labor and business agreed to temporary controls on wages and prices in return for a commitment to strict fiscal discipline and continued structural reform. The approach was successful. Inflation dropped to 52 percent in 1988—with most of the price rise in the first three months of the year—and GDP grew a modest 1 percent. Although the peso appreciated in real terms and the non-interest current account surplus dropped by $4 billion, the reform process was well underway.

The Reform Process

The key elements in Mexico's reform have been fiscal austerity, the opening of the economy, and a changing role for government. Reform efforts were strengthened under the presidency of Carlos Salinas de Gortari, who took office in December 1988, and growing confidence in Mexico's economy is shown in sizeable capital inflows and a sharp reduction in real interest rates from 1990 to early 1992.

Fiscal adjustment has been remarkable. The fiscal stance has remained firm since 1983, with the primary surplus registering an improvement equivalent to 16 percentage points of GDP. The main changes have been in expenditures. Non-interest expenditures, almost 35 percent of GDP in 1981, were cut to 28 percent by 1983 and then gradually reduced to 22 percent by 1990. Capital expenditures were halved over the same period. While the cuts brought about increased efficiency in government operations by eliminating most of the dubious large projects of the late 1970s, expenditures on maintenance and social sectors were also sharply, and probably excessively, reduced.

Interest payments were reduced sharply by 1990/91 with the reduction in the debt burden. From 1982 to 1990 interest payments ranged from 12 to 20 percent of GDP. While foreign interest payments have been relatively stable at about 4 percent of GDP, real domestic interest payments fluctuated from about 4 percent of GDP over 1983–86 to zero in 1987. They then rose to 7.3 percent of GDP in 1988/89 when real interest rates were high at the start of the disinflation program and its sustainability was in question. Real domestic interest payments fell to less than 3 percent of GDP in 1990, and were below 0.5 percent in 1991.

The efficiency of the tax system has been substantially improved. A major tax reform in 1987 expanded the tax base, simplified the tax system, reduced rates, and modernized tax administration. Personal and corporate tax rates have been brought in line with international levels. The highest personal tax rate and the flat corporate tax rate are now 35 percent, compared to 60.5 percent and 42 percent in 1986. A value added tax—now set at 10 percent—was introduced. The excise tax on gasoline and gasoline prices were sharply increased in 1990-92.

Political support for the stabilization efforts has been carefully engineered by periodically renewing the Pact negotiated in 1987. The seventh phase of the Pact, running from October 1992 to December 1993, was announced in October 1992.

The Pact has been highly successful. Inflation was below 20 percent in 1991 and 11.9 percent in 1992; single-digit levels are expected in 1993. The prices of about 90 percent of private production now are free of regulation. The Pact continues to set two key prices, the minimum wage and a band for the peso. While minimum wage adjustments have consistently lagged behind inflation, it is estimated that more than 90 percent of the labor force now earns more than the minimum wage. The average manufacturing real wage has risen since 1989 at an average annual rate of 6.3 percent.

Until 1992 exchange rate policy under the Pact was to set a daily nominal devaluation of the official rate. This was originally at a rate of one peso a day relative to the dollar; it was reduced to 80 centavos a day in the May 1990 renewal, 40 centavos in the November 1990 renewal and 20 centavos in the November 1991 renewal. These daily nominal devaluations were not large enough to offset inflation, however, so the real exchange rate appreciated—by 9 percent in 1991 and a further 5 percent in 1992. Mexico moved to a different system under the Pact renewal announced in October 1992. An explicit band system was announced under which the ceiling of the band was adjusted 40 centavos a day, while the floor of the band was kept fixed. The new band system marks a significant change in policy, and although the band itself is still relatively narrow, the new system moves toward a more market-determined mechanism for setting the exchange rate.

A fast and far-reaching trade reform has been at the center of structural adjustment. In 1983 virtually all merchandise imports were subject to quantitative restrictions. Now, Mexico is one of the more open economies in the world. Less than 20 percent of tradable production is subject to quantitative controls. The maximum tariff is 20 percent and the weighted average is 12.5 percent, about one-fifth and half of what they were in 1985. Since mid-1989 a major effort has been made to modernize and improve customs procedures. The Free Trade Agreement would cap this trade reform process, and ensure it is not soon reversed.

The restructuring of Mexico's foreign debt boosted confidence in the reform process. Agreement was reached in mid-1989 with the commercial bank advisory committee to restructure about $48 billion in debt. About 42.6 percent of the debt was exchanged for 35 percent principal reduction bonds at LIBOR plus 13/16 percent; about 46.6 percent for par bonds at a below-market 6.25 percent fixed rate of interest, and 9.1 percent was maintained at full value, but with the last group of lenders providing new money totalling 25 percent of their existing loans. The debt deal reduced annual transfers abroad by about $4 billion a year, reducing pressure on the exchange rate. More importantly, the increased confidence as a result of the debt deal, in conjunction with the rest of the reform program, was reflected in a drop of 20 percentage points in domestic interest rates, reducing the annual cost of government's domestic debt service by 4 percent of GDP and stimulating a resumption of investment.

The financial sector has been liberalized and private sector intermediation is rapidly increasing. In the mid-1980s the banking system was burdened with interest rate controls, compulsory lending to targeted activities, and high reserve requirements to finance the government's deficit. Interest rates and portfolio restrictions have been eliminated, while prudential regulations and supervision of financial intermediaries have been substantially improved and modernized. Restrictions on foreign participation in the financial sector have been partially relaxed and legislation allowing private ownership of banks and the establishment of financial groups enacted. The commercial banks nationalized in 1982 have been re-privatized and the financial system has been growing rapidly. In just five years, 1988 to 1992, private sector claims on the financial system jumped from 34 percent to 45.7 percent of GDP. The stock market has boomed; the Bolsa Mexicana de Valores increased by 266 percent in real terms from end-1988 to end-1991; it increased a further 18 percent in real terms by May, 1992, but there has been a partial correction that reduced it by 19 percent by January 1993.

Privatization has been comprehensive. In 1982 there were 1,155 public enterprises; by June 1992 there were only 220. This has had important implications for the government budget. Transfers to public enterprises were reduced from 3.5 percent of GDP in 1983 to 1 percent in 1990. Privatization receipts totalled $21.9 billion from 1984 to mid-1992. The bulk of privatization has been concentrated in recent years: privatization receipts were $3.2 billion in 1990, $10.8 billion in 1991 and $6.3 billion in the first half of 1992. The largest sale has been of the national telephone company; in late 1990, a 20.4 percent controlling interest was sold to a Mexican-French-US consortium for $1.8 billion. Since then the government has sold most of its remaining holdings in the company to employees, to the controlling group, and to Mexican and foreign investors for an extra $4.5 billion, including a $1.9 billion placement in foreign stock markets.

The sale of Mexican commercial banks was completed in the first half of 1992 and raised about $13 billion for the government. Prices received for banks ranged from 2.5 to 4 times book value. The largest sales were Banamex for $3.2 billion equivalent and Bancomer for $3 billion. The government has not used the sale proceeds from the privatizations for current expenditures, but for reducing debt—mainly domestic debt, which dropped from around 20 percent of GDP in 1990 to 12.1 percent at the end of 1992.

An improved regulatory framework and increased confidence have stimulated foreign investment. In May

1989 regulations on foreign investment were modified to encourage investment by introducing automaticity and transparency, and by harmonizing the tax system. In most sectors 100 percent foreign ownership is allowed; in some sectors, where foreign participation was previously banned, a 49 percent minority stake is permitted, with the exception of brokerage houses and banks, where the limit is 30 percent. These limits would be further liberalized under the Free Trade Agreement. Foreigners are allowed to purchase securities, including government paper, in the stock market. Direct and portfolio foreign investment in 1992 was $18.9 billion, compared with $3.5 billion in 1989 and $2.5 billion in 1988.

Deregulation has also been extended to industry and transportation, and Mexico's interventionist industrial policy is being dismantled. Trade restriction and requirements for computers, pharmaceuticals, steel, and automobiles are being phased out. A cumbersome transportation licensing system has been streamlined and the sector opened to competition. Those public enterprises that will remain in public hands are being reformed. Enterprises targeted for major restructurings include rail services and the food distribution company. Oil production will continue to be a government monopoly, but foreign participation in the petrochemical sector is now being extended as the list of petrochemicals reserved for the public sector has been very significantly narrowed.

A profound transformation of the agricultural sector is being pursued. The system constructed after the Mexican revolution centered on communal land ownership and heavy government intervention in output and input prices. The system was further distorted by government control of agricultural marketing and subsidized credit. Agricultural reforms have moved toward more reliance on market forces. Subsidies on inputs such as fertilizer, electricity and water have been reduced. The rural financial system has been reformed—although more remains to be done—and credit subsidies have been curtailed. Output pricing has been substantially liberalized and protection to agriculture reduced, with the notable exceptions of maize, beans, and wheat. This protection would, however, be phased out under the Free Trade Agreement.

In November 1991 the government announced the end of the land redistribution program initiated after the revolution and proposed a modification of the constitution to permit—but not require—the sale and leasing of ejido and communal land. In early 1992 the constitution was amended, and the government issued a new Agrarian Law and created the legal framework for privatizing ejido lands and ensuring rural property rights. The old law theoretically provided every Mexican with the right to land, and set restrictions on land use and farm size. Ejido land could not be pledged as collateral for credit and could not be rented or exploited through sharecropping or other tenancy arrangements. The constitutional reforms firmly establish private property rights to land by abolishing the constitutional obligation to distribute land and allowing domestic and foreign investment in agriculture. Under the new system, the ejidatarios have security of tenure, and the option to remain on communal property or become individual proprietors. They are allowed to lease their land, and can enter into joint ventures with other ejidatarios or the private sector. The implementation of these reforms is expected to boost productivity by stimulating investment and promoting more efficient land use.

Poverty and the Environment

Some 20 percent of Mexico's population is still below a poverty line of $350 a year. The government is attacking poverty through its growth-oriented economic strategy and public expenditure programs targeted to the poor. The Programa Nacional de Solidaridad initiated in 1988 targets health, education, nutrition, housing, employment, infrastructure and other projects to the poor in disadvantaged areas. The program's budget tripled from $500 million in 1989 to more than $1.5 billion in 1991; it is estimated that in 1992 it increased a further 30 percent in real terms, and a further substantial real increase is programmed in the 1993 budget. The government also provides targeted urban and rural food subsidies.

Mexico's environmental problems are a result of decades of explosive growth of vehicular traffic, unchecked industrialization, ranching's invasion of forests, and subsidized consumption of natural resources. The government has begun to establish the institutional capability to implement a comprehensive ecological policy. The central agency for environmental policy has been strengthened and a pricing policy conducive to energy savings is being adopted.

Privatization

Mexico is increasing private sector participation in financing, building, and operating infrastructure services. Objectives include increased efficiency and reversing the declining infrastructure investment from fiscal retrenchment in the 1980s. The program that has proceeded most quickly in privatizing toll roads; by the end of 1992 about 1,500 kilometers of private toll roads were in operation, and a further 2,500 kilometers under construction. Since 1990 the private sector has also participated, in a limited way, in financing and building but not operating, electricity plants under build-lease-transfer contracts. And under a law passed in December 1992, the private sector will now be permitted to own and operate electric generation plant. At the municipal level, the private sector has been involved in building, financing and operating water treatment plants.

The Free Trade Agreement

If the Free Trade Treaty is ratified in the second half of 1993 it could go into effect on January 1, 1994. The treaty envisages a phased elimination — over a period of up to 15 years in some areas — of tariff and non-tariff barriers for important categories of trade between the three countries. Agriculture is being liberalized over an extended period because some 2 million Mexicans and their dependents will be strongly affected, and rapid liberalization could cause strong rural-urban migration pressures. Although there will be important liberalization in the automotive and textile sectors, restrictive rules of origin requirements will limit progress. In the services sectors, including the financial sector, the opening is gradual until the year 2000, after which full competition under each country's laws will be allowed. Mexico's oil parastatal will maintain its monopoly for oil exploration, extraction, and import licenses for crude oil, but competition will allowed in much of the petrochemical sector.

Deep and sustained structural reform has been critical to Mexico's success in tapping international capital markets over recent years. After being negative in 1987 and 1988, Mexico's capital account showed a surplus of $8.2 billion in 1990, $20.2 billion in 1991 and $26 billion in 1992. Until the early spring of 1992, these private foreign capital inflows were associated with declining interest rates in Mexico. An important feature of the inflows was the growing share of non-debt creating capital inflows (direct and portfolio investment), which rose from 56 percent in 1990 to 73 percent in 1992. Another feature was the growing share of bonds issued by public and private firms in new debt issues; new syndicated commercial bank lending was virtually non-existent. Finally, unlike in the early 1980s, most of the capital inflows financed private rather than public spending.

Recent Developments

Economic growth slowed from roughly 4 percent between 1989 and the first half of 1991 to around 2.8 percent in the second half of 1991 and 2.6 percent in 1992. Nominal interest rates continued their decline until March 1992; since then they increased from less than 11 percent—roughly zero percent in real terms—to almost 20 percent in October 1992. They have declined since then to a 15 to 17 percent range (depending on the maturity) in May 1993. The peso appreciated 9 percent in real terms in 1991, and a further 5 percent in 1992. In part as a consequence, the current account deficit grew from $4.0 billion in 1989 and $7.1 billion in 1990, to $13.3 billion in 1991 and $22.8 billion in 1992, about 6.9 percent of GDP, based on the 1992 real exchange rate. Capital inflows have been large and have financed, despite large current account deficits, foreign reserve accumulation equivalent to $7.8 billion in 1991 and $1.2 billion in 1992. Until about March 1992 foreign capital inflows coincided with falling domestic interest rates, but since then the necessary inflows were obtained only with a substantial increase in real domestic interest rates. Real interest rates on government paper dropped from 9.1 percent in 1990 to 2 percent in 1991 on average; they rebounded to about 6 percent in real terms during the second half of 1992. Interest rates have dropped somewhat since March 1993, possibly as a consequence of a deepening of the economic slowdown; nevertheless, they remain high in real terms, particularly for the private sector.

Fiscal policies have remained tight. In 1990 the primary surplus reached 7.9 percent of GDP, approximately the same as in 1989. Lower interest payments brought the overall fiscal deficit to 2.3 percent of GDP. Strong fiscal performance continued in 1991; although the primary surplus declined due to the drop in oil prices to 6 percent of GDP, the overall fiscal balance turned into a surplus of 0.2 percent of GDP (excluding privatization proceeds), due to lower domestic and foreign interest payments. In 1992 the overall fiscal balance increased to a surplus of 1.8 percent of GDP. Including proceeds from privatization, the surplus in 1992 was 3.1 percent of GDP. The proceeds from the oil windfall of 1990 and bank privatization were invested in an oil contingency fund. In September 1991 the government used 20 billion pesos (about $6.6 billion) from the fund to reduce domestic public debt held by the central bank. A further 14 billion pesos (about $4.5 billion) of the fund were used for domestic debt reduction in February and March 1992. Over the past 18 months Mexico repurchased about $7.2 billion of its Brady bonds at an average discount of 25 percent.

Despite tight monetary policy, strong demand for domestic financial assets and reduced credit to the government led to fast rates of growth in monetary aggregates and credits to the private sector. In 1991 private sector claims on the financial system, measured by M4, increased 9.2 percent in real terms, and consolidated bank credit to the non-financial private sector expanded by 32 percent in real terms. In 1992 M4 increased 7 percent in real terms and consolidated bank credit to the non-financial private sector increased 32 percent in real terms. Fast growth in credit to the private sector was facilitated only in part by increased deposits; more important were the contraction in credit to the public sector and the elimination of the domestic liquidity requirements of commercial banks. Despite the large increase in external reserves during 1991, the monetary base only increased 7.6 percent in real terms. The expansion of foreign assets was offset by a $6.2 billion reduction in central bank net credit to the non-financial public sector. Central bank credit to the financial system, mainly development banks, increased $2.6 billion, so that credit to the public sector and financial system (the other sources of base money growth) declined $3.6 billion, de-facto sterilizing about half the reserve accumulation. In 1992 reserve accumulation slowed and monetary base growth dropped to 2 percent in real terms.

The recent slowdown of economic growth can be traced to a combination of slow productivity growth, a weak US economy, tight fiscal and monetary policies, and real exchange rate appreciation. The real peso appreciation has resulted from tight anti-inflation policies including the use of the exchange rate as a nominal anchor to reduce inflation, and a massive portfolio reallocation of foreign and Mexican investors into domestic assets. The effect on producers of import de-substitution brought about by the real peso appreciation has been compounded by the acceleration of trade liberalization. The real peso appreciation has affected growth by reducing external competitiveness in Mexico's tradeable sector, reflected in a sharp deterioration of the manufacturing resource balance. The main source of the economic slowdown has not been falling demand — consumption, investment, and exports all show strong growth, although exports slowed down in 1992 — but growing substitution of imports for domestically produced goods.

The government's tight anti-inflation commitment and trade liberalization strategy had visible effects on gross labor manufacturing productivity: it increased 5.9 percent in 1992 and averaged 4 percent over 1989-92. Estimates of total factor productivity for the economy as a whole, though, at less than 1 percent, give cause for concern. It is possible that, in view of the rapid opening of the economy and changes in relative prices associated with the real peso appreciation, production technologies have become economically obsolete. This would imply that much of the new investment is going to replace the existing capital stock, rather than adding to it; if so, a rebound in output growth can be expected.

Medium-Term Prospects

In view of ongoing tight anti-inflation policies, a deceleration in domestic aggregate demand and a further slowdown of output growth appears likely in the short term. Increases in the share of non-performing assets of commercial banks to more than 7 percent in March 1993 are likely to lead to sharp reduction in credit growth to the private sector. In this context, the single-digit inflation target for 1993 appears likely. Inflation in the first four months of 1993 was about 30 percent less than in the same period during 1992; extrapolating this trend would lead to inflation of 8.5 percent in 1993.

With continued tight monetary and fiscal policies designed to reduce inflation and the high interest rates needed to induce foreign capital inflows to finance the current deficit, growth is expected to slow further in 1993. In 1992 about two-thirds of the widening of the current account deficit can be ascribed to lower private saving. Public saving has improved but has only partially offset this trend, and a growing share of consumption and investment is being financed by capital inflows. If this trend continues it could renew fears about Mexico's ability to generate enough foreign exchange to service debt or remit dividends. Over the medium term, sustainable growth will require higher domestic and, in particular, private savings. The relaxation of liquidity constraints in 1988/90 unlocked pent up consumer demand that is likely to return to normal levels and lead to a recovery in private savings. In the short run, however, a side effect of an increase in private saving could be continued downward pressure on GDP growth.

Despite relatively fast growing fixed capital formation total factor productivity growth has been relatively slow, and the loss of external competitiveness implied by the real peso appreciation has only been partially offset.

The growth in the current account deficit to over 7 percent of GDP is cause for concern. The sharp deterioration in the manufacturing trade balance suggests that major areas of manufacturing are having serious problems of competitiveness. The strongest impact of the peso appreciation has so far been on the import-competing manufacturing sector, which grew only 1.8 percent in 1992. The risk that Mexico now faces is that slowdown pressures from the peso appreciation could be compounded by a cyclical correction of private consumption and possibly investment. Under these circumstances a real peso depreciation, an improvement in foreign demand conditions, or a combination of the two would be needed to offset slowdown pressures.

External Debt

Mexico's gross external debt increased slightly from $99.7 billion in 1990 to $104.1 billion in 1991. However, in relation to GDP it fell from 41.8 percent to 37.9 percent, due mainly to the real appreciation of the exchange rate. The debt service to exports ratio fell from 41.4 percent in 1989 to 33 percent in 1990 and 32 percent in 1991. The fundamental changes that have taken place in the economy have reduced Mexico's vulnerability to external shocks. Dependency on oil exports has been reduced, and they now represent less than one-third of exports compared to two-thirds in the early 1980s. Furthermore, almost half of the debt renegotiated with commercial banks was exchanged for fixed 6.25 percent interest rate bonds, reducing vulnerability to interest rate shocks. External public debt declined from $80 billion in 1991 to $75.8 billion in 1992, due mainly to the cancellation of Brady bonds.

Mexico

Population mid-1991 (millions)	83.3
GNP per capita 1991 (US$)	3,030

Income group: **Upper-middle**
Indebtedness level: **Severe**

KEY RATIOS

	1980	1985	1990	1991	1992
Gross domestic investment/GDP	27.2	21.2	21.9	22.4	23.2
Exports of goods and nfs/GDP	10.7	15.4	15.8	13.9	13.6
Gross domestic savings/GDP	24.9	26.3	20.7	19.3	16.7
Gross national savings/GDP	21.6	21.6	18.5	17.6	15.3
Current account balance/GDP	-4.8	0.4	-2.9	-4.6	-6.9
Interest payments/GDP	2.0	5.1	2.4	2.2	1.9
Total debt/GDP	25.7	53.1	39.9	35.5	29.9
Total debt/exports	258.1	323.8	222.8	224.1	211.0

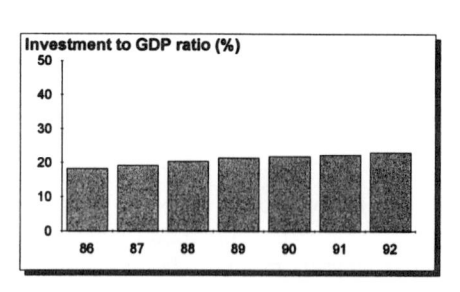

GDP: PRODUCTION
(% GDP)

	1980	1985	1990	1991	1992
Agriculture	8.2	9.1	8.0	7.7	8.4
Industry	32.8	33.3	30.7	30.0	28.4
Manufacturing	22.1	23.4	22.8	22.3	20.4
Services	59.0	57.6	61.3	62.2	63.2

(Growth rates)

	1980-85	1985-90	1990	1991	1992
Agriculture	2.0	-0.8	6.0	1.0	-0.2
Industry	0.1	2.5	5.7	3.4	2.7
Manufacturing	0.1	3.2	6.1	4.0	1.7
Services	1.8	1.4	3.6	4.1	3.0
GDP	1.2	1.6	4.6	3.6	2.6

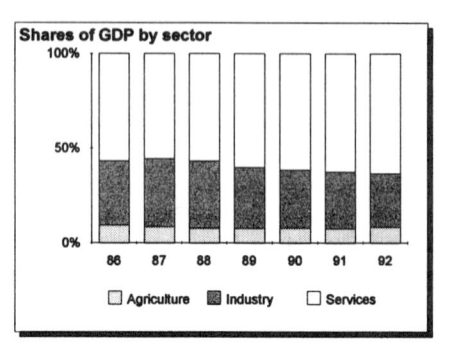

GDP: EXPENDITURE
(% GDP)

	1980	1985	1990	1991	1992
Private consumption	65.1	64.5	70.9	71.7	74.3
General government consumption	10.0	9.2	8.4	9.0	9.0
Gross domestic investment	27.2	21.2	21.9	22.4	23.2
Exports of goods and nfs	10.7	15.4	15.8	13.9	13.6
Imports of goods and nfs	13.0	10.3	16.9	17.0	20.1

(Growth rates)

	1980-85	1985-90	1990	1991	1992
Private consumption	-0.7	3.7	7.7	6.1	8.2
General government consumption	4.1	0.1	2.3	3.9	2.2
Gross domestic investment	-9.7	3.7	10.8	7.3	8.6
Exports of goods and nfs	10.0	5.4	3.6	5.4	0.3
Imports of goods and nfs	-13.9	15.5	19.8	16.4	21.2
Gross national product	0.9	2.1	5.4	4.4	2.9
Gross national income	-0.1	2.1	7.3	3.8	2.9

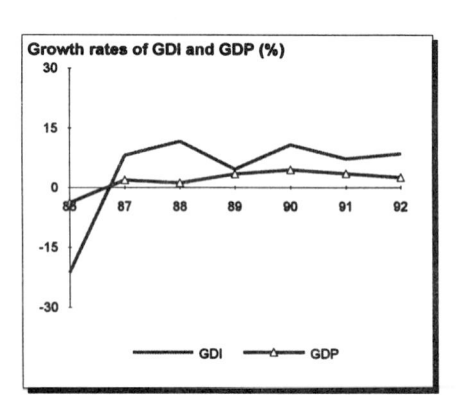

PRICES and GOVERNMENT FINANCE

	1980	1985	1990	1991	1992
Domestic prices					
(% change)					
Consumer prices	26.4	57.8	26.7	22.7	15.5
Wholesale prices	24.5	53.6	23.3	20.5	13.4
Implicit GDP deflator	26.7	56.5	29.3	21.7	14.7
Government finance					
(% GDP)					
Current budget balance	3.1	-2.0	2.7	4.2	5.3
Overall surplus/deficit	-2.7	-2.2	1.8	3.6	..

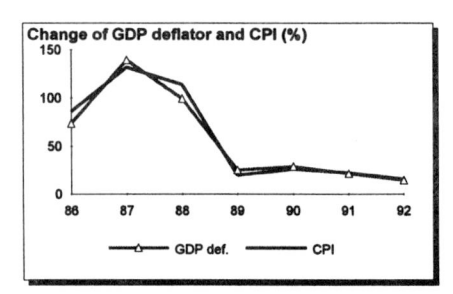

Mexico

POVERTY and SOCIAL
(annual growth rates)

	1980-85	1985-91
Population	2.2	1.8
Labor force	3.2	3.1

most recent estimate (mre)

Headcount index (% of population)	10.1
Energy consumption per capita (kg oil equivalent)	1,300.3
Infant mortality (per thousand live births)	36.0
Access to safe water (% of population)	70.0
Child malnutrition (% of children under 5)	14.0
Illiteracy (% of population age 15+)	12.7
Secondary enrollment (% of school-age population)	53.0

Development diamond

TRADE
(millions US$)

	1980	1985	1990	1991	1992
Total exports (fob)	15,512	21,664	26,839	27,120	27,516
Fuel	10,441	14,767	10,104	8,167	8,307
n.a.	..	..	..	..	..
Manufactures	3,030	4,978	13,956	16,035	16,740
Total imports (cif)	18,897	13,212	31,272	38,184	48,192
Food	2,448	1,082	5,099	5,639	7,744
Fuel and energy	..	..	..	..	..
Capital goods	5,174	3,165	6,790	8,471	11,556
Export price index (1987=100)	145	123	111	102	103
Import price index (1987=100)	83	98	113	113	114
Terms of trade (1987=100)	175	126	98	90	90
Openness of economy	15	19	24	23	23

Export and import levels (mill. US$)

BALANCE of PAYMENTS
(millions US$)

	1980	1985	1990	1991	1992
Exports of goods and nfs	20,844	27,609	38,351	40,008	41,363
Imports of goods and nfs	25,189	19,796	41,214	48,666	59,680
Resource balance	-4,345	7,813	-2,863	-8,658	-18,317
Net factor income	-6,669	-8,898	-7,716	-6,866	-6,876
Net current transfers	275	1,799	3,465	2,242	2,385
Current account balance					
Before official transfers	-10,739	714	-7,114	-13,282	-22,808
After official transfers	-10,700	1,387	-7,114	-13,096	-22,808
Long-term capital inflow	10,535	-632	5,674	17,286	26,816
Total other items (net)	-573	1,059	1,391	3,732	-1,974
Changes in net reserves	738	-1,814	49	-7,922	-2,034
Memo:					
Reserves excluding gold (mill. US$)	2,960	4,906	9,863	17,726	18,942
Reserves including gold (mill. US$)	4,175	5,679	10,217	18,052	19,171
Official exchange rate (local/US$)	0.0	0.3	2.8	3.0	3.1

Current account balance to GDP ratio (%)

EXTERNAL DEBT

	1980	1985	1990	1991	1992
Export ratios					
Long-term debt/exports	185.4	295.6	185.8	184.8	177.7
IMF credit/exports	0.0	9.9	15.0	14.9	12.7
Short-term debt/exports	72.7	18.2	22.1	24.4	20.7
Total debt service/exports	49.3	51.1	27.7	30.9	27.5
GDP ratios					
Long-term debt/GDP	18.4	48.5	33.2	29.3	25.1
IMF credit/GDP	0.0	1.6	2.7	2.4	1.8
Short-term debt/GDP	7.2	3.0	3.9	3.9	2.9
Long-term debt ratios					
Private nonguaranteed/long-term	17.7	17.8	5.4	6.5	5.3
Public and publicly guaranteed					
Private creditors/long-term	71.4	72.2	66.5	63.5	62.9
Official creditors/long-term	10.9	10.0	28.1	30.0	31.8

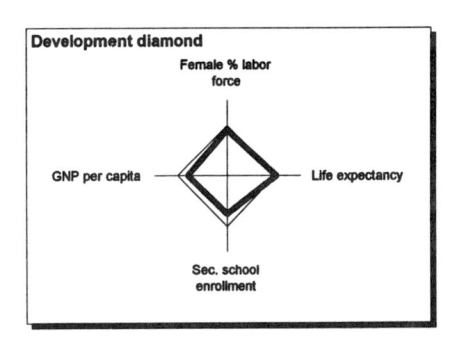

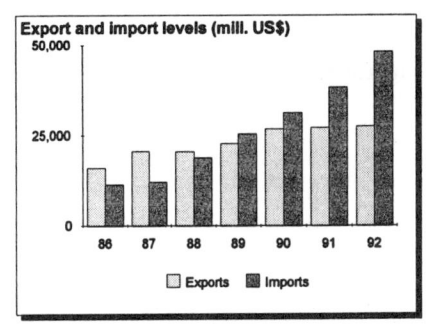

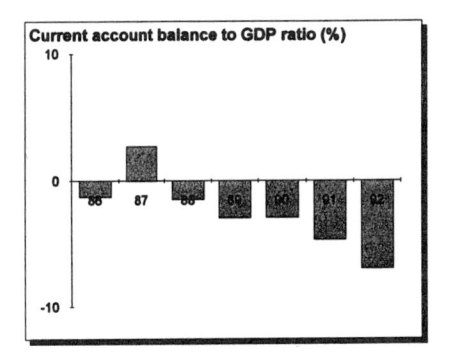

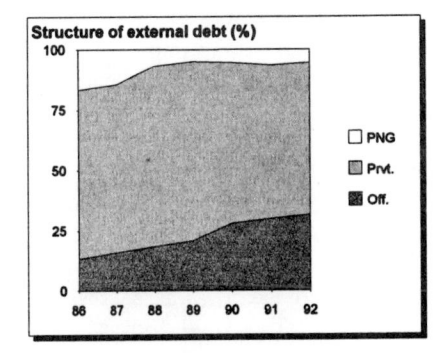

Structure of external debt (%)

Nigeria

Nigeria is the largest country in Sub-Saharan Africa, containing some 20 percent of the region's population. Its wealth of natural resources—including major oil and gas deposits—vibrant private sector, and large labor force and market endow it with considerable economic potential. When Nigeria became independent in 1960 it inherited institutions, ways of thinking, and processes that have evolved into robust professional associations, an inquisitive press, a cultural commitment to freedom, and a competent bench and bar. But it also inherited ethnic and regional tensions that reflected the colonial artificiality of Nigeria's borders and constituencies. Nigeria has recently completed elections for state and federal government assemblies and state executives. A presidential election was held in June 1993, but subsequently voided, creating a political turmoil that remains unresolved at the end of July.

Petroleum production provides 25 percent of Nigeria's GDP, over 90 percent of foreign exchange receipts, and 70 percent of budgetary revenues. Nigeria has also vast reserves of natural gas, which are only beginning to be exploited. Agriculture employs two-thirds of the labor force and provides 30 percent of GDP. Ninety percent of agricultural output comes from the crop sector, which is largely based on small-scale farming. Yams, cassava, and grains are the main food crops; cocoa, oil palm, rubber, groundnuts, and cotton are the principal cash crops. Productivity is low, but there is considerable scope for improvement through extending irrigation, improving technology, and expanding cultivated areas. Manufacturing accounts for less than 10 percent of GDP. The service sector, dominated by wholesale and retail trade, accounts for the remaining 30 percent of GDP.

The oil boom of the 1970s financed massive increases in public investment. These were designed to increase the economy's productive capacity and human capital and heal the wounds of the civil war that ravaged Nigeria in the late 1960s. But many of the investments were undertaken without sufficient attention to their economic viability. In addition, shifts in the terms of trade and fiscal expansion raised relative prices for non-tradables and undermined the non-oil export base in cocoa, groundnuts, and cotton. When the oil market weakened in the early 1980s the government continued spending. Foreign debt accumulated, including sizable trade arrears.

In late 1983 a new military government imposed fiscal austerity using across the board budgetary cuts and administrative restrictions on imports and foreign exchange. The austerity measures reduced the fiscal and external deficits, but failed to address the economy's structural weaknesses. The latter included the legacy of sustained agricultural decline, an uncompetitive, import-dependent, manufacturing sector, and a cumbersome regulatory framework. Uneven implementation notwithstanding, the measures exacted a heavy economic toll. They also proved politically unsustainable.

Structural Adjustment

A new government came to power in mid-1985 and declared its intention to move from "austerity alone to austerity with structural adjustment." With a further collapse in oil prices adding urgency, in 1986 the government adopted a far-reaching reform program and, in parallel, a multi-year transition program for the return to civilian rule. The structural adjustment program combined exchange rate and trade policy reforms aimed at revitalizing the non-oil economy with stabilization policies designed to restore balance of payments equilibrium and price stability. The program emphasized downsizing the public sector and improving the efficiency of public asset management. Import licenses and agricultural marketing boards were eliminated, price controls were lifted, and the banking deregulation was initiated.

These exchange rate and trade reforms remain basically intact, although they have been unevenly implemented over the past six years. The centerpiece of the reform effort was the replacement of import licensing by a foreign exchange market in 1986. This facilitated a cumulative depreciation in the real effective exchange rate of 51 percent between September 1986 and August 1992. The gap between the official and parallel rates has periodically widened, but was usually narrowed again by devaluations. In the latter part of 1992, however, official foreign exchange sales were suspended as the system came under severe inflationary pressure and declining reserves. Since February 1993 currency sales have been rationed and the official rate revalued to naira

21 to the dollar by the end of April. The parallel rate has subsequently appreciated somewhat but a spread of approximately 50 percent remains.

Other reforms, such as the creation of domiciliary accounts, abolition of surrender requirements, and the licensing of exchange bureaus, have improved incentives for repatriating foreign exchange receipts from non-oil exports and other activities. The tariff reforms that accompanied the adjustment program reduced the cascading protection that had encouraged assembly operations based on imported raw materials and other inputs.

Since the adoption of the adjustment program the government has taken steps to encourage private sector development. It has simplified the regulatory environment for private investment, reduced limitations on foreign investment, and introduced a debt equity conversion program. Nevertheless, major constraints to private sector development remain. These include a cumbersome regulatory framework that raises the cost of doing business in Nigeria, and an incentive structure that favors domestic production over exports and short-term activities over long-term investment. Nor has the erratic provision of critical infrastructure services, such as power and telecommunications, been supportive of private sector activity, reflecting ongoing difficulties with the management of public utilities. The investment response on the part of the private sector, both foreign and domestic, has been muted due to unstable macro-management and considerable political uncertainty.

An important start has been made on much-needed financial sector and monetary policy reforms. Intermittent reversals notwithstanding, interest rates and spreads have been largely deregulated. The 1991 Banking Act introduced stricter supervision and provisioning, and there has been considerable progress in meeting the new requirements. In the last year, however, there has been a proliferation of non-bank financial institutions that fall outside the purview of central bank supervision and regulation. While the central bank and the National Deposit Insurance Corporation have begun to address the difficult task of restructuring banks with non-performing loans, considerable uncertainty remains concerning the closure of some of these banks and the financing of the restructurings. The recent decision to convert state government debts to state-owned banks into securities is a first step toward addressing the latter's serious portfolio problems. Meanwhile, the government is divesting its equity participation in commercial and merchant banks.

Some 86 enterprises have been privatized under the adjustment program, mostly through public offers—or deferred public offers—on the Nigerian Stock Exchange. Although this is an important achievement, the planned privatization of several large enterprises has been delayed. Less success has been achieved with the commercialization program. Eleven parastatals were slated for full commercialization. However, only limited progress has been made with the partial commercialization of the Nigerian Electric Power Authority and Nigerian Telecommunications. Institution-building efforts and the creation of appropriate regulatory frameworks have stalled. Services remain intermittent, raising operating costs to public and private sector users.

The adjustment program also aimed to improve public expenditure planning and budgetary procedures, including the adoption of a rolling plan process, but these reforms did not adequately deal with deep-rooted weaknesses in public expenditure management. Fiscal policy reversals have jeopardized the sustainability of the reform process and introduced uncertainty that has delayed the recovery of private investment. Increased off-budget spending and continued financing of non-viable investment projects since 1990 have eroded fiscal and monetary discipline. The temporary revenue windfall accruing from the jump in oil prices associated with the Gulf Crisis facilitated the re-emergence of large-scale spending of oil revenues through devices outside the statutory budgetary and accounting framework. These additional expenditures were generally not directed at basic social services and infrastructure.

Despite implementation difficulties and overspending, adjustment has produced results. Real GDP grew by about 5 percent a year between 1986 and 1992, primarily reflecting recovery in agriculture and manufacturing. There also is evidence of growth in non-traditional exports. This has been associated with a realignment in the structure of consumption and production to be more consistent with Nigeria's factor endowments. Some of the anti-export bias in manufacturing has disappeared, and producers have switched from imported to local inputs. There is now greater use of locally produced materials, particularly in agro-processing and textile manufacturing.

Following a shift in relative prices in favor of the rural sector, net cash-crop exports revived, as did the production of traditional food crops. Agricultural output has grown at an average rate of 5 percent since 1987. Cocoa production, like cotton and other export crops, had almost come to a halt before adjustment due to the overvalued exchange rate, the marketing boards, and low producer prices but, between 1986 and 1990, output increased by 122 percent in volume terms. Food production has shown a similar upswing and Nigeria's food import bill has been considerably reduced.

Medium-Term Prospects

The adjustment program has reduced some of the grave distortions in the incentives framework and diminished macroeconomic imbalances. These actions nevertheless represent only the beginning. Nigeria has continued to be affected by significant slippages in macroeconomic management and political uncertainties. Both 1991 and 1992 have seen considerable increases in the federal budget deficit, money supply, and inflation. The oil windfall of 1990/91 was followed by rapid growth in government spending reinforced by political pressures. Supplementary and extra-budgetary outlays increased more than sixfold from 1990, to reach 25 percent of total federal expenditures in 1991. As the oil market weakened in 1991 and 1992, large fiscal deficits emerged.

The federal deficit worsened from 2.8 percent of GDP in 1990 to 6 percent in 1991 and 9 percent in 1992. Extra-budgetary outlays that year were equivalent to 8 percent of GDP. Their financing required a 55 percent increase in the money supply during 1992, which was mirrored in a rapid depreciation of the naira and an increase in the average annual rate of inflation from 13 percent in 1991 to 45 percent in 1992. Early returns from 1993 indicate that the inflationary fiscal and monetary expansion has continued unabated: by March 1993 the inflation rate had accelerated to 79 percent. With the expiration of the Paris Club agreement in March 1992, significant arrears to official creditors have accumulated.

If recent policies continue, real GDP growth is projected to continue at an average of 4 percent a year. This should enable consumption per capita to increase marginally while the private sector investment/GDP ratio rises to a level more compatible with long-term sustainable growth. Meanwhile, oil continues to represent 90 percent of Nigeria's exports. Economic performance and government revenues will continue to be directly linked to the state of the world oil market. Medium-term growth in oil production (including condensates) is projected to average 4 percent for 1993 through 1996, reflecting significant increases in oil sector investment associated with new joint venture agreements signed in early 1991. Long-run oil sector growth will be somewhat slower, averaging 2 percent over 1993–2000. Real growth in non-oil GDP is projected to continue at about 4 to 5 percent a year.

Poverty and the Environment

Although the adjustment program revived growth, that growth has so far been insufficient to compensate for the large drop in purchasing power associated with the collapse of international oil markets. Per capita income is $340, down from $1,000 in 1980. In real per capita terms, consumption and income are now no higher than they were in the early 1970s before the oil boom. Basic social indicators place Nigeria among the 20 poorest countries worldwide. Infant mortality rates are around 100 per 1,000 live births; half of all children aged 2 to 5 show signs of persistent malnutrition; and only about two-thirds of the relevant age group are enrolled in primary schools—down from 90 percent in the early 1980s. Meanwhile, population is growing an estimated 2.9 percent a year, outstripping the capacity to provide basic education and health services.

The government has adopted comprehensive and far-sighted policies for education, health, and population. These policies accord preference to primary health and education services; provide access to universal primary education free of charge; encourage adoption of cost recovery measures in health care; and aim to improve the health of women and children through birth spacing. The devolution of responsibilities for delivering primary social services to local government authorities presents new opportunities for strengthening administrative capacities. However, without a commensurate increase in budgetary provisions, notably for recurrent and, within recurrent budgets, for supplies and maintenance, insufficient funding will remain a critical constraint on implementation.

While some women play a dynamic role in political and economic life in parts of the country, women generally tend to be seriously disadvantaged, particularly in rural areas. Legal, cultural, and social barriers limit their access to land, credit, farming inputs, technology, and support services and constrain their earning capacity. They spend long hours on low-output, physically demanding activities such as water and fuelwood transport, manual crop processing, and headloading of farm produce, in addition to their responsibilities for household and family maintenance tasks. They are often illiterate and poorly nourished and face extreme health risks because of frequent pregnancies starting at a young age.

The diversity of Nigeria's climatic zones and ecology terms translates into a host of environmental issues. The most important problems are soil degradation, water contamination, and deforestation. These and other environmental problems could cost the economy an estimated $5 billion a year over the long term. Many of the problems are directly related to rapid population growth, which has reduced the viability of traditional land-extensive farming systems. The result has been exhausted soils and continuing loss of forest cover. Soil degradation affects about 50 million people and could have long-term impact in excess of $3 billion a year. Surface and groundwater contamination—and in urban areas, problems of solid waste disposal—are strongly associated with increased health risks and reduced productivity; 40 million people are potentially at risk if ground and surface water contamination continues unchecked. Deforestation, which has been proceeding at the rate of 2.2 percent per year, is resulting in the loss not only of wood but also non-wood products such as foods, spices, and medicines. More broadly, deforestation affects soil and water retention; these losses raise costs from flooding and sedimentation. It also jeopardizes wildlife and biodiversity, and increases the time rural women must spend gathering firewood.

The government has formulated a national environmental policy and established an Ecological Fund, aimed at promoting sustainable development. Specific projects and programs are being developed.

External Debt

The Nigerian economy is highly exposed to price fluctuations in world oil markets and, to a much lesser extent, economic developments in neighboring countries. Another key parameter with both domestic and external dimensions affecting Nigeria's economic development over the medium term is its external debt overhang.

Nigeria's net transfer position has been persistently negative, averaging 4.5 percent of GDP over 1986-92 for a cumulative total of $11 billion. Nonetheless, over this period, Nigeria's stock of medium- and long-term external debt has doubled, from $14.6 billion at end-1985 to an estimated $31 billion by end-1992. This increase was principally due to a combination of cross-currency revaluations, recognition as public debts of a large stock of private trade arrears incurred in the early-1980s, and the capitalization of interest through successive rescheduling agreements. Notwithstanding a recently completed debt and debt service reduction agreement with the commercial banks, Nigeria's total debt service burden, two-thirds of which is due to official creditors, will remain virtually unchanged until 1997.

While there is growing recognition among official creditors that continued reschedulings on conventional terms will not provide Nigeria with a sustainable solution to its debt problem, deteriorating performance in macromanagement, particularly the lack of fiscal transparency, the absence of a medium-term economic reform program, and the sheer size of Nigeria's debt stock are impediments to progress toward debt and debt service reduction. At the same time even though Nigeria's status as a low-income country was recognized when it was declared IDA eligible in 1988, a historical trend of very low levels of concessional bilateral support continues. Concessional aid flows thus have not been a factor in mitigating Nigeria's difficult negative net transfer position.

Nigeria

Population mid-1991 (millions)	99.0
GNP per capita 1991 (US$)	340

Income group: **Low**
Indebtedness level: **Severe**

KEY RATIOS

	1980	1985	1990	1991	1992
Gross domestic investment/GDP	22.2	9.0	14.6	16.3	18.2
Exports of goods and nfs/GDP	29.0	16.1	39.7	35.9	39.1
Gross domestic savings/GDP	32.3	12.6	29.5	22.7	22.7
Gross national savings/GDP	27.0	8.7	20.3	15.6	14.3
Current account balance/GDP	4.8	-0.2	4.2	-2.9	-4.8
Interest payments/GDP	0.6	1.6	5.2	6.5	6.8
Total debt/GDP	9.7	24.0	97.5	101.1	105.0
Total debt/exports	33.0	148.5	241.6	272.1	262.1

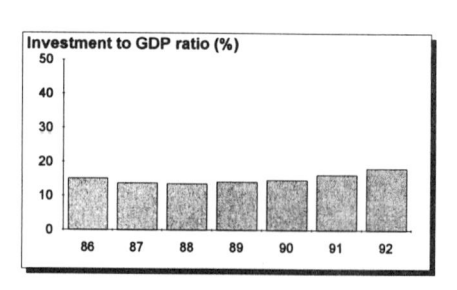

GDP: PRODUCTION

(% GDP)	1980	1985	1990	1991	1992
Agriculture	27.4	37.3	36.2	36.8	36.5
Industry	40.3	29.2	38.4	37.6	38.2
Manufacturing	8.0	8.7	..	..	..
Services	32.3	33.5	25.4	25.5	25.3

(Growth rates)	1980-85	1985-90	1990	1991	1992
Agriculture	-1.0	4.6	4.1	4.0	4.0
Industry	-6.0	3.5	6.4	4.3	2.0
Manufacturing	-4.3	4.4	..	..	..
Services	-1.2	6.3	5.1	6.3	4.1
GDP	-3.1	4.8	5.6	5.1	5.5

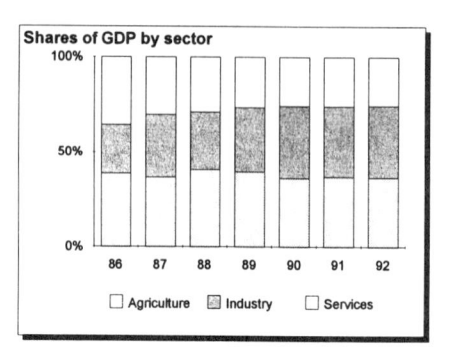

GDP: EXPENDITURE

(% GDP)	1980	1985	1990	1991	1992
Private consumption	55.8	73.8	59.1	64.8	..
General government consumption	11.9	13.5	11.4	12.6	6.4
Gross domestic investment	22.2	9.0	14.6	16.3	18.2
Exports of goods and nfs	29.0	16.1	39.7	35.9	39.1
Imports of goods and nfs	19.0	12.4	24.9	29.6	34.6

(Growth rates)	1980-85	1985-90	1990	1991	1992
Private consumption	-2.5	0.3	3.3	5.5	18.1
General government consumption	-4.2	1.1	19.9	16.5	-49.7
Gross domestic investment	-21.4	1.0	10.6	7.8	2.0
Exports of goods and nfs	-7.8	3.8	8.8	3.7	1.3
Imports of goods and nfs	-13.5	-10.0	13.7	12.2	1.3
Gross national product	-2.8	3.9	3.8	8.5	-20.7
Gross national income	-7.4	0.9	11.8	1.0	-23.0

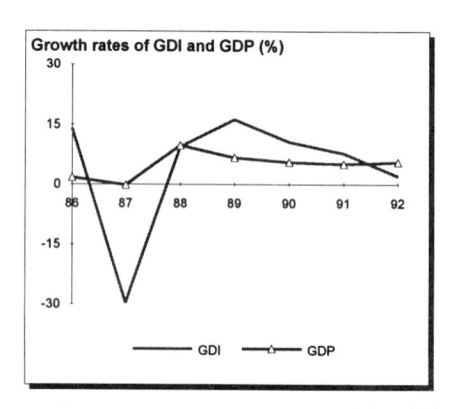

PRICES and GOVERNMENT FINANCE

	1980	1985	1990	1991	1992
Domestic prices (% change)					
Consumer prices	10.0	7.4	7.4	13.0	44.6
Wholesale prices	..	..	..	..	..
Implicit GDP deflator	14.1	4.1	17.3	12.9	48.4
Government finance (% GDP)					
Current budget balance	12.5	2.7	3.4	1.8	1.4
Overall surplus/deficit a/	-1.2	-4.3	-2.8	-6.0	-9.0

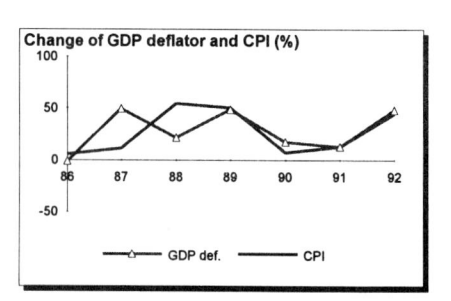

Nigeria

POVERTY and SOCIAL (annual growth rates)	1980-85	1985-91
Population	3.1	2.9
Labor force	2.6	2.7

most recent estimate (mre)

Headcount index (% of population)	..
Energy consumption per capita (kg oil equivalent)	138.3
Infant mortality (per thousand live births)	85.0
Access to safe water (% of population)	36.0
Child malnutrition (% of children under 5)	..
Illiteracy (% of population age 15+)	49.3
Secondary enrollment (% of school-age population)	20.0

Development diamond
(Female % labor force, Life expectancy, Sec. school enrollment, GNP per capita)

TRADE
(millions US$)

	1980	1985	1990	1991	1992
Total exports (fob)	25,956	12,566	13,923	12,071	11,972
Fuel	24,942	12,203	13,510	11,655	11,495
Cocoa	606	310	166	183	..
Manufactures	..	..	..	..	..
Total imports (cif)	16,312	9,165	7,300	8,387	9,354
Food	..	..	..	..	..
Fuel and energy	..	..	..	..	..
Capital goods	5,464	3,199	3,511	3,187	..
Export price index (1987=100)	203	151	136	114	121
Import price index (1987=100)	81	77	113	115	120
Terms of trade (1987=100)	251	196	120	99	101
Openness of economy	46	27	60	60	69

Export and import levels (mill. US$) — chart 86-92

BALANCE of PAYMENTS
(millions US$)

	1980	1985	1990	1991	1992
Exports of goods and nfs	27,006	13,032	14,083	12,324	12,171
Imports of goods and nfs	17,648	10,070	9,341	10,376	10,977
Resource balance	9,358	2,962	4,742	1,948	1,194
Net factor income	-4,472	-2,916	-3,287	-2,969	-2,714
Net current transfers	-409	-244	26	27	29
Current account balance					
Before official transfers	4,477	-198	1,481	-994	-1,491
After official transfers	4,496	-180	1,610	-964	-1,491
Long-term capital inflow	-273	-787	-2,592	-1,960	-5,430
Total other items (net) b/	322	1,663	3,490	2,974	5,469
Changes in net reserves c/	-4,545	-696	-2,508	-50	1,452
Memo:					
Reserves excluding gold (mill. US$)	10,235	1,667	3,864	4,435	967
Reserves including gold (mill. US$)	10,640	1,892	4,129	4,678	1,196
Official exchange rate (local/US$)	0.6	0.9	8.0	9.9	17.2

Current account balance to GDP ratio (%) — chart 86-92

EXTERNAL DEBT

	1980	1985	1990	1991	1992
Export ratios					
Long-term debt/exports	19.9	110.6	230.6	264.9	252.0
IMF credit/exports	0.0	0.0	0.0	0.0	0.0
Short-term debt/exports	13.1	37.9	11.0	7.2	10.1
Total debt service/exports	4.3	34.2	23.6	26.6	26.4
GDP ratios					
Long-term debt/GDP	5.8	17.9	93.0	98.4	100.9
IMF credit/GDP	0.0	0.0	0.0	0.0	0.0
Short-term debt/GDP	3.8	6.1	4.5	2.7	4.1
Long-term debt ratios					
Private nonguaranteed/long-term	20.4	9.7	1.2	1.0	0.8
Public and publicly guaranteed					
Private creditors/long-term	60.9	75.0	48.1	43.1	37.4
Official creditors/long-term	18.7	15.3	50.7	55.9	61.8

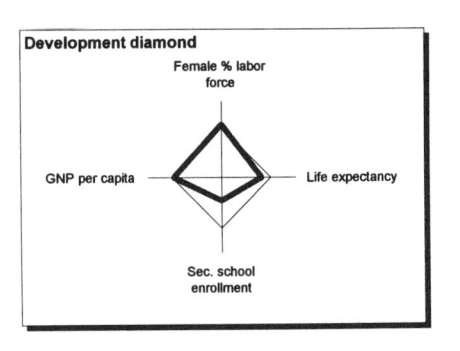

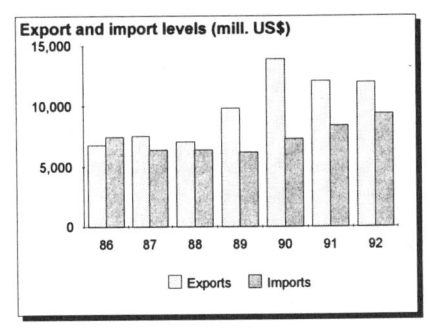

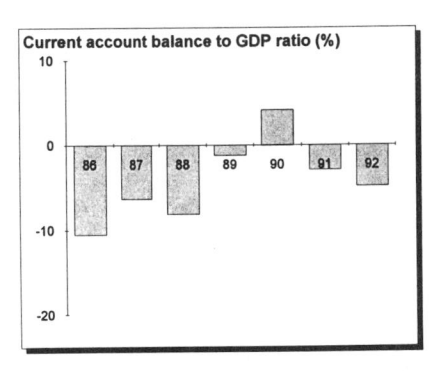

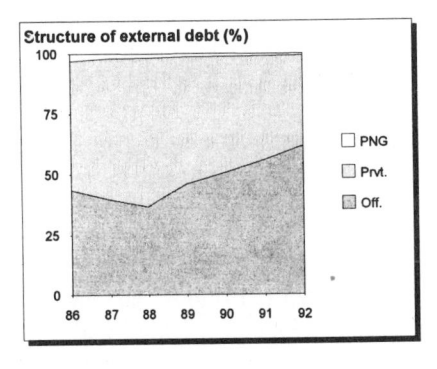

Structure of external debt (%) — chart 86-92 (PNG, Prvt., Off.)

a. Deficit is computed on a commitment basis. b. 1989 includes transactions associated with the sale of oil production equity. c. 1992 change in reserves includes collateralization for commercial bank and debt service reduction operation.

Pakistan

Pakistan's growth performance has been strong, with GDP growing about 6.5 percent a year in real terms for most of the 1980s, and averaging over 5 percent over 1950–85. This performance reflects agricultural production that averaged over 3 percent growth in the 1970s and over 4 percent in the 1980s. Pakistan's industrial sector has also developed rapidly, with manufacturing value added growing on average over 7 percent since the late 1970s. Access to substantial external financing and favorable markets for Pakistan's exports also played a crucial role in maintaining high GDP growth. Despite this growth, poverty is widespread: per capita income remains low at $400 in fiscal 1991, and the benefits of growth have not been widely shared. Basic social services are weak and social indicators poor. Population growth of over 3 percent a year has increased pressures on the environment and constrained rapid improvements in living standards.

Pakistan's production and export base has undergone only limited diversification, with agriculture contributing about 23 percent of GDP, employing half the labor force and providing 70 percent of exports, including agriculture-based manufactures. Industry remains concentrated in cotton processing, textiles, petroleum refining and food processing. Despite recent policy reforms, industry still suffers from poor product quality, outdated technology, and an untrained labor force. The narrow industrial base and inefficiencies in production reflect continued distortions in the industrial incentive system and high levels of protection.

Pakistan also faces serious macroeconomic constraints, marked by high fiscal and current account deficits. These macroeconomic problems, which reached unsustainable levels in the late 1980s, prompted the government to embark upon a medium-term macroeconomic and structural reform program in 1988. While progress has been good in privatization and financial market liberalization, attempts to reduce fiscal deficits and improve the revenue base were largely unsuccessful. The balance of payments has become more vulnerable due to a deterioration in the terms of trade and lower inflows of remittances and foreign aid. Macroeconomic management has also suffered from political changes.

Development Issues

Pakistan's high population growth and poor record in social development have undermined the pace of development and contributed negatively to improving income distribution. Estimates indicate that 29 percent of households fall below the poverty line, with poverty more prevalent in rural areas and small towns than in the cities. The past decade has seen an increase in average incomes and some success in allocating more resources to the social sectors. Nevertheless, Pakistan's literacy rate of 26 percent ranks among the lowest in the world, and few countries record a poorer literacy rate for rural females than Pakistan's 6 percent. Infant mortality and life expectancy indicators are similarly poor. Health care is heavily biased in favor of urban areas and hospital-based curative care.

The persistence of poverty in Pakistan is mainly due to very inadequate basic social services, high population growth, and limited access to productive assets. Aside from insufficient budgets, major constraints to improved access to basic services include a shortage of primary school teachers and paramedical staff—especially females—and a lack of commitment by local administrations to improving primary education and health care. Rapid population growth in rural areas has increased the number of landless, and reduced the average size of farms operated by the poor. Both trends have adverse implications for poverty.

Economic growth has concentrated on a limited number of profitable crops and a narrow range of industrial products. Even after a major policy shift in 1991 towards deregulating industrial sector activity there are still important direct and indirect price controls, subsidy programs, and regulatory policies that affect resource allocation. Above all, economic incentives are still heavily distorted due to a highly protective and discriminatory trade regime.

The concentration of exports in rice and cotton, which have uncertain price prospects, and in low value added cotton textiles subject to protectionist pressures from industrialized countries has made Pakistan's balance of payments fragile and vulnerable to external shocks.

Physical infrastructure bottlenecks also constitute important obstacles to growth and private sector development. Continued high levels of spending on defense, large debt-servicing needs, and weak resource mobilization efforts have made it difficult to expand public investment in priority areas, including basic infrastructure. Public sector management constraints and project implementation bottlenecks have also slowed public investment efforts.

Adjustment and Structural Reform

Although substantial progress has been made since 1988 in implementing reforms in a number of areas, the overall pace of reform has been slower than expected, partly because of changes in government in 1990 and 1993, the Gulf Crisis in 1991, and the flood of 1992. There has also been a lack of resolve in implementing adjustment measures, especially in fiscal reform.

GDP growth remained strong throughout the fiscal 1989-92 adjustment program, peaking at 6.4 percent in fiscal 1992. Efforts to reduce the fiscal deficit, however, have been disappointing, with the deficit increasing sharply to 8.7 percent of GDP in fiscal 1991 and remaining at 7.5 percent of GDP in fiscal 1992 because of slow progress in tax reform and insufficient control of expenditures. To finance these large deficits, borrowing from the banking system rose sharply, to 4.2 percent and 5.9 percent of GDP in fiscal 1991 and fiscal 1992, putting pressure on monetary aggregates. As a result of these factors and the sharp increase in energy prices in fiscal 1991, inflation remained above target at 13.1 percent in fiscal 1991 and 9.1 percent in fiscal 1992.

Exports have exhibited strong growth, increasing on average by 14.1 percent in dollar terms between fiscal years 1989 and 1992, which in part reflects Pakistan's flexible exchange rate policy. The current account deficit declined from 4.4 percent of GDP in fiscal 1988 to 3.1 percent of GDP in fiscal 1992. The latter figure is largely due to an increase in foreign currency deposits of residents, which have been accounted for as private transfers since fiscal 1991. Had these deposits been accounted for in the capital account—as those of non-residents continue to be—the current account would show a deterioration to 5.1 percent of GDP in fiscal 1992. Greater reliance on financing from foreign currency deposits has made the economy more vulnerable to external shocks.

Several terms of trade shocks, mainly due to increases in the prices of oil products, the depressed state of world cotton market, and liberalization of the import regime contributed to a weakening of the balance of payments position. An important factor behind the weak external position has been that domestic demand policies, in particular fiscal policy, have been too expansionary.

Despite continued difficulties in strengthening macroeconomic management, the government has made considerable progress in opening the economy and improving the environment for private sector activity. The important reforms in industrial deregulation, lifting foreign exchange controls, and eliminating investment sanctions, which were implemented in fiscal 1991, have developed a more hospitable framework for the private sector. Progress has also been made in reducing non-tariff barriers to imports and the maximum tariff. Nevertheless, Pakistan's trade regime remains heavily protective and distortionary and has negative impact on domestic competitiveness.

The government has continued financial sector reform, introducing an auction system for government securities and improving competition by approving several new private financial institutions and privatizing the nationalized commercial banks, two of which have already been sold. These reforms are important elements for promoting a stronger private sector, improving overall resource mobilization and allocation, and helping to pave the way for the needed increase in the savings rate. Recent rulings of the Shariat Court create some uncertainties on future financial sector policies, however, and the government is seeking further judicial review.

Considerable progress has been made in privatization. Of the 103 industrial units put up for sale, 49 have been sold to the private sector, and another three sales are in process. The government has made regulatory changes to prepare for privatizing the Pakistan Telecommunications Corporation. It is also pursuing initiatives to increase private sector participation in the energy sector. These include development by the power authority of a privatization strategy for some of its activities—including establishing a national regulatory authority—and actions to reduce the government's ownership share in energy sector enterprises.

Pakistan has launched a Social Action Program aimed at providing a coherent framework for basic social services, primary education, basic health care, family planning, and rural water supply and sanitation. The goal is to develop a realistic action program with achievable targets, adequate resources, and enabling policy and institutional measures.

Medium-Term Prospects

Economic performance in fiscal 1993 is expected to be considerably weaker, largely due to the impact of the September 1992 floods, but also because compensatory policy measures were not implemented effectively. Fiscal policy progress, especially in revenue mobilization, has been constrained by political uncertainties. The floods resulted in substantial loss of life and widespread damage to crops, infrastructure and property, with damages estimated at $2.4 billion. GDP growth is projected at only about 3 percent, as compared with the 4.6 percent expected earlier, mainly reflecting losses in cotton, rice, and sugar cane. Additional expenditures for relief operations and infrastructure rehabilitation were incurred without cutting planned expenditures, so that, combined with revenue shortfalls, the fiscal deficit is expected to exceed 9 percent of GDP.

Losses in production of exportables and higher imports of fertilizer and materials adversely affected the current account balance, which is expected to result in a deficit of about 5.3 percent of GDP, or about $2.53 billion. The weakening of the balance of payments in fiscal 1993 has caused a substantial further deterioration in gross reserves.

Over the medium term growth is expected to remain strong and could return to an average of 6 percent if satisfactory progress is made in policy reform program and improving macroeconomic management. On the demand side, exports and investment are expected to be the main sources of growth. The trade and industry reform program, together with the flexible exchange rate policy, are expected to benefit export-oriented industries, particularly in manufactures. Increased investment in infrastructure will directly benefit the construction industry, although other sectors such as agriculture and transportation will also benefit from lower costs.

Despite Pakistan's good growth potential, there are substantial risks posed by its vulnerability to external shocks and policy slippages. On the external front, the main sources of risks are fluctuations in cotton and oil prices, slow growth in the OECD countries, and changes in international interest rates.

External Debt

Pakistan's debt/GDP and debt service ratios stood at 49 percent and 26 percent respectively in 1991 and are expected to decline moderately as the government's adjustment program continues.

Pakistan

Population mid-1991 (millions)	115.8
GNP per capita 1991 (US$)	400

Income group: **Low**
Indebtedness level: **Moderate**

KEY RATIOS

	1980	1985	1990	1991	1992
Gross domestic investment/GDP	18.5	18.3	18.9	18.7	18.7
Exports of goods and nfs/GDP	12.5	11.2	16.3	16.3	17.2
Gross domestic savings/GDP	6.9	6.7	11.8	11.9	12.3
Gross national savings/GDP	13.7	22.0	19.8	18.3	14.9
Current account balance/GDP	-4.8	-5.4	-4.7	-4.8	-5.1
Interest payments/GDP	1.0	1.0	1.3	1.3	1.4
Total debt/GDP	41.9	42.9	51.6	50.3	46.2
Total debt/exports	208.8	228.0	249.7	244.9	226.5

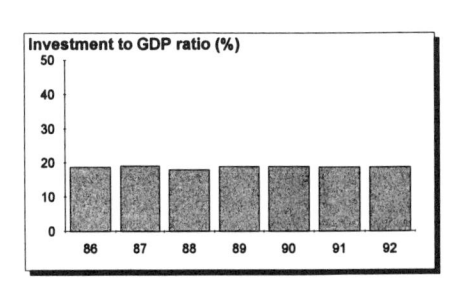

GDP: PRODUCTION
(% GDP)

	1980	1985	1990	1991	1992
Agriculture	29.5	28.5	26.0	25.6	..
Industry	24.9	22.5	25.2	25.6	..
Manufacturing	15.9	15.9	17.4	17.5	..
Services	45.6	49.0	48.9	48.7	..

(Growth rates)

	1980-85	1985-90	1990	1991	1992
Agriculture	3.9	3.8	0.5	4.5	..
Industry	6.2	7.8	9.8	7.8	..
Manufacturing	7.7	7.3	9.2	6.2	..
Services	7.8	5.2	3.6	5.4	..
GDP	6.4	5.8	4.3	5.5	7.8

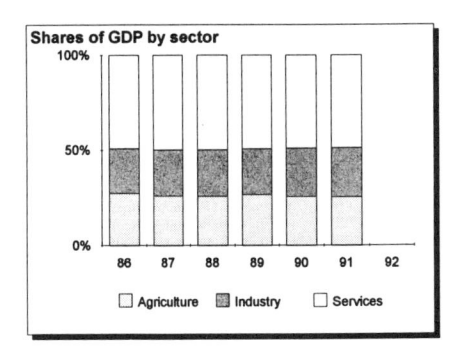

GDP: EXPENDITURE
(% GDP)

	1980	1985	1990	1991	1992
Private consumption	83.1	81.2	73.1	74.7	73.8
General government consumption	10.0	12.1	15.1	13.5	13.8
Gross domestic investment	18.5	18.3	18.9	18.7	18.7
Exports of goods and nfs	12.5	11.2	16.3	16.3	17.2
Imports of goods and nfs	24.1	22.8	23.5	23.1	23.6

(Growth rates)

	1980-85	1985-90	1990	1991	1992
Private consumption	4.1	4.5	5.8	5.9	6.2
General government consumption	10.6	8.7	-5.9	-6.2	9.9
Gross domestic investment	7.9	3.5	4.3	4.2	7.8
Exports of goods and nfs	7.1	8.4	9.8	8.5	19.2
Imports of goods and nfs	2.2	2.3	5.5	-0.4	11.4
Gross national product	8.3	5.0	4.3	4.5	4.6
Gross national income	7.6	5.1	4.3	3.6	3.9

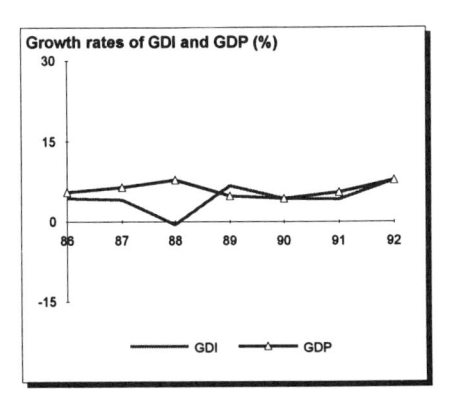

PRICES and GOVERNMENT FINANCE

	1980	1985	1990	1991	1992
Domestic prices *(% change)*					
Consumer prices	11.9	5.6	9.1	11.8	9.5
Wholesale prices	13.4	2.9	8.6	12.0	7.2
Implicit GDP deflator	8.9	4.6	6.7	13.1	9.1
Government finance *(% GDP)*					
Current budget balance	1.9	-0.8	0.1	-2.1	-1.5
Overall surplus/deficit	..	..	..	-8.6	..

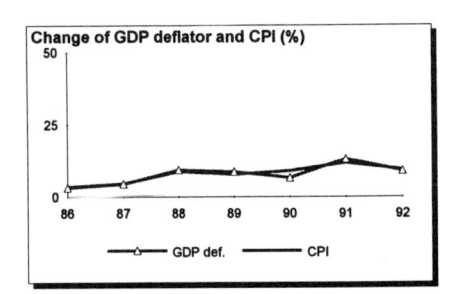

65

Pakistan

POVERTY and SOCIAL
(annual growth rates)

	1980-85	1985-91
Population	3.1	3.1
Labor force	3.2	2.5

most recent estimate (mre)

Headcount index (% of population)	31.0
Energy consumption per capita (kg oil equivalent)	233.1
Infant mortality (per thousand live births)	97.0
Access to safe water (% of population)	56.0
Child malnutrition (% of children under 5)	40.0
Illiteracy (% of population age 15+)	65.2
Secondary enrollment (% of school-age population)	20.0

Development diamond: Female % labor force, Life expectancy, Sec. school enrollment, GNP per capita

TRADE
(millions US$)

	1980	1985	1990	1991	1992
Total exports (fob)	2,342	2,457	4,926	5,902	..
Rice	422	220	239	346	..
Cotton	335	288	443	412	..
Manufactures	..	..	..	..	..
Total imports (cif)	5,563	6,531	8,055	9,094	..
Food	359	525	714	..	..
Fuel and energy	1,080	1,398	1,186	1,691	..
Capital goods	1,663	1,910	2,244	2,846	..
Export price index (1987=100)	72	62	141	149	149
Import price index (1987=100)	..	..	157	185	185
Terms of trade (1987=100)	..	..	90	81	81
Openness of economy	33	29	32	33	..

BALANCE of PAYMENTS
(millions US$)

	1980	1985	1990	1991	1992
Exports of goods and nfs	2,958	3,247	6,217	7,450	8,361
Imports of goods and nfs	5,709	7,113	9,351	10,563	11,436
Resource balance	-2,751	-3,867	-3,134	-3,113	-3,075
Net factor income	-281	-506	-966	-1,160	-1,141
Net current transfers	1,895	2,688	2,210	2,102	1,735
Current account balance					
Before official transfers	-1,137	-1,685	-1,890	-2,171	-2,481
After official transfers	-869	-1,282	-1,352	-1,558	-2,037
Long-term capital inflow	823	460	1,017	881	2,014
Total other items (net)	55	-225	335	677	221
Changes in net reserves	-279	1,048	0	0	-198
Memo:					
Reserves excluding gold (mill. US$)	496	807	296	527	850
Reserves including gold (mill. US$)	1,568	1,429	1,046	1,220	1,524
Official exchange rate (local/US$)	9.9	15.2	21.4	22.4	24.8

EXTERNAL DEBT

	1980	1985	1990	1991	1992
Export ratios					
Long-term debt/exports	179.2	180.8	201.1	189.2	180.8
IMF credit/exports	14.2	24.8	10.1	11.4	9.4
Short-term debt/exports	15.5	22.4	38.6	44.3	36.3
Total debt service/exports	17.9	24.2	22.9	21.1	21.4
GDP ratios					
Long-term debt/GDP	36.0	34.0	41.5	38.8	36.9
IMF credit/GDP	2.8	4.7	2.1	2.3	1.9
Short-term debt/GDP	3.1	4.2	8.0	9.1	7.4
Long-term debt ratios					
Private nonguaranteed/long-term	0.2	0.2	0.8	0.6	1.2
Public and publicly guaranteed					
Private creditors/long-term	6.3	7.6	4.1	3.2	5.1
Official creditors/long-term	93.5	92.2	95.1	96.2	93.7

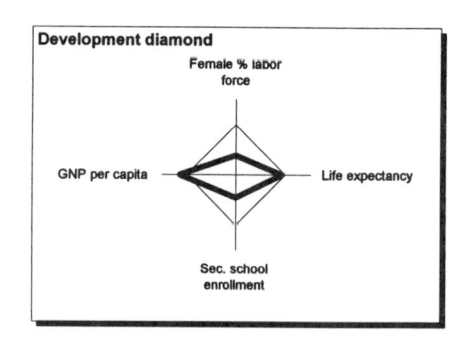

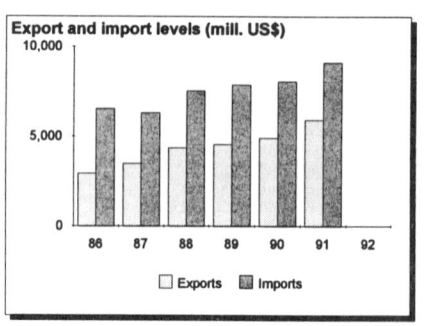

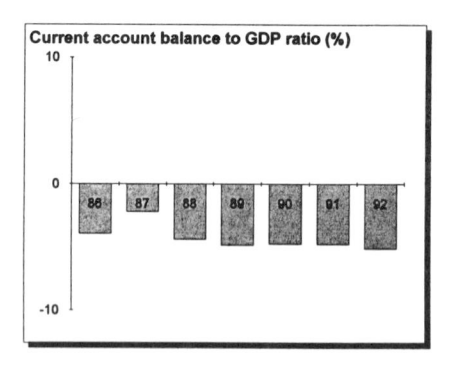

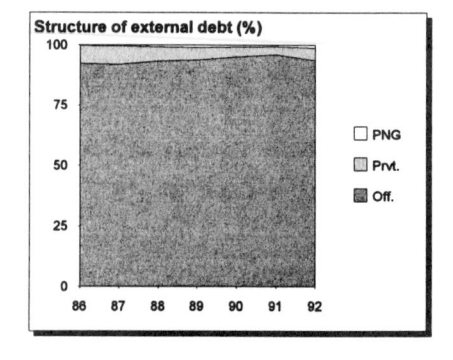

Philippines

The Philippines marked its first orderly democratic transition of power in more than 20 years in June 1992. In the year since, the Fidel Ramos administration has sought to develop a growth-oriented program focusing on improved international competitiveness and people empowerment. The government has continued stabilization and structural reform programs to maintain a stable macroeconomic framework and achieve greater integration into the world economy. Foreign exchange transactions have been fully liberalized. And in December 1992 it completed a comprehensive agreement to restructure medium- and long-term external debt held by commercial banks.

Although the Philippine economy grew about 6 percent a year in the 1970s, the need for structural adjustment was evident by the end of the decade. External debt had accumulated to 53 percent of GDP by 1980, and heavy investment requirements to generate growth had produced unsustainable current account deficits above 5 percent. Since 1980 and particularly since the change in government in 1986, the Philippines has made concerted efforts to correct a wide array of structural problems. Reforms in agricultural pricing and marketing, the financial sector, investment incentives, and direct and indirect taxes have been undertaken, along with some liberalization of the trade regime, and privatization. Sugar and coconut monopolies have been disbanded, interest rates are now determined by market forces, the bias towards capital intensity in investment incentives has been effectively removed, and a value added tax and improved income tax measures have reduced tax distortions.

Despite successes in structural reform and an initial recovery between 1986 and 1989, the goal of sustainable growth has eluded the Philippines. It has lagged behind its dynamic neighboring countries in foreign investment inflows, export performance, and income growth. This failure in the 1980s can be attributed to a number of factors. Macroeconomic policy slippages were frequent, with delayed responses by the government to shocks such as higher oil prices or revenue shortfalls. Despite substantial policy reforms since 1980, the private sector response was slow because of deep-rooted oligopoly, low private savings and investment rates, and a narrow tax base. High foreign debt added to public deficits and created worries about future disruptions of trade and capital flows. A string of major natural disasters in 1990 and 1991 pummelled the economy. Domestic political turmoil, especially the political crisis of the mid-1980s, depressed private investment.

Recent Developments

The Philippines began a successful two-year macroeconomic program, supported by the IMF, in February 1991. The government made considerable progress in achieving its stabilization goals, even accommodating within the original targets major expenditures for disaster relief. The consolidated public sector deficit was reduced from 5.5 percent of GDP in 1990 to 2.4 percent in 1991—as the national government deficit fell from 3.5 percent to 2.1 percent of GDP—a significant accomplishment and in excess of the program target. This effort was sustained through 1992, and the consolidated public sector deficit was squeezed to an estimated 1.7 percent of GDP.

The cost of sustained fiscal and monetary tightening has been economic stagnation. GDP declined by 1 percent in 1991 and stagnated in 1992, aggravated by serious energy shortages that disrupted productive activity across all sectors. The counterpart of low growth has been a substantial improvement in external balances. Restrained import demand and a modest increase in merchandise exports reduced the current account deficit from 7.0 percent of GDP in 1990 to 3.2 percent in 1991. In 1992 a worsening of the trade balance as imports recovered was more than offset by gains in service receipts, resulting in further improvements in the current account deficit to around 2 percent of GDP.

Successful implementation of stabilization policies through 1991 and 1992 has created an emerging track record of sound macroeconomic management. Inflation as measured by the consumer price index fell from 18.7 percent in 1991 to 8.9 percent in 1992. Returning flight capital, attracted by high peso interest rates, has allowed the central bank to purchase over $3 billion since 1991 in foreign exchange markets, causing unaccustomed problems of sterilization and an appreciating currency. The macroeconomic situation in the first half of 1993 remained encouraging: inflation fell below 8 percent;

the exchange rate started to depreciate in an orderly fashion, and private investment showed a modest pickup.

Progress on structural issues has also continued. Since mid-1991, further substantial reforms have been carried out. The Foreign Investment Act of 1991 substantially liberalized the environment for foreign investment, allowing investment into all but a few sectors on a short negative list and 100 percent foreign equity in most sectors. A tariff code introduced in August 1991 is being implemented in stages reducing tariff dispersion and the number of tariff bands and lowering overall protection. The average import-weighted tariff will be reduced to 14 percent by July 1995. Quantitative restrictions have been removed from all but a few products. In 1992 the foreign exchange market was fully deregulated, allowing free use of foreign exchange funds for current and capital transactions.

In 1992, in response to the continuing power crisis, the government adopted a national action plan for the energy sector, set up a Department of Energy responsible for policy, oversight, and planning for the sector, and made progress in depoliticizing energy prices. In April 1993 the president secured "calamity powers" on the energy sector from the Congress to ensure that bottlenecks do not become a binding constraint on implementation over the next 12 months. The government also made substantial improvements in transport policies in 1992 by promoting competition on major routes and liberalizing rate setting. Decentralization of significant fiscal powers and responsibilities from national to local government units was mandated at the end of 1991, providing an opportunity to increase local autonomy and improve service delivery.

Taken together, these measures have substantially opened the economy to external competition and corrected major policy-induced distortions, leaving the Philippines with a business environment that compares favorably to its neighbors and to other reforming countries. Structural adjustment has not been achieved as smoothly and quickly as might have been desired, and further consolidation of reforms is required in a number of areas, notably revenue generation, energy, transport, and capital markets, but the remaining problems are viewed mostly as a matter of improving implementation effectiveness. The speed and depth of policy reform have been significant.

An important further success was the government's completion of a broad debt restructuring agreement with its creditor banks in 1992. The Brady-type agreement, implemented in December, restructured $4.5 billion of Philippine medium- and long-term commercial bank debt through a package of cash buybacks and issuance at par of principal-collateralized interest reduction bonds, temporary interest rate reduction bonds, and new money and conversion bonds. The debt agreement will generate gross interest savings of about $1.5 billion and gross deferred principal savings of around $1.8 billion over the next five years. As a result, total debt service as a share of exports, which peaked at 44 percent in 1982, is projected at around 18 percent for the medium term.

The Brady agreement, along with continued macroeconomic stability and rising foreign exchange reserves—at $6.7 billion as of end-April 1993—have regained the government and some large Philippine companies access to international capital markets. The government's $150 million Eurobond issue (at 320 basis points above US Treasuries) was fully subscribed in February 1993; sizeable private financing packages for power generation, oil refining, and telecommunications investments have been put together. Portfolio investment inflows in 1992 reached $375 million, up threefold from 1991. The April 1993 price of Philippine new money bonds on the secondary market was 71 cents on the dollar, up from 50 cents in 1991 and marginally above the investment grade threshold of 70 cents.

Poverty and the Environment

Poverty alleviation continues as a central concern of the Philippine government. The official poverty line used in the past in the Philippines was much higher than that used in other countries. Recent modification has corrected that problem, and estimates under the new definition show that poverty incidence decreased between 1985, when 44 percent of families lived below the poverty line, to 41 percent in 1991; most of these gains accrued to the poorest. Poverty alleviation should be helped by a population growth rate projected at 1.8 percent a year over the next decade, compared to 2.5 percent in the 1980s.

The Philippines has a rich but fragile biodiversity, which is at risk from natural disasters, such as the 1991 eruption of Mt. Pinatubo, and from uncontrolled exploitation and pressures from a growing population. The government has formulated a plan with four planks: stronger preservation of natural resources, especially forests and national parks; controlling industrial air and water pollution; reducing urban degradation through better systems of human and industrial waste management, including the eradication of toxic wastes; and strengthening protection of coastal waters and fisheries.

Medium-Term Prospects

The government has prepared a 1993-98 medium-term development plan containing its strategy for restoring and sustaining robust growth led by a competitive private sector while addressing high poverty incidence. First and foremost, the government recognized that bolstering investor confidence required two essential ingredients in addition to macroeconomic stability: an improved law and order situation and an expanded infrastructure base that can provide investors with the ingredients found in neighboring countries. While concentrating on attracting investment and encouraging export growth, the government also realizes the importance of environmental sustainability and poverty alleviation to underpin growth over the long term and distribute its benefits more fairly.

After a decade of reform effort, the Philippines is in a position to resume growth on a sustained path. The ongoing stabilization program has reduced inflation and built up international reserves. The recent debt restructuring operation reduced the burden of foreign debt service on external payments and fiscal balances. Thus, the Philippines can realistically aim over the medium term for a target GDP growth rate of about 5.5 percent.

Although improved efficiency of investment and increased domestic savings can be expected to cover some part of the financing needs, the mobilization of foreign resources will be critical for Philippine development over the medium term, given the substantial volume of infrastructure spending required. The country aims to secure direct foreign investment flows to all sectors in excess of $1 billion annually over the medium term. The bulk of such flows in the short term will likely be linked to the many build-operate-transfer contracts for power generation and other infrastructure projects that the government has negotiated.

President Ramos has announced that the Philippines will push for a strong export drive as the engine of sustained growth. The medium-term development plan places international competitiveness at center stage and proposes specific policies to reach that goal, such as appropriate wage and anti-monopoly policy and greater emphasis on product quality and export-promotion activities. In addition to liberalizing foreign exchange markets and the foreign investment and trade regimes, important institutional changes have cleared the way for export growth. The Export and Investment Development Council, chaired by the president, is addressing bottlenecks for exporters. Procedures for customs inspections, for duty drawbacks, and for foreign investors to obtain visas and work permits have been streamlined. Privately-owned industrial parks can now be licensed as export processing zones; and the government is actively encouraging such private financing of industrial infrastructure.

Philippines

Population mid-1991 (millions)	62.9
GNP per capita 1991 (US$)	730

Income group: **Lower-middle**
Indebtedness level: **Moderate**

KEY RATIOS

	1980	1985	1990	1991	1992
Gross domestic investment/GDP	29.1	15.3	24.9	20.9	22.6
Exports of goods and nfs/GDP	23.6	24.0	28.0	30.1	29.0
Gross domestic savings/GDP	24.2	17.4	19.3	19.5	18.0
Gross national savings/GDP	24.9	15.2	20.6	21.9	21.2
Current account balance/GDP	-6.3	-0.8	-7.0	-3.2	-2.6
Interest payments/GDP	1.8	3.1	3.5	3.2	3.5
Total debt/GDP	53.7	86.6	68.7	70.6	63.0
Total debt/exports	212.3	331.6	228.8	216.5	188.3

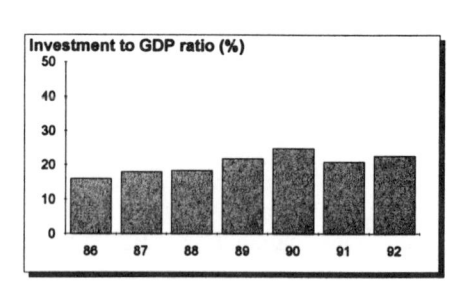

GDP: PRODUCTION
(% GDP)

	1980	1985	1990	1991	1992
Agriculture	25.1	24.6	22.1	21.1	21.7
Industry	38.8	35.1	34.9	34.3	33.3
Manufacturing	25.7	25.2	25.0	25.5	24.5
Services	36.1	40.4	43.0	44.6	45.0

(Growth rates)

	1980-85	1985-90	1990	1991	1992
Agriculture	-0.7	2.8	0.5	-0.2	-0.4
Industry	-3.6	5.5	2.3	-2.9	-0.6
Manufacturing	-3.1	5.4	3.1	-0.4	-1.7
Services	1.2	5.4	4.0	0.6	0.7
GDP	-1.1	4.8	2.6	-0.8	0.0

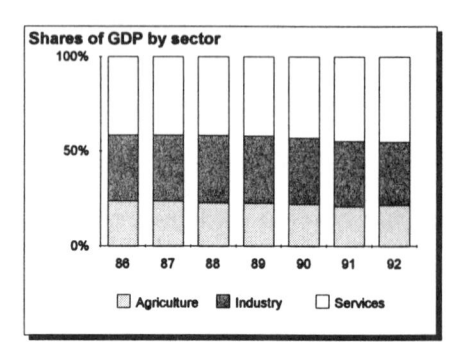

GDP: EXPENDITURE
(% GDP)

	1980	1985	1990	1991	1992
Private consumption	66.7	75.0	70.5	70.3	72.3
General government consumption	9.1	7.6	10.2	10.2	9.7
Gross domestic investment	29.1	15.3	24.9	20.9	22.6
Exports of goods and nfs	23.6	24.0	28.0	30.1	29.0
Imports of goods and nfs	28.5	21.9	33.5	31.6	33.7

(Growth rates)

	1980-85	1985-90	1990	1991	1992
Private consumption	0.3	4.6	2.1	0.9	3.5
General government consumption	-3.0	5.7	8.1	0.7	-4.3
Gross domestic investment	-10.8	14.4	14.6	-17.0	9.3
Exports of goods and nfs	-1.6	9.7	1.3	6.6	1.2
Imports of goods and nfs	-6.9	16.4	10.0	-2.0	13.2
Gross national product	-1.7	5.4	4.4	0.0	1.0
Gross national income	-1.8	5.6	3.2	1.5	1.3

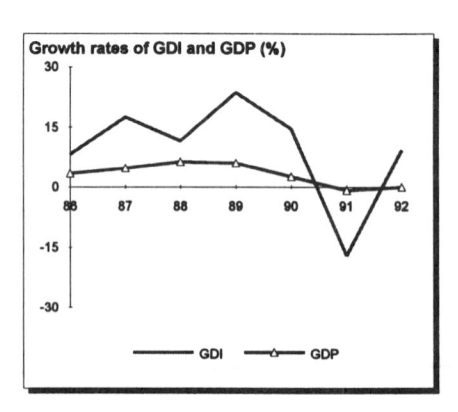

PRICES and GOVERNMENT FINANCE

	1980	1985	1990	1991	1992
Domestic prices					
(% change)					
Consumer prices	18.2	23.1	14.1	18.7	8.9
Wholesale prices	18.3	18.2	10.2	13.4	4.5
Implicit GDP deflator	14.3	17.6	12.7	17.0	7.8
Government finance					
(% GDP)					
Current budget balance	4.2	2.4	0.3	2.1	2.9
Overall surplus/deficit	-1.4	-1.9	-3.5	-2.1	-1.2

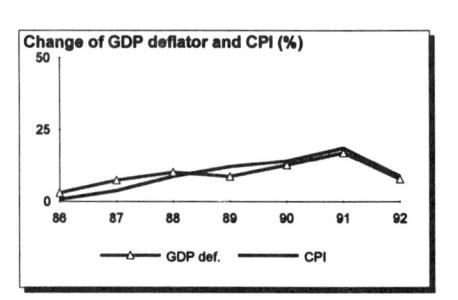

70

Philippines

POVERTY and SOCIAL (annual growth rates)	1980-85	1985-91
Population	2.5	2.3
Labor force	2.5	2.5

most recent estimate (mre)

Headcount index (% of population)	61.8
Energy consumption per capita (kg oil equivalent)	215.0
Infant mortality (per thousand live births)	41.0
Access to safe water (% of population)	81.0
Child malnutrition (% of children under 5)	19.0
Illiteracy (% of population age 15+)	10.3
Secondary enrollment (% of school-age population)	73.0

TRADE
(millions US$)

	1980	1985	1990	1991	1992
Total exports (fob)	5,788	4,629	8,186	8,839	9,824
Timber	425	199	95	73	62
Sugar	657	185	133	136	111
Manufactures	1,996	2,539	5,706	6,432	7,203
Total imports (cif)	7,727	5,111	12,206	12,052	14,520
Food	242	256	656	494	529
Fuel and energy	2,248	1,452	1,842	1,784	2,003
Capital goods	1,900	769	3,122	2,957	3,925
Export price index (1987=100)	..	100	107	109	..
Import price index (1987=100)	..	120	116	119	..
Terms of trade (1987=100)	..	83	92	92	..
Openness of economy	42	32	46	46	46

BALANCE of PAYMENTS
(millions US$)

	1980	1985	1990	1991	1992
Exports of goods and nfs	7,236	6,864	11,106	12,087	14,244
Imports of good and nfs	9,147	5,961	13,832	13,699	16,699
Resource balance	-1,911	903	-2,726	-1,612	-2,455
Net factor income	-439	-1,317	-762	-306	573
Net current transfers	299	172	397	494	492
Current account balance					
Before official transfers	-2,051	-242	-3,091	-1,424	-1,390
After official transfers	-1,903	-35	-2,695	-1,035	-994
Long-term capital inflow	1,748	1,757	-1,099	-95	-495
Total other items (net)	1,060	-1,990	3,749	2,885	1,479
Changes in net reserves	-904	268	45	-1,755	10
Memo:					
Reserves excluding gold (mill. US$)	2,846	615	924	3,246	4,403
Reserves including gold (mill. US$)	3,978	1,098	2,036	4,436	5,336
Official exchange rate (local/US$)	7.5	18.6	24.3	27.5	25.5

EXTERNAL DEBT

	1980	1985	1990	1991	1992
Export ratios					
Long-term debt/exports	107.5	203.0	188.4	175.7	156.7
IMF credit/exports	12.7	14.6	6.9	7.4	5.3
Short-term debt/exports	92.1	114.1	33.5	33.4	26.3
Total debt service/exports	26.6	31.8	26.9	23.3	22.5
GDP ratios					
Long-term debt/GDP	27.2	53.0	56.6	57.3	52.5
IMF credit/GDP	3.2	3.8	2.1	2.4	1.8
Short-term debt/GDP	23.3	29.8	10.1	10.9	8.8
Long-term debt ratios					
Private nonguaranteed/long-term	27.8	16.0	4.8	5.3	1.7
Public and publicly guaranteed					
Private creditors/long-term	42.3	41.2	34.7	29.7	35.7
Official creditors/long-term	29.9	42.8	60.5	65.0	62.7

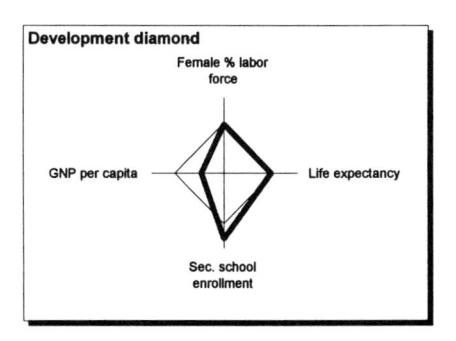

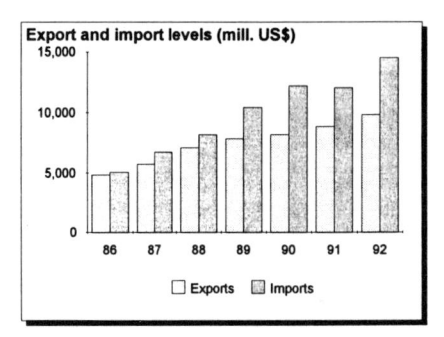

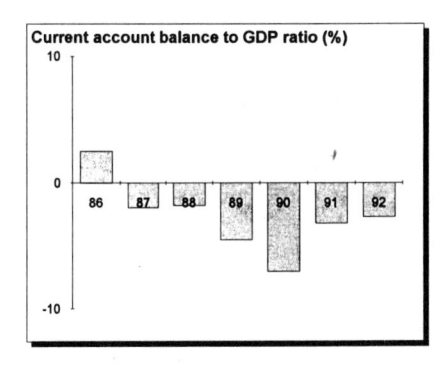

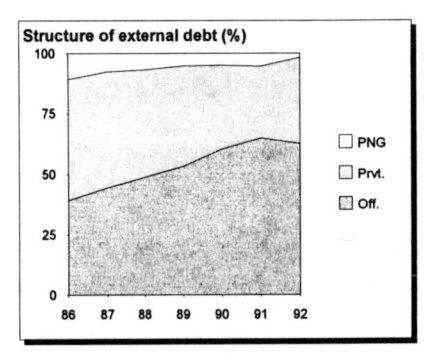

Thailand

By the close of the last decade Thailand was one of the world's fastest growing economies. This remarkable growth rate—founded on a sound economic base developed in the 1970s and 1980s—has been accompanied in recent years by a fiscal surplus and an overall external surplus. Significant progress has been made in reducing poverty and expanding employment. At the same time, the transformation of the economy from dependence on natural resources and agriculture to industrial production and services has provided a more diversified base of economic activity. Thailand provides an excellent example of the dividends to be obtained through an outward orientation, receptivity to foreign investment, and a market-friendly philosophy backed up by conservative macroeconomic management and cautious external borrowing policies.

The Thai economy has undergone considerable change over the last decade. At the end of the 1970s agriculture employed more than two-thirds of the labor force and produced more than a quarter of GDP; manufacturing's share was 20 percent. By 1981 manufacturing had overtaken agriculture, and in 1990 it contributed well over a quarter of GDP. Agricultural value added has now declined to about 12 percent. Services, including trade, finance and tourism and government services remain the largest sector in the economy. These features provide Thailand with a broadly diversified activity base for development. The Thai economy is also strongly export-oriented. In recent years, exports of manufactures have grown particularly quickly, with exports of goods and non-factor services increasing from 25 percent of GDP in 1980 to almost 40 percent in 1992 while the share of manufactures in total merchandise exports rose from 35 to 75 percent. Rice, the leading export commodity of Thailand for many years, was surpassed by textile products in 1985, and textile exports are now almost four times the value of rice exports.

Early in the 1980s the Thai economy faced a period of serious imbalance and painful adjustment. Because of its heavy dependence on imported oil, Thailand was seriously affected by both the 1973 and 1979 oil price shocks, but it did not immediately pass on increased prices to domestic users. This was partly because the first oil price rise coincided with the general commodity price boom, which cushioned the economy from the full impact of the price stock. When the second oil shock hit in 1979, however, a relatively expansionary fiscal stance combined with delays in taking appropriate action to correct the fundamental imbalances contributed to a sharp deterioration in the fiscal and external accounts. From 1979 to 1983 the current account deficit averaged about 7 percent of GDP, and the public sector deficit hovered around 5 percent of GDP for an even longer period. Long-term external debt rose sharply from $2.7 billion in 1978 to $13.2 billion in 1985.

The Thai government took a number of actions in the first half of the 1980s toward stabilization and structural reform. These involved fiscal retrenchment, stronger tax collection, competitive exchange rate management, vigorous export promotion, and reduced external borrowing. Initially, the economy responded slowly to these policy changes, in part because of the unfavorable global economic situation, and in part because the adjustment was relatively gradual. From 1985, however, the cumulative effect of policy measures, including a 14 percent devaluation of the baht in late 1984, combined with more propitious external economic conditions, stimulated a rapid turnaround and recovery. This turnaround was sustained by effective exchange rate management and an increasingly attractive market for Thai exports. Accompanied by improvements in the terms of trade, the economy grew faster and the fiscal and external deficits both fell rapidly. Between 1987 and 1990 real GDP growth was among the highest in the world, averaging almost 12 percent.

While the economic rebound in the latter half of the 1980s was directly attributable to a more favorable international environment—including the depreciation of the dollar against the yen, rising cost pressures elsewhere in East Asia and Japan, and lower oil prices—it was reinforced by prudent macroeconomic and structural policies. Conservative fiscal management, competitive exchange rate policy, and a general shift in the incentive system from import substitution toward export promotion have strengthened investor confidence in the Thai economy and significantly boosted exports.

Recent Developments

Despite the deepening recession in the world economy, GDP growth in 1991/92 was 8 percent. While this was lower than the double-digit growth rates during the latter part of the 1980s, this performance is more sustainable. Lower domestic demand due in part to monetary and fiscal tightening has been the main factor in slowing GDP growth. Private fixed investment in particular, was almost stagnant in 1992 after having risen by over 15 percent a year over 1988–91. Even with rapid economic growth, consumer price index inflation has remained below 6 percent, while the public sector maintained a current budget surplus for four consecutive years. And although tax revenues fell in 1992, because the new 7 percent value added tax was not revenue-neutral, an overall budget balance is forecast for 1992/93.

The external current account deficit rose to 9.2 percent in 1990. Given the Gulf Crisis, oil price rises and a significant decline in visitor arrivals, the deficit for 1991 was expected to be even higher, but fell to 8.5 percent. The deficit fell slightly to 8.2 percent in 1992. As in the past, despite strong foreign investment, the financing of the current account deficit relied heavily on short-term capital inflows.

Trade liberalization has continued, particularly for raw materials and intermediates. Agreement was reached on establishing an Association of Southeast Asian Nations Free Trade Area as of January 1, 1993, to promote regional economic integration. New tax reforms raised indirect taxes through a value added tax and cut income and company taxes. There was also a slight easing of monetary policy to accompany these fiscal changes, which resulted in a fall in interest rates.

Monetary arrangements have also been liberalized, and the regulatory and supervisory framework of financial transactions strengthened. Deposit interest rates, except savings deposit rates, have been completely freed. Lending rates have been substantially liberalized, essentially by raising the ceiling rates. The foreign exchange regime and controls, already quite liberal, have also been further relaxed and the authorities have signed the Article VIII Agreement of the IMF. The net result has been to make the system more open and to integrate Thailand more fully into the international financial market.

Along with overheating, signs of infrastructure deficiencies began to emerge in 1990. Infrastructure is under strain, especially roads, ports, sewerage and telecommunications in the Bangkok Metropolitan Region. Reduced public investment for several years has aggravated this situation, but the shortcomings are being addressed in the 1992–96 Seventh National Development Plan. It is expected that investment will remain high but that its composition will shift from private expenditures on construction and equipment to public and private provision of infrastructure services.

Rapid economic growth has led to an improvement in income levels for most sections of the population, but income distribution appears to have worsened during the 1980s despite rapid growth. Falling rural incomes, reflecting international prices and structural factors within the rural sector, started to recover in the late 1980s but have since regressed. Many farm households are also facing increasing problems of access to principal factors of production such as irrigation water—after a series of drought years in the north—and land.

The urban labor market has expanded very rapidly, at an average of 0.5 million new jobs each year, but it has been next to impossible for public housing, health care, and transport services to keep pace with growing demand. The government is giving increased priority to ensuring affordable access to such social services by lower-income groups, while encouraging greater reliance on private service provision for those able to afford it. Widening urban/rural income differentials have become a politically sensitive issue, and the government is also considering ways to improve public services and to encourage more private investment in the less developed regions such as the Northeast, and to increase local community participation in managing public resources.

Thailand's natural resource base has been depleted and the quality of the urban environment has deteriorated in the last two decades. This has been the result of uncontrolled exploitation of common resources such as timber and fisheries, pressure on agricultural land for urban and residential development, and the pace of industrial and commercial growth. The results are visible in the loss of most of Thailand's natural forests during the last 20 years, increasing water shortages, deteriorating water quality, and air pollution. Government has recently begun to give much greater attention to environmental concerns, and in 1992 there was an overhaul of the legislative and regulatory system for protecting the environment.

Medium-Term Prospects

Thailand's Seventh National Development Plan attaches priority to sustained economic growth and maintaining economic and financial stability. It also encourages a more even distribution of income and the sharing of prosperity between regions. The plan seeks an improvement in the quality of life, including the preservation of the country's environment. The primary economic objective is to sustain a growth rate sufficient to absorb expected growth in the labor force while keeping budgetary and balance of payment deficits under control.

Thailand's development strategy focuses on industrial deepening and greater sophistication to maintain a strong export-led industrial growth. In manufacturing, particular emphasis is being placed on the role of small and medium enterprises, many of which supply parts and components to final assemblers or exporters in the high technology segments of industry. The government believes that Thailand's export competitiveness in the more advanced industries is directly related to the improved efficiency of these smaller firms. The emphasis on smaller firms also derives from a belief that this will lead to a more equitable distribution of income and assets, and a further diminution in poverty by creating greater employment. In pursuing this strategy, the government has begun to remove biases against smaller firms embedded in the tariff system, the structure of investment incentives, the financial system, and infrastructure services.

For the medium-term gross investment will remain a high share of GDP as infrastructure gaps are filled. Hence, the need to mobilize domestic savings to supplement external financing is likely to increase. In terms of mobilizing foreign savings, Thailand remains highly creditworthy and still enjoys a favorable market perception. Gross official reserves at the end of 1991 represented close to half a year's imports of goods and services.

Despite the political instability last year, the Thai business community and international investors appear optimistic about Thailand's medium-term economic outlook. Two factors that justify this confidence are Thailand's strong economic performance over the past five years in a period of varying international fortunes, and the general sense that the right economic environment for private sector export-led industrial growth has been created. If the current government can restore political stability, the Thai economy remains well placed for continued industrial growth, with policies being adopted to further strengthen competitiveness and to increase the pace of privatization.

Steps are also being taken to develop more diversified financial services and to improve the industrial infrastructure. Given the present skills bottlenecks and the desire to better serve the needs of a newly industrializing economy, the education and training system is being adapted to produce more engineers and science and technical manpower in general within a vocational setting.

External Debt

The total debt to GDP ratio peaked at 47 percent in 1985 and, despite rising since 1989, was around 44 percent in 1992. The ratio of debt service to exports has declined continuously since 1988, to about 13 percent in 1992.

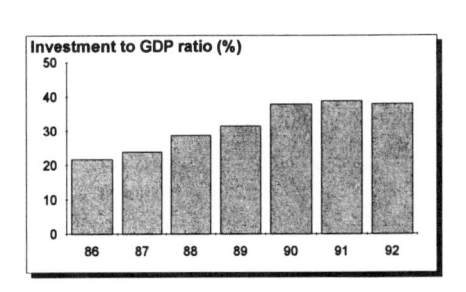

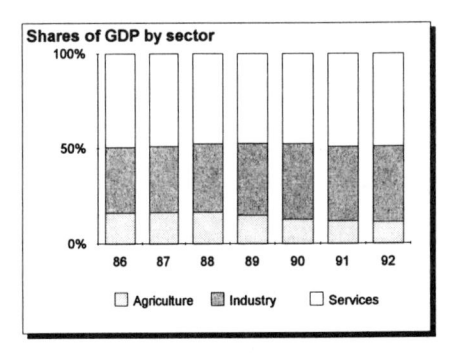

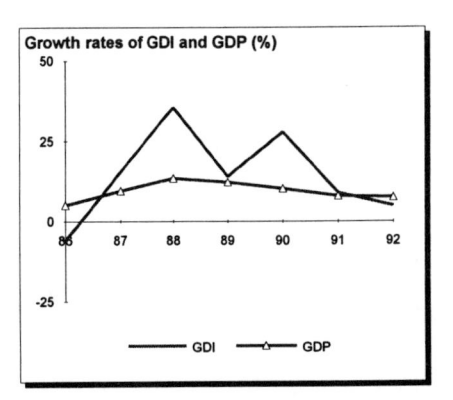

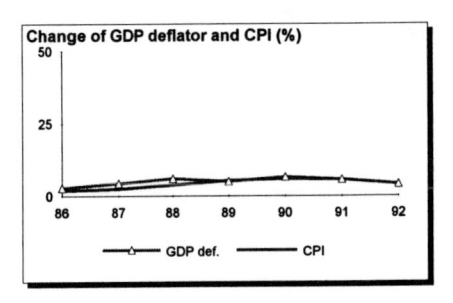

Thailand

Population mid-1991 (millions)	57.2
GNP per capita 1991 (US$)	1,570

Income group: **Lower-middle**
Indebtedness level: **Below average**

KEY RATIOS

	1980	1985	1990	1991	1992
Gross domestic investment/GDP	26.4	24.0	37.9	38.9	37.9
Exports of goods and nfs/GDP	24.3	24.2	35.7	38.0	..
Gross domestic savings/GDP	20.1	21.2	29.9	31.7	34.1
Gross national savings/GDP	19.5	19.6	28.7	30.4	32.6
Current account balance/GDP	-6.9	-4.4	-9.2	-8.6	-8.2
Interest payments/GDP	1.5	2.4	1.7	1.9	1.3
Total debt/GDP	25.8	47.0	34.6	38.4	27.1
Total debt/exports	96.8	171.7	90.2	94.8	..

GDP: PRODUCTION

(% GDP)	1980	1985	1990	1991	1992
Agriculture	23.2	16.7	12.7	11.9	11.4
Industry	30.8	34.0	39.7	39.1	39.8
Manufacturing	21.2	22.1	25.7	27.3	..
Services	46.0	49.2	47.6	49.0	48.8

(Growth rates)	1980-85	1985-90	1990	1991	1992
Agriculture	4.6	3.4	-4.0	3.6	3.5
Industry	5.4	13.5	16.1	10.8	9.6
Manufacturing	4.9	13.4	14.3	9.5	9.3
Services	6.2	9.7	10.4	6.9	7.0
GDP	5.6	10.1	10.3	8.0	7.6

GDP: EXPENDITURE

(% GDP)	1980	1985	1990	1991	1992
Private consumption	67.5	64.7	60.5	58.5	56.2
General government consumption	12.4	14.1	9.6	9.8	9.7
Gross domestic investment	26.4	24.0	37.9	38.9	37.9
Exports of goods and nfs	24.3	24.2	35.7	38.0	..
Imports of goods and nfs	30.6	27.0	43.7	45.2	..

(Growth rates)	1980-85	1985-90	1990	1991	1992
Private consumption	3.9	9.2	6.0	7.7	..
General government consumption	7.0	1.6	1.3	6.4	6.0
Gross domestic investment	4.9	16.8	27.9	9.0	4.9
Exports of goods and nfs	7.3	19.1	13.7	11.0	..
Imports of goods and nfs	2.9	20.2	17.8	10.9	..
Gross national product	5.6	10.3	10.7	7.2	7.7
Gross national income	4.9	9.6	6.6	8.1	..

PRICES and GOVERNMENT FINANCE

	1980	1985	1990	1991	1992
Domestic prices (% change)					
Consumer prices	19.7	2.4	5.9	5.7	4.1
Wholesale prices	20.1	0.0	3.5	6.8	..
Implicit GDP deflator	12.6	0.8	6.5	5.6	4.1
Government finance (% GDP)					
Current budget balance	..	-0.6	7.8	7.4	..
Overall surplus/deficit	..	..	..	..	..

Thailand

POVERTY and SOCIAL
(annual growth rates)

	1980-85	1985-91
Population	2.0	1.7
Labor force	2.5	2.1

most recent estimate (mre)

Headcount index (% of population)	21.8
Energy consumption per capita (kg oil equivalent)	352.0
Infant mortality (per thousand live births)	27.0
Access to safe water (% of population)	64.0
Child malnutrition (% of children under 5)	25.7
Illiteracy (% of population age 15+)	7.0
Secondary enrollment (% of school-age population)	32.0

Development diamond
(Female % labor force, GNP per capita, Life expectancy, Sec. school enrollment)

TRADE
(millions US$)

	1980	1985	1990	1991	1992
Total exports (fob)	6,505	7,120	23,053	28,437	33,126
Rice	953	829	1,085	1,196	..
Other food	727	552	904	955	..
Manufactures	2,271	2,920	13,911	16,871	..
Total imports (cif)	9,280	9,248	33,006	37,576	41,116
Food	302	348	1,312	1,643	..
Fuel and energy	2,868	2,696	5,175	5,762	..
Capital goods	2,250	2,598	13,611	15,236	..
Export price index (1987=100)	113	83	114	118	121
Import price index (1987=100)	100	99	125	131	132
Terms of trade (1987=100)	113	84	91	90	92
Openness of economy	49	44	69	71	71

Export and import levels (mill. US$) — bar chart, 86–92

BALANCE of PAYMENTS
(millions US$)

	1980	1985	1990	1991	1992
Exports of goods and nfs	7,939	9,100	29,230	35,502	41,665
Imports of goods and nfs	9,966	10,160	35,700	42,532	..
Resource balance	-2,027	-1,060	-6,471	-7,030	..
Net factor income	-259	-643	-1,024	-993	..
Net current transfers	0	0	26	153	0
Current account balance					
Before official transfers	-2,212	-1,656	-7,469	-7,978	-8,598
After official transfers	-2,070	-1,537	-7,282	-7,870	-8,440
Long-term capital inflow	2,084	1,606	3,489	4,706	5,347
Total other items (net)	-175	13	7,022	7,618	5,947
Changes in net reserves	161	-82	-3,230	-4,454	-2,854
Memo:					
Reserves excluding gold (mill. US$)	1,560	2,190	13,305	17,517	20,359
Reserves including gold (mill. US$)	3,026	3,003	14,258	18,393	21,183
Official exchange rate (local/US$)	20.5	27.2	25.6	25.5	25.4

Current account balance to GDP ratio (%) — bar chart, 86–92

EXTERNAL DEBT

	1980	1985	1990	1991	1992
Export ratios					
Long-term debt/exports	65.8	129.4	63.6	61.8	..
IMF credit/exports	4.1	11.0	0.0	0.0	..
Short-term debt/exports	26.9	31.3	26.6	33.1	..
Total debt service/exports	18.9	31.9	17.0	13.1	..
GDP ratios					
Long-term debt/GDP	17.6	35.4	24.4	25.0	18.8
IMF credit/GDP	1.1	3.0	0.0	0.0	0.0
Short-term debt/GDP	7.2	8.6	10.2	13.4	8.3
Long-term debt ratios					
Private nonguaranteed/long-term	30.2	25.5	36.8	43.0	29.0
Public and publicly guaranteed					
Private creditors/long-term	31.5	31.3	22.9	21.0	28.9
Official creditors/long-term	38.4	43.2	40.3	35.9	42.2

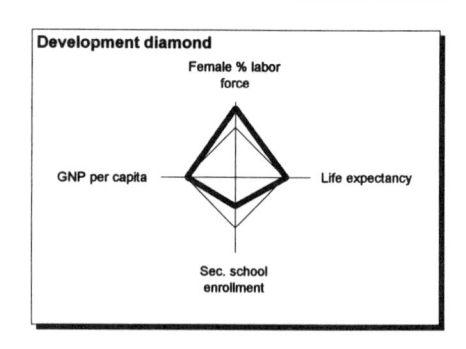

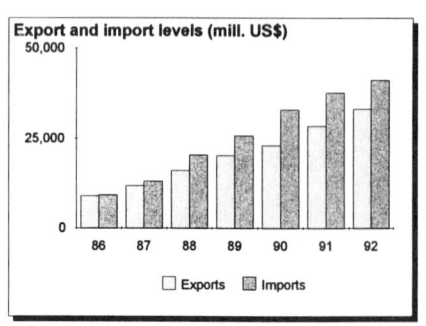

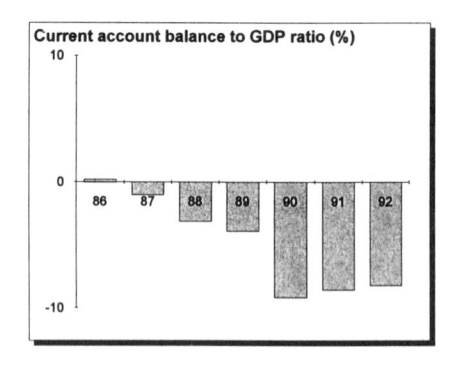

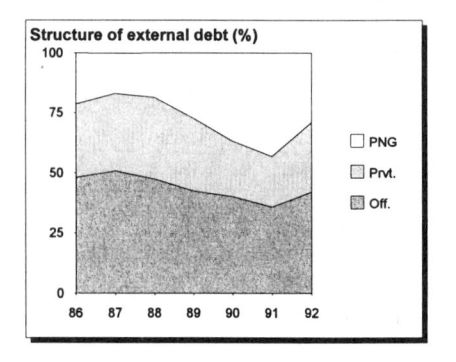

Structure of external debt (%) — area chart, 86–92 (PNG, Prvt., Off.)

Turkey

Turkey's population of about 57 million, with a per capita income of $1,780 in 1991, grew at an average of about 2.3 percent a year in the 1980s. Population density is low, and about 60 percent of the population lives in urban centers. Unemployment has remained slightly above 10 percent through most of the past decade. There is little absolute poverty, but income inequality is high, with considerable differences in income between regions and between rural and urban communities. Data for 1987 indicate that only 4 percent of income accrues to the lowest 20 percent of households, while 55 percent goes to the richest 20 percent. Educational enrollment at the primary level has increased considerably. Most health indicators, including infant mortality rates, have shown substantial improvement over the past two decades, but here too, regional disparities remain significant.

In 1980, following a serious external crisis, Turkey embarked on a stabilization and reform program that was a major break with past policies favoring import substitution, market intervention and reliance on state enterprises. Between 1980 and 1986 growth averaged about 5 percent per year, inflation was reduced to 25 percent, and, as a result of an outward-oriented strategy, exports as a share of GDP increased threefold, substantially improving Turkey's creditworthiness. After 1986 there was further progress in integrating Turkey into the world economy, but most of the previous gains in reducing inflation were lost with the reemergence of serious fiscal imbalances. External liberalization continued as import restrictions were reduced, export subsidies curtailed, and controls on capital transactions substantially diminished. The process culminated in a reform of the exchange rate system that left it largely free of restrictions on external transactions.

These achievements have been overshadowed by persistently high budget deficits and inflation. After being lowered successfully from a three-digit level in 1980, inflation started rising again in 1987 and reached 60 percent in 1990. The fundamental cause was the public sector deficit. Fueled by the poor performance of state-owned enterprises, the public sector borrowing requirement reached 11.6 percent of GNP by 1990. External performance remained strong, with the current account shifting into surplus in the late 1980s, aided by growing revenues from tourism and worker remittances, and continued export growth. Foreign direct investment also surged, and Turkey was able to diversify its sources of foreign financing while repaying the last of its IMF and rescheduled commercial debt.

The 1980s also witnessed substantial political changes. After three years of military government, an elected civilian government took over in 1983. Since the political liberalization, economic policy has had to operate in an increasingly complex political environment. The Motherland Party stayed in power till October 1991, when it gave way to a coalition between the True Path and Social Democrat Populist Parties. The new Government announced its intention to stabilize the economy and maintain the outward-looking and market-oriented policy stance of the 1980s. Nationwide local elections are scheduled in March 1994.

Economic Performance

Economic performance in 1991 was influenced by three major events: the Gulf War; a change in government in mid-year; and national elections in October. These events heightened uncertainty, depressed investment and economic activity, and disrupted the exchange and financial markets. After expanding by 9.2 percent in 1990, GNP grew by only 0.4 percent in 1991. As domestic political events unfolded, electoral considerations dominated the policy agenda, and the fiscal deficit widened. The public sector borrowing requirement rose to 16.9 percent of GNP, and consumer price inflation rose to an average of 66 percent. The underlying causes of the fiscal deterioration, which stemmed from the political agenda, included generous wage increases for civil servants and public sector workers, agricultural support policies, and the poor performance of parastatal enterprises.

The coalition Government which took office in late 1991 inherited an economy with a high fiscal deficit and rising inflation. The Government's program was aimed at reducing public borrowing by accelerating tax collection—coupled with a partial tax amnesty—implementing a centralized cash management scheme for extra-budgetary funds, accelerating privatization and improving parastatal financial performance. The implementation of the anti-inflationary strategy was, and continues to be, complicated by wage rigidity, a large domestic debt burden, a public investment program that had already been substantially cut since 1987, and significant individual and corporate tax evasion.

In 1992 there was only limited progress in dealing with key structural issues, including subsidies, in particular for agriculture. Parastatal divestiture and restructuring, and tax reform also lagged. Economic activity picked up and GNP growth is estimated at 5.6 percent, but was consumption-led and reflected wage increases granted in 1991 and 1992.

Private investment remained weak. The extra-budgetary funds were subjected to financial discipline and some fiscal adjustment took place. The public borrowing requirement, excluding grants, is estimated to have declined from 16.9 percent of GNP in 1991 to 13.4 percent. However, inflation remained high at 70 percent, as labor settlements continued to reflect past inflation rates, and inflationary expectations embodied in interest rates remained high.

Without the needed fiscal adjustment, Central Bank credit to the public sector expanded rapidly, and the authorities concentrated on maintaining stability in the foreign currency markets.

Turkey's situation has not changed significantly in the past year. Reducing the fiscal deficit remains the priority. Past policy slippage has increased the rigidity of inflationary expectations. Currency substitution, which accelerated in the last two years, has not shown signs of reversing, and has reduced the room for noninflationary financing of the deficit through monetary expansion. Given the openness of Turkey's capital account, attempts in 1992 to reduce the Government's interest burden by resorting to central bank financing and interfering with interest rate determination only reinforced currency substitution. As Central Bank reserves declined in 1992, the authorities shifted to domestic borrowing to finance the deficit, raising interest rates to reverse the decline in foreign reserves.

Turkey's goals in 1993 are to maintain GNP growth of 5 percent while reducing inflation. The main instrument is a reduction of the fiscal deficit by about 4 percent of GNP. No monetary program was announced for 1993. A 5 percent growth rate is well within the reach of the Turkish economy, but achieving both the growth and inflation targets will be difficult, given the uncertainties surrounding the fiscal outcome and its impact on monetary policy. If fully implemented, the 1993 fiscal program will be an important step towards restoring macroeconomic stability.

The spillover effects of domestic imbalances on the external accounts have been mitigated by a flexible exchange rate policy that helped maintain the competitiveness of Turkish goods. Although in 1990 domestic policies and the Gulf Crisis led to a marked deterioration in the external accounts, in 1991 Gulf Crisis-related grants of 1.8 percent of GNP and a decline in the trade deficit, mostly due to a slowdown in private demand, compensated for the decline in tourism revenues and worker remittances and led to a small current account surplus.

Overall, the external sector adjusted well to the shocks. The loss of traditional export markets, such as Iraq, was compensated by inroads into other markets. The same resilience was apparent in the tourism and service sectors, where new markets were explored, and service contractors aggressively and successfully tapped new business opportunities.

In 1992, in spite of the good performance of the export and tourism sectors, large import growth and lower inflows from Gulf crisis-related grants led to a current account deficit that is estimated to have reached $1.3 billion, compared to a $0.3 billion surplus in 1991. Increases in foreign direct investment, from around $100 million net a year in the mid- and late-1980s to over $800 million over 1990–92, have reduced external borrowing requirements. In 1992 Turkey was active in the bond markets, successfully tapping the German, United States, and Japanese markets.

Turkey has gained substantial market access and has succeeded in developing strong and broad-based trading links with its European and Middle Eastern trading partners. The OECD countries are Turkey's main trading partners, representing about two-thirds of both exports and imports. Turkey is also actively exploring trade links with the new republics in Central Asia.

Development Issues

Following the adjustment program of the 1980s, the major economic challenge facing Turkey in the 1990s include stabilization and acceleration of productivity growth. Turkey still has almost half its labor force in agriculture, a high unemployment rate, and a rapidly growing population. On the positive side, a much more robust and outward-oriented economy, with a dynamic private sector, puts Turkey in a strong position to meet these challenges.

External Debt

Turkey's external debt at the end of 1992 was estimated at $52.4 billion. The debt service ratio has fallen from an average of about 35 percent in 1988/89 to about 30 percent in 1991/92, and the debt-to-GDP ratio declined from about 55 percent to about 47 percent over the same period. The falling share of official and multilateral financing, however, has been accompanied by a reduction in the average maturity of long-term debt. Reflecting recent increases in short-term debt, particularly for the private sector, short-term debt as a percentage of total debt increased from about 14.8 percent in 1988–89 to about 18.4 percent in 1991–92.

Turkey

Population mid-1991 (millions)	57.3
GNP per capita 1991 (US$)	1,780

Income group: **Lower-middle**
Indebtedness level: **Moderate**

KEY RATIOS

	1980	1985	1990	1991	1992
Gross domestic investment/GDP	21.9	21.0	23.1	19.0	18.8
Exports of goods and nfs/GDP	6.4	20.6	18.6	19.8	21.5
Gross domestic savings/GDP	14.1	17.8	18.3	16.4	15.7
Gross national savings/GDP	15.9	18.6	19.6	17.2	17.0
Current account balance/GDP	-6.0	-2.3	-3.5	-1.8	-2.0
Interest payments/GDP	0.9	2.5	2.6	2.6	2.9
Total debt/GDP	33.6	49.3	45.3	46.6	47.7
Total debt/exports	332.9	198.1	195.1	194.7	185.1

GDP: PRODUCTION
(% GDP)

	1980	1985	1990	1991	1992
Agriculture	22.6	18.8	18.1	17.8	17.6
Industry	30.2	35.3	33.3	34.0	34.6
Manufacturing	21.1	25.1	23.5	23.9	24.4
Services	47.2	45.9	48.6	48.2	47.8

(Growth rates)

	1980-85	1985-90	1990	1991	1992
Agriculture	2.5	2.6	11.8	-0.8	3.5
Industry	5.8	5.2	5.8	3.2	6.6
Manufacturing	7.6	5.6	8.0	2.9	6.6
Services	4.4	5.7	7.9	0.8	4.6
GDP	4.7	5.3	8.7	1.2	5.0

GDP: EXPENDITURE
(% GDP)

	1980	1985	1990	1991	1992
Private consumption	73.4	73.6	67.6	67.6	66.8
General government consumption	12.6	8.6	14.1	16.0	17.5
Gross domestic investment	21.9	21.0	23.1	19.0	18.8
Exports of goods and nfs	6.4	20.6	18.6	19.8	21.5
Imports of goods and nfs	14.2	23.8	23.4	22.5	24.6

(Growth rates)

	1980-85	1985-90	1990	1991	1992
Private consumption	4.8	6.4	14.4	4.1	6.7
General government consumption	1.3	4.4	12.0	1.0	1.8
Gross domestic investment	2.0	2.3	16.0	-17.0	0.7
Exports of goods and nfs	25.6	12.4	10.3	6.2	10.2
Imports of goods and nfs	14.4	11.5	35.5	-2.0	10.4
Gross national product	4.6	5.4	9.6	0.4	5.6
Gross national income	4.3	5.2	10.1	0.8	5.3

PRICES and GOVERNMENT FINANCE

	1980	1985	1990	1991	1992
Domestic prices					
(% change)					
Consumer prices	110.2	45.0	60.3	66.0	70.1
Wholesale prices	..	43.2	52.3	55.3	..
Implicit GDP deflator	102.2	44.0	55.1	57.1	59.9
Government finance					
(% GDP)					
Current budget balance	0.5	1.2	-0.6	-5.3	..
Overall surplus/deficit	..	..	-4.2	..	..

Turkey

POVERTY and SOCIAL
(annual growth rates)

	1980-85	1985-91
Population	2.5	2.2
Labor force	2.3	2.1

most recent estimate (mre)

Headcount index (% of population)	..
Energy consumption per capita (kg oil equivalent)	857.4
Infant mortality (per thousand live births)	58.0
Access to safe water (% of population)	..
Child malnutrition (% of children under 5)	..
Illiteracy (% of population age 15+)	19.3
Secondary enrollment (% of school-age population)	54.0

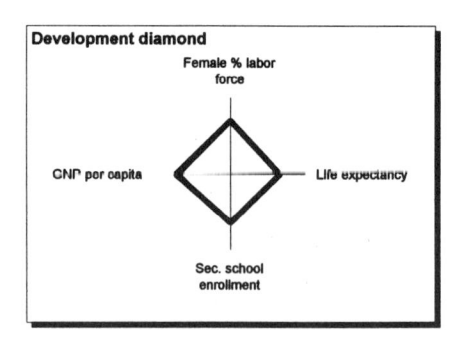

Development diamond
- Female % labor force
- GNP per capita
- Life expectancy
- Sec. school enrollment

TRADE
(millions US$)

	1980	1985	1990	1991	1992
Total exports (fob)	2,910	7,958	12,959	13,594	15,122
Agriculture	1,541	1,454	2,074	2,376	2,393
Textiles	474	..	4,061	4,328	5,231
Manufactures	1,047	5,995	8,294	6,336	7,059
Total imports (cif)	7,909	11,343	22,302	21,038	22,907
Food	50	375	1,319	808	1,055
Fuel and energy	2,953	3,487	3,519	2,456	2,727
Capital goods	1,435	2,252	5,264	5,614	5,818
Export price index (1987=100)	119	99	135	..	..
Import price index (1987=100)	125	112	116	..	..
Terms of trade (1987=100)	95	88	116	..	..
Openness of economy	19	37	33	32	35

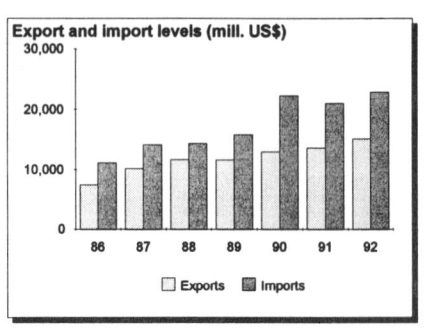

Export and import levels (mill. US$)

BALANCE of PAYMENTS
(millions US$)

	1980	1985	1990	1991	1992
Exports of goods and nfs	3,621	10,873	20,301	21,331	23,637
Imports of goods and nfs	8,082	12,563	25,652	24,216	27,042
Resource balance	-4,461	-1,690	-5,351	-2,885	-3,405
Net factor income	-1,118	-1,307	-1,767	-1,942	-1,755
Net current transfers	2,153	1,762	3,349	2,854	3,000
Current account balance					
Before official transfers	-3,426	-1,235	-3,769	-1,973	-2,160
After official transfers	-3,408	-1,013	-2,625	272	-1,250
Long-term capital inflow	2,916	262	1,005	623	2,200
Total other items (net)	565	643	2,563	-2,094	350
Changes in net reserves	-72	108	-943	1,199	-1,300
Memo:					
Reserves excluding gold (mill. US$)	1,077	1,056	6,050	5,144	6,159
Reserves including gold (mill. US$)	3,298	2,318	7,626	6,616	7,508
Official exchange rate (local/US$)	76.0	522.0	2,608.6	4,171.8	6,872.4

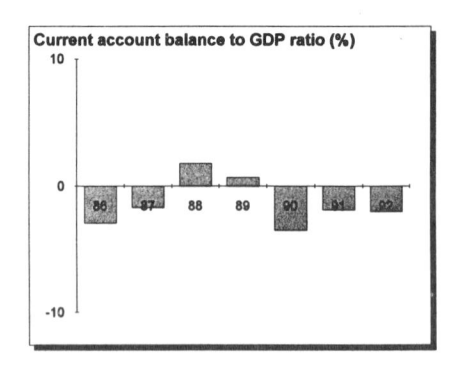

Current account balance to GDP ratio (%)

EXTERNAL DEBT

	1980	1985	1990	1991	1992
Export ratios					
Long-term debt/exports	271.2	151.7	157.4	159.4	150.5
IMF credit/exports	18.4	10.1	0.0	0.0	0.0
Short-term debt/exports	43.4	36.2	37.7	35.3	34.6
Total debt service/exports	28.0	34.9	29.2	30.5	29.5
GDP ratios					
Long-term debt/GDP	27.4	37.7	36.6	38.1	38.8
IMF credit/GDP	1.9	2.5	0.0	0.0	0.0
Short-term debt/GDP	4.4	9.0	8.8	8.5	8.9
Long-term debt ratios					
Private nonguaranteed/long-term	3.4	1.8	2.7	4.7	2.4
Public and publicly guaranteed					
Private creditors/long-term	34.7	36.5	51.6	49.7	53.9
Official creditors/long-term	61.9	61.7	45.7	45.6	43.7

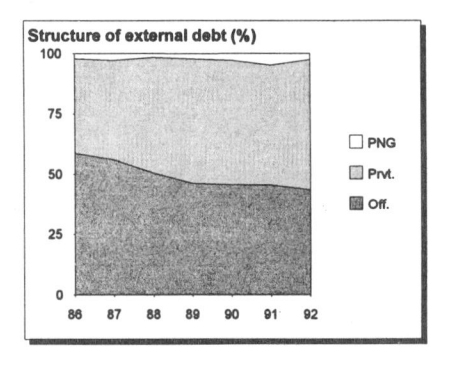

Structure of external debt (%) — PNG, Prvt., Off.

Venezuela

When Carlos Andrés Pérez took office as Venezuela's president in February 1989 his government inherited a mature statist economy and an economic crisis after 15 years of economic mismanagement. During this period oil revenues were poorly invested, the economy became increasingly regulated, infrastructure maintenance was neglected, and costly and misdirected subsidies failed to alleviate poverty. The new government's answer to the crisis was a program of broad structural reforms: deregulation and subsidy elimination, and democratization of the political process drastically changed the rules of the game, and in two years Venezuela was transformed into one of Latin America's most deregulated economies. Despite good economic results from the reform program, Venezuela's future remains uncertain, as the speed of reform has slowed significantly and oil prices are unlikely to increase significantly in the near term.

Growth rates were relatively high from 1950 to 1973 and by the early 1970s per capita output was the highest in Latin America. Following the 1974 oil boom, Venezuela actively promoted state-led industrial development, investing heavily in steel, aluminum, and petrochemicals. The accompanying policies resulted in price distortions, resource misallocation, and wide variations in sectoral performance. Regulation aggravated basic structural problems and led to inefficiencies and inequities. Starting in 1976 growth rates declined and by 1980 had turned negative. In 1988 Venezuela was in crisis: foreign reserves fell sharply, inflation was 60 percent, the fiscal deficit was 9.4 percent of GDP, and Venezuela could not service its external obligations. Living standards plunged: between 1980 and 1985 per capita income fell every year, and income distribution deteriorated and the percentage of the population living in poverty increased throughout the decade.

Economic Policies and Performance

The cornerstones of the comprehensive reform program begun early in 1989 were stabilization, trade and financial sector liberalization, price deregulation, privatization, and new social sector programs.

The key stabilization element was a change from multiple foreign exchange rates to a unified floating exchange system. The exchange rate reached 43 bolivars to the dollar by end 1989, three times the official rate on the eve of the program; this large real devaluation increased the bolivar value of oil revenues and the taxes paid by the state oil company grew from 11.4 percent of GDP in 1988 to 20.5 percent in 1989. The prices of publicly supplied goods and services—including fuel and electricity—were also raised, and most state-owned enterprise prices for tradeable goods were fully liberalized. A further small fiscal improvement was realized by cutting central government capital spending. From end-1988 through the third quarter of 1989 real money supply (M1) fell 47 percent because of the reduction in the nominal money supply and price increases.

Unifying and floating the exchange rate—combined with abolishing foreign exchange controls and reducing the number and level of import tariffs—were the main ingredients in trade reform. Non-tariff barriers now affect only about 2 percent of domestic production, the average tariff has been cut from 37 to 16 percent, and the highest tariff from 135 to 20 percent. Agricultural import licensing has been greatly reduced. Financial sector reforms are reducing the government role in financial intermediation and limiting the central bank's role in providing liquidity and money management. Interest rates were freed within a non-binding range in April 1990, and real rates rose sharply. Other financial reforms include eliminating portfolio requirements—except in agriculture—liquidating development banks, and eliminating preferential credit, except in housing and agriculture.

The government has privatized seven major enterprises, including three banks, the telephone company, and the international airline. It has liquidated the national ports agency, privatized cargo handling and stevedoring, and transferred port administration to new regional authorities. Through 1992 the government had received some $2.3 billion in privatization proceeds and eliminated transfers to most of the largest state-owned enterprises.

Although Venezuela's per capita income is among the highest in Latin America, large sections of its population still live in poverty. In 1989 general food subsidies were replaced with programs targeted to lower-income groups. Existing targeted programs were expanded, and in 1992 about 2.5 million of 2.9 million children were helped by nutritional supplements for pregnant women and their children.

The reform program quickly corrected Venezuela's major economic imbalances, and growth resumed after a year. Inflation fell from 80 percent in the first half of 1989 to 27 percent in December, but GDP also fell—by 8.6 percent over the whole year. To counteract the recession restrictive macroeconomic policies were discontinued toward the end of the year, and a fiscal deficit appeared in the first quarter of 1990. Inflation accelerated to an annual rate of about 32 percent. While oil prices continued to play a major role in economic performance during the reform years, the non-oil sectors clearly responded positively to the reforms. In 1990 GDP grew 6.5 percent—oil by 13.9 percent and non-oil activities by 4.6 percent—and the fiscal and external accounts showed large surpluses, due in part to windfall oil earnings because of the Gulf War. Economic recovery continued in 1991, with oil GDP growing 10.4 percent, and non-oil GDP 8.9 percent.

Major domestic and external events influenced 1992 policy and economic performance. Since a—failed—military coup attempt in February 1992 the speed of reform has slowed significantly because of political instability and public administration problems. Economic performance in 1992 was generally good, except on the fiscal side. GDP grew 7.3 percent as non-oil activities rose 9.5 percent while oil GDP fell 1.9 percent. Central government expenditures declined by about 3 percent of GDP, but the fiscal accounts showed a 6.1 percent deficit, mainly because of falling oil prices; they were also hurt by congressional refusal to pass tax legislation. Foreign exchange reserves remained high at about $13.4 billion—about 11 months of imports.

A second coup attempt in November 1992 has affected 1993 performance, as capital flight in the first quarter reduced reserves by about $1 billion. To avoid further losses, and because the pre-specified bands had become binding, commercial interest rates were linked to the market-determined zero-coupon bond rate. Although domestic real interest rates have remained high, this has prevented speculatory changes in the nominal exchange rate. The change to market-determined exchange and interest rates has been critical and, faced with major domestic and external shocks, the economy has been adjusting with only minimum policy intervention.

In late May President Pérez was suspended pending trial on embezzlement charges and succeeded—until December, when presidential and congressional elections are scheduled—by Ramon Vclasquez. These events and election year maneuvering have undercut political support for proposed tax and financial sector reform legislation, and for ending the gasoline price freeze; electricity and a number of other utility prices have, however, been raised. GDP growth of about 3 percent is expected for 1993; inflation is expected to be in the 30 to 35 percent range. Fiscal and current account deficits of 5 percent and $3 billion are expected. The current account deficit will be financed by foreign investment, external debt, and international reserves.

Medium-Term Prospects

While Venezuela is rich in natural resources, and its new economic framework is promising, prospects in the medium and longer term will depend in part on political developments over the next few months. If the reform agenda is maintained after the December elections, these prospects are favorable. A pro-reform government would be expected to deepen the reforms through new non-oil taxes and increasing user charges, improving public administration and the financial sector, and restructuring and privatizing public utilities. As the reforms show positive results and investment expands, GDP could grow at an annual rate of about 5 percent during the mid-1990s. Sustained economic growth would sharply reduce the debt burden and improve creditworthiness over the medium term.

External Debt

In 1990 Venezuela concluded an external debt and debt service reduction agreement covering $19.7 billion of commercial bank debt.

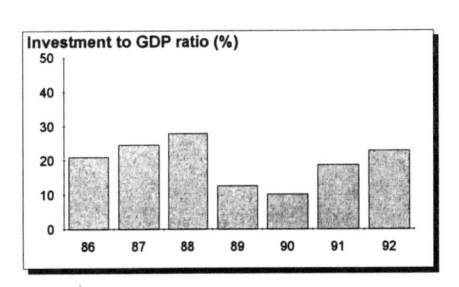

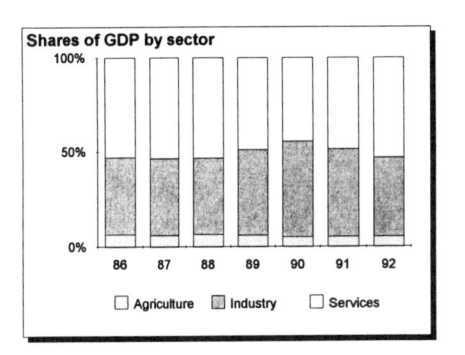

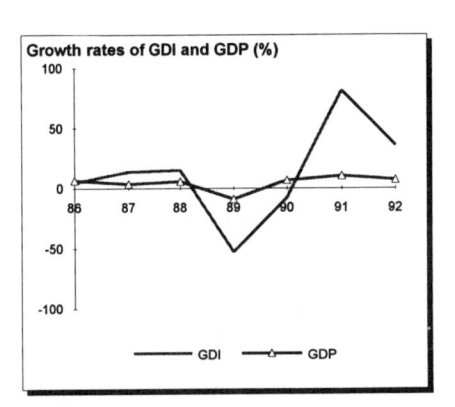

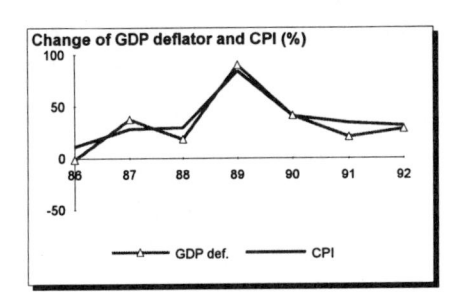

Venezuela

Population mid-1991 (millions): **19.8**
GNP per capita 1991 (US$): **2,730**

Income group: **Upper-middle**
Indebtedness level: **Moderate**

KEY RATIOS

	1980	1985	1990	1991	1992
Gross domestic investment/GDP	26.4	18.5	10.2	18.7	22.9
Exports of goods and nfs/GDP	28.8	25.0	39.4	30.9	25.5
Gross domestic savings/GDP	33.3	27.7	29.5	23.4	19.9
Gross national savings/GDP	33.2	24.0	26.0	20.8	16.5
Current account balance/GDP	6.8	6.0	17.1	2.9	-5.9
Interest payments/GDP	2.1	2.9	6.2	3.9	3.9
Total debt/GDP	42.3	57.0	68.5	64.3	58.2
Total debt/exports	132.0	198.7	156.4	188.8	209.6

GDP: PRODUCTION
(% GDP)

	1980	1985	1990	1991	1992
Agriculture	4.8	5.8	5.4	5.5	5.5
Industry	46.4	43.0	50.2	46.0	41.4
Manufacturing	16.0	21.9	14.7	15.4	15.6
Services	48.8	51.3	44.4	48.5	53.1

(Growth rates)

	1980-85	1985-90	1990	1991	1992
Agriculture	1.9	1.7	-1.8	3.2	2.3
Industry	-1.1	2.6	10.3	12.4	5.8
Manufacturing	5.0	-5.5	7.4	10.8	12.0
Services	-1.5	1.5	5.3	9.6	9.1
GDP	-1.2	2.0	6.9	10.4	7.3

GDP: EXPENDITURE
(% GDP)

	1980	1985	1990	1991	1992
Private consumption	54.9	61.8	62.1	67.2	71.2
General government consumption	11.8	10.4	8.4	9.4	8.9
Gross domestic investment	26.4	18.5	10.2	18.7	22.9
Exports of goods and nfs	28.8	25.0	39.4	30.9	25.5
Imports of goods and nfs	21.8	15.8	20.2	26.2	28.5

(Growth rates)

	1980-85	1985-90	1990	1991	1992
Private consumption	0.6	2.2	3.3	8.4	8.7
General government consumption	-0.3	4.4	5.0	9.5	4.7
Gross domestic investment	-9.3	-10.9	-7.9	81.5	35.8
Exports of goods and nfs	-1.1	5.5	14.5	5.0	-5.9
Imports of goods and nfs	-4.8	-3.0	-7.9	46.1	20.5
Gross national product	-2.1	1.9	8.0	11.6	6.7
Gross national income	-0.9	1.2	9.3	6.1	6.1

PRICES and GOVERNMENT FINANCE

	1980	1985	1990	1991	1992
Domestic prices (% change)					
Consumer prices	21.6	11.4	40.8	34.2	31.4
Wholesale prices	20.0	15.2	27.2	22.3	23.6
Implicit GDP deflator	26.0	10.4	41.2	20.7	28.3
Government finance (% GDP)					
Current budget balance	..	..	13.3	9.3	5.4
Overall surplus/deficit	..	..	1.1	0.6	-6.1

Venezuela

POVERTY and SOCIAL
(annual growth rates)

	1980-85	1985-91
Population	2.8	2.5
Labor force	3.4	3.1

most recent estimate (mre)

Headcount index (% of population)	31.3
Energy consumption per capita (kg oil equivalent)	2,582.3
Infant mortality (per thousand live births)	34.0
Access to safe water (% of population)	89.0
Child malnutrition (% of children under 5)	5.0
Illiteracy (% of population age 15+)	11.9
Secondary enrollment (% of school-age population)	35.0

Development diamond

TRADE
(millions US$)

	1980	1985	1990	1991	1992
Total exports (fob)	19,275	14,660	17,278	15,127	..
Fuel	18,301	13,144	13,912	12,122	..
Aluminum	..	..	661	548	..
Manufactures	424	997	786	710	..
Total imports (cif)	10,652	7,304	6,543	10,181	..
Food	1,249	..	..	..	..
Fuel and energy	104	..	939	1,213	..
Capital goods	3,022	2,464	2,231	3,303	..
Export price index (1987=100)	..	..	..	..	..
Import price index (1987=100)	..	..	..	..	..
Terms of trade (1987=100)	..	..	..	..	..
Openness of economy	43	35	49	47	..

Export and import levels (mill. US$)

BALANCE of PAYMENTS
(millions US$)

	1980	1985	1990	1991	1992
Exports of goods and nfs	19,968	15,863	18,723	16,262	15,431
Imports of goods and nfs	15,130	9,930	9,284	13,575	16,981
Resource balance	4,838	5,933	9,439	2,687	-1,550
Net factor income	329	-2,137	-877	-817	-1,641
Net current transfers	-418	-102	-259	-310	-415
Current account balance					
Before official transfers	4,749	3,694	8,303	1,560	-3,606
After official transfers	4,728	3,668	8,279	1,528	-3,606
Long-term capital inflow	2,060	-1,617	449	2,715	2,813
Total other items (net)	-3,025	-324	-6,056	-1,025	-332
Changes in net reserves	-3,763	-1,727	-2,672	-3,218	1,125
Memo:					
Reserves excluding gold (mill. US$)	6,604	10,251	8,321	10,666	9,562
Reserves including gold (mill. US$)	13,360	13,998	12,733	14,719	13,381
Official exchange rate (local/US$)	4.3	7.5	46.9	56.8	68.4

Current account balance to GDP ratio (%)

EXTERNAL DEBT

	1980	1985	1990	1991	1992
Export ratios					
Long-term debt/exports	62.0	148.4	132.8	158.4	184.7
IMF credit/exports	0.0	0.0	14.2	17.9	17.0
Short-term debt/exports	69.9	50.3	9.4	12.5	7.9
Total debt service/exports	27.2	24.2	23.5	18.9	29.3
GDP ratios					
Long-term debt/GDP	19.9	42.6	58.2	54.0	51.3
IMF credit/GDP	0.0	0.0	6.2	6.1	4.7
Short-term debt/GDP	22.4	14.4	4.1	4.3	2.2
Long-term debt ratios					
Private nonguaranteed/long-term	23.1	32.8	12.9	12.7	10.8
Public and publicly guaranteed					
Private creditors/long-term	72.8	65.6	80.2	78.5	78.9
Official creditors/long-term	4.1	1.6	6.9	8.9	10.3

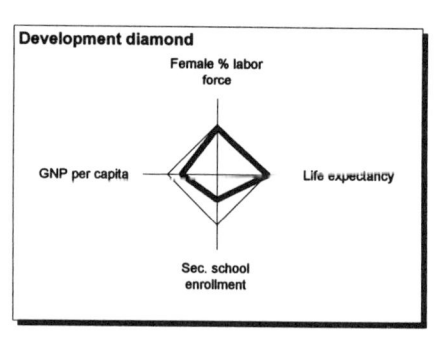

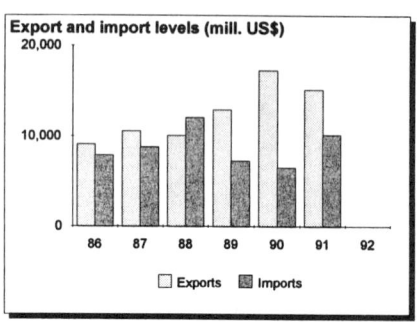

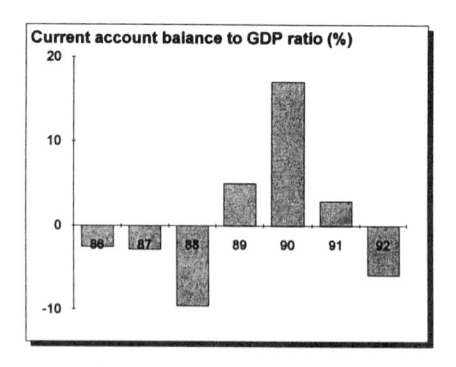

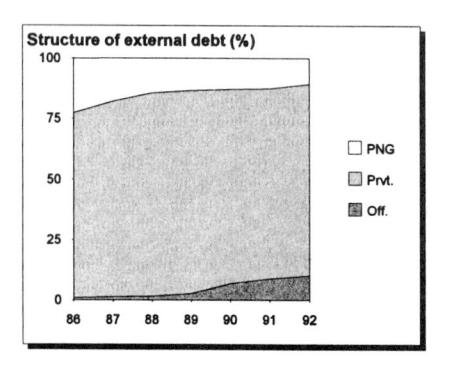

Structure of external debt (%)

Zimbabwe

Zimbabwe is a landlocked country of about 390,000 square kilometers bordered by Mozambique on the east, Botswana on the southwest, Zambia on the northwest, and the Republic of South Africa on the south. Estimated GNP per capita was $650 in 1991, but has fallen in 1992 due to the combined effect of the worst drought to hit Southern Africa this century and real depreciation of the Zimbabwe dollar. Its population of 10.4 million is growing at about 3.2 percent a year.

Economic Performance in the 1980s

At independence in 1980 Zimbabwe inherited a diversified economy, with good potential for growth and well-developed administrative and physical infrastructure. Zimbabwe's government faced a number of difficult issues as the population expected rapid progress in redressing severe inequalities in income, capital, land-holding, and access to social services. At the same time, physical infrastructure and the capital stock had been depleted by foreign exchange shortages over the previous 15 years and the war of liberation. There were significant shortages of skilled labor, largely due to the emigration of white Zimbabweans and the educational policies of the pre-independence government. The government also faced internal and external security problems that affected business confidence and the transport of exports and imports.

The government effectively left the inherited economic structure intact, with predominantly private ownership of productive sectors, and maintained an extensive system of economic controls. To promote growth, it sharply increased foreign exchange allocations in 1980 and 1981, raised agricultural producer prices, and invested heavily in the road and rail systems to repair war damage. To promote equity, it undertook a rapid expansion of education and health services, increased minimum wages, initiated a major reorientation of agricultural services toward communal smallholder areas, and introduced an agricultural resettlement program. The combination of these policies and very favorable weather conditions resulted in bumper crops and an economic boom in 1980 and 1981, with GDP growth averaging 10 percent, but unsustainable external and internal imbalances developed.

Zimbabwe's development strategy produced mixed results during the 1980s. While the country made great strides in education, health, and smallholder agriculture, its per capita income remained stagnant because of disappointing economic growth averaging 3.8 percent. Private sector investment as a share of GDP fell to below 10 percent, and total investment, at less than 18 percent of GDP, was insufficient to expand Zimbabwe's capital stock and raise productivity. Labor force growth outpaced the expansion of employment opportunities, so that by the end of the 1980s only one in three school leavers was being absorbed into the formal sector. Most formal sector employment growth during the 1980s was in the public sector. Government deficits averaging 9 percent of GDP crowded out private investment and fueled inflation.

After a period of large foreign borrowing in the early 1980s the current account deficit of the balance of payments was kept in check through a strict system of direct foreign exchange allocations, avoiding excessive foreign borrowing and debt buildup. The debt service ratio rose to around 35 percent for the period 1985-88, due to a hump in repayment obligations to commercial banks and the IMF, before falling back to the low 20s for 1989 and 1990. However, the resulting shortages of imported goods constrained investment and productivity.

Adjustment in 1990 and 1991

Toward the end of the 1980s it became increasingly clear that sustained income growth would require fundamental changes in economic management. The fiscal deficit had to be reduced to a sustainable level, trade policy liberalized, and domestic regulations greatly reduced. Bolstered by the successful elections of 1990, the government prepared a wide-ranging program of policy reform that was presented to donors in early 1991. The adjustment program, which is phased over five years, addresses the key policy constraints that hampered Zimbabwe's development in the 1980s and aims to increase public sector efficiency, private sector development, and employment creation.

The program's main components are fiscal deficit reduction and monetary policy reform, trade liberalization, deregulation of private sector activities, sector-specific policy initiatives, and measures to alleviate the impact of reforms on vulnerable groups. The program constitutes a movement from pervasive direct controls to market forces. Its fundamental objective is to improve living conditions, especially for the poorest segments of society.

Structural adjustment began well in 1991. A system of open general import licensing, covering 15 percent of imports, was established and the export retention scheme was increased to 15 percent of export earnings to provide additional incentives to exports and access to license-free imports. To support demand management measures in maintaining a reasonable balance of payments position, the real depreciation of the exchange rate was accelerated.

The government accelerated its program of fiscal reform by adopting a budget that aimed to reduce the deficit from 10.7 percent of GDP in fiscal 1991 to 7.1 percent of GDP in fiscal 1992—a target that could not be met because of the need for extraordinary financing to counter that year's severe drought. Initial steps were taken to liberalize marketing and pricing and the Labor Relations Act was amended to formalize a transparent and quick mechanism for retrenching labor.

While good progress was made in initiating the adjustment process, macro-economic balances deteriorated later in 1991. The current account of the balance of payments deteriorated, from 4.2 percent of GDP in 1990 to 8.7 percent of GDP in 1991. Export receipts remained sluggish, due to disappointing agricultural export performance resulting from below-average rainfall and the world economic slowdown, aggravated by the Gulf Crisis. Imports grew rapidly because of pent-up demand and speculation about further exchange rate movements.

The authorities initially hesitated to tighten monetary policy but when pressure on foreign exchange mounted, decisive steps were taken during the second half of 1991 to contain aggregate demand. Money supply growth was slowed, interest rates were liberalized and became positive in real terms, and aggressive exchange rate policy resulted in a 35 percent real depreciation of the Zimbabwe dollar between July and September 1991.

Despite the emergence of a number of stabilization problems, these reforms appeared to raise confidence in the economy, and private investment, output, and foreign aid flows increased in 1991. Non-traditional exports, such as horticultural products, textiles and garments increased significantly, albeit from a relatively low base. The supply response was, however, less than expected, and GDP grew only 3.6 percent. Continued investment licensing and excessive regulation of marketing and pricing were recognized as impediments to reaping the full benefits of foreign trade liberalization and fiscal reform. It was also felt that further action was needed to shield the poor and other vulnerable groups from transitional hardships, partly to improve the reform program's longer-term sustainability.

Dealing with Drought in 1992

Southern Africa was hit in 1992 by the worst drought in living memory. Drought negated the economic benefits arising from the 1991 policy adjustments and the further steps taken in 1992. That the program was continued, despite the adverse economic circumstances, indicates the government's commitment to adjustment. As a result of the drought Zimbabwe's GDP fell by 8 percent in 1992, with agricultural sector output falling by 25 percent. Manufacturing investment and output also fell due to the combined effect of agricultural input shortages, a drastic decline in domestic demand, shortages of power and water, and the tight credit policies used to contain inflation and support the balance of payments. Inflation peaked at over 40 percent, fueled by agricultural commodity shortages, currency devaluation, and liberalization of administered prices. Real incomes and consumption fell, as wages did not keep pace with the much higher cost of living. The government implemented a broad drought relief and recovery program that provided free food for much of the population, agricultural inputs for smallholder farmers, and electricity and water rehabilitation projects. The program's fiscal burden led to a larger than expected fiscal 1993 budget deficit of more than 10 percent of GDP.

Because of the unprecedented need for food imports and much lower exports of agricultural products, external balances deteriorated sharply during 1992. The current account deficit rose to 15 percent of GDP and the accumulation of external debt was much higher than anticipated, rising from $2.5 billion at the end of 1990 to $3.9 billion—70 percent of GDP—at the end of 1992. Monetary and credit policy remained tight, and interest rates remained positive in real terms at around 40 percent. After the major depreciation of the Zimbabwe dollar in the third quarter of 1991, the nominal exchange rate was held constant during 1992, before falling by another 20 percent between December 1992 and February 1993. Large amounts of bilateral and multilateral financial support were disbursed during 1992 to assist Zimbabwe in its drought relief and recovery program and help keep its economic reform program on track.

Recent Economic Developments

Recovery began in the second half of 1993. The year's maize crop is expected to exceed 2 million tons—about enough to meet domestic needs. Cotton is expected to recover fully, water resources will be replenished, and electricity shortages. Livestock, sugar and treecrop industries will, however, take another couple of good seasons to recover completely. Growth in agriculture is not, however, expected to be matched in other sectors, and overall 1993 GDP growth is unlikely to exceed 2 percent. The current account deficit on the balance of payments is projected to fall in 1993 to about 12 percent of GDP as the need for emergency imports declines.

There seem to be two main reasons for Zimbabwe's weak recovery from the drought: continued macroeconomic imbalances and weak investor confidence. In fiscal 1993 the government had to rely primarily on tight monetary policy to restrain inflation, as drought-related expenditures and large shortfalls in expected external financial assistance led to a large government borrowing requirement from domestic sources. A further complicating factor is the collapse of the world tobacco market in 1993, which will defer full export recovery for another two or three years.

Despite the serious economic and social difficulties created by the devastating drought, Zimbabwe continued with structural adjustment in 1992 and 1993. Import liberalization proceeded in line with program targets, with the export retention scheme rate being increased to 50 percent in April 1993. Decontrol and adjustment of prices proceeded more quickly than targeted. Investment licensing was relaxed in April 1993, and the government now allows automatic and unrestricted dividend remittance for foreign investments made after May 1, 1993, through the export retention scheme market. Foreign investment made after September 1979 is eligible for unrestricted repatriation—through the export retention market—of foreign exchange injected as capital. The fiscal 1994 budget calls for a significantly reduced deficit. Monetary restraint has limited inflation to about 20 percent, albeit at some cost in terms of economic growth.

Poverty and Employment

Zimbabwe has made only limited progress in developing an effective social safety net for the poor and those suffering from the transitional effects of structural adjustment. The government initially focused more on the economic that the social aspects of adjustment; the 1992 drought relief program then diverted manpower and budget resources from planned social programs toward continuing subsidies for maize, maize meal, and bread, and a significant expansion of the rural food for work program. While the government has established an effective program to exempt the rural poor from school fees, cumbersome and costly administrative structures prevent social programs from serving more than a fraction of population targeted for exemption from fees for health or urban schools. Budget pressures have also caused the government to defer plans to move to selectively targeted food subsidies.

Average per capita incomes have been stagnant since the early 1980s, but there have been significant poverty-related improvements in two areas. First, a supportive policy on agricultural pricing and a reorientation of agricultural services toward the communal areas have improved smallholder incomes, apart from in drought years. Second, there has been a substantial expansion of basic services in health, family planning, education, and urban services.

Inadequate employment growth has become a major concern in Zimbabwe. Although there are 200,000 new entrants to the work force each year, formal employment has expanded very slowly. This problem should be eased as structural reforms and deregulation lead to an expansion of small- and medium-sized enterprises.

External Debt

Assuming that gradual but decisive structural reforms take place, Zimbabwe's total outstanding debt is projected to decline from its peak of 70 percent of GDP in 1992. and to decline thereafter. Long-term debt servicing rose to 30 percent in 1992 and is projected to fall back to 24 percent by 1995, provided a large share of the external finance needed is provided on a concessional and long-term basis.

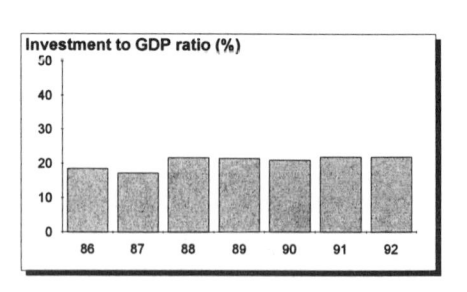

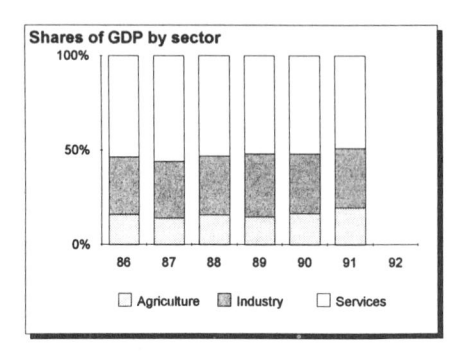

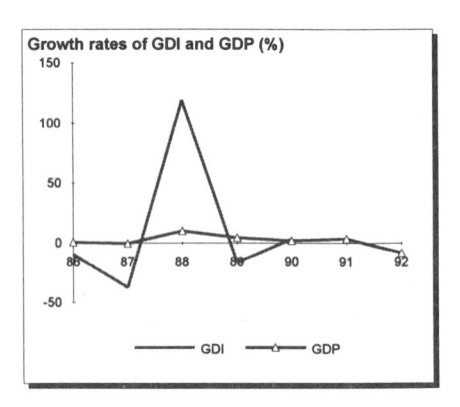

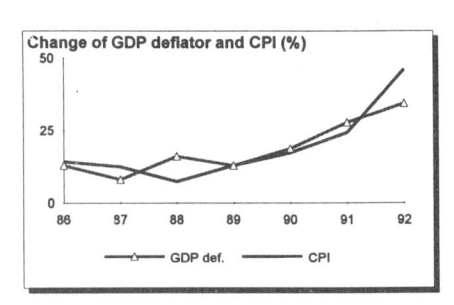

Zimbabwe

Population mid-1991 (millions)	10.1
GNP per capita 1991 (US$)	650

Income group: **Low**
Indebtedness level: **Below average**

KEY RATIOS

	1980	1985	1990	1991	1992
Gross domestic investment/GDP	18.8	19.8	21.1	22.0	22.0
Exports of goods and nfs/GDP	30.3	28.8	30.2	32.5	34.7
Gross domestic savings/GDP	15.8	21.0	21.4	18.1	10.2
Gross national savings/GDP	12.2	16.1	17.3	13.4	13.3
Current account balance/GDP	-5.6	-3.4	-3.9	-8.7	-17.2
Interest payments/GDP	0.2	2.8	2.2	4.0	3.5
Total debt/GDP	14.6	53.3	48.6	54.3	64.9
Total debt/exports	45.4	186.9	159.1	164.7	184.4

GDP: PRODUCTION

(% GDP)	1980	1985	1990	1991	1992
Agriculture	14.0	20.2	16.5	19.5	..
Industry	33.7	28.0	31.8	31.7	..
Manufacturing	24.9	22.9	25.5	25.5	..
Services	52.3	51.8	51.7	48.8	..

(Growth rates)	1980-85	1985-90	1990	1991	1992
Agriculture	3.6	-0.8	-6.6	3.1	..
Industry	-1.2	3.6	4.9	3.1	..
Manufacturing	0.9	4.3	6.1	2.5	..
Services	4.8	4.2	2.8	4.0	..
GDP	3.4	3.8	2.0	3.6	-8.3

GDP: EXPENDITURE

(% GDP)	1980	1985	1990	1991	1992
Private consumption	64.5	57.5	55.7	60.9	69.2
General government consumption	19.7	21.5	22.9	21.0	20.5
Gross domestic investment	18.8	19.8	21.1	22.0	22.0
Exports of goods and nfs	30.3	28.8	30.2	32.5	34.7
Imports of goods and nfs	33.3	27.6	29.9	36.4	46.5

(Growth rates)	1980-85	1985-90	1990	1991	1992
Private consumption	1.8	..	..	..	..
General government consumption	8.7	13.8	..	..	..
Gross domestic investment	-1.7	4.6	3.4	..	..
Exports of goods and nfs	3.6	..	..	..	..
Imports of goods and nfs	-1.0	..	..	..	..
Gross national product	2.9	3.9	1.1	2.8	-6.0
Gross national income	2.9	..	..	..	..

PRICES and GOVERNMENT FINANCE

	1980	1985	1990	1991	1992
Domestic prices (% change)					
Consumer prices	5.4	8.5	17.4	24.3	46.2
Wholesale prices	..	..	..	..	..
Implicit GDP deflator	10.0	6.9	18.8	27.9	34.6
Government finance (% GDP)					
Current budget balance	..	-4.8	-2.0	-0.4	-2.1
Overall surplus/deficit	..	..	..	..	..

Zimbabwe

POVERTY and SOCIAL (annual growth rates)	1980-85	1985-91
Population	3.7	3.0
Labor force	2.7	2.8

most recent estimate (mre)

Headcount index (% of population)	40.3
Energy consumption per capita (kg oil equivalent)	531.4
Infant mortality (per thousand live births)	48.0
Access to safe water (% of population)	..
Child malnutrition (% of children under 5)	12.0
Illiteracy (% of population age 15+)	33.1
Secondary enrollment (% of school-age population)	50.0

Development diamond

Female % labor force — Life expectancy — Sec. school enrollment — GNP per capita

TRADE
(millions US$)

	1980	1985	1990	1991	1992
Total exports (fob)	1,445	1,120	1,753	1,785	1,506
Cotton	192	223	395	532	425
Gold	180	121	239	225	164
Manufactures	..	..	425	385	361
Total imports (cif)	1,641	1,040	1,849	2,150	..
Food	49	35	42	20	..
Fuel and energy	271	192	288	268	..
Capital goods	706	402	689	883	..
Export price index (1987=100)	166	101	106	113	..
Import price index (1987=100)	141	87	124	124	..
Terms of trade (1987=100)	118	116	85	91	..
Openness of economy	57	48	54	62	..

Export and import levels (mill. US$)

BALANCE of PAYMENTS
(millions US$)

	1980	1985	1990	1991	1992
Exports of goods and nfs	1,612	1,229	2,018	2,056	1,820
Imports of goods and nfs	1,721	1,211	2,002	2,301	2,438
Resource balance	-109	18	16	-245	-618
Net factor income	-72	-126	-272	-305	-298
Net current transfers	0	-45	-2	2	11
Current account balance					
Before official transfers	-302	-153	-258	-548	-905
After official transfers	-244	-98	-150	-407	-608
Long-term capital inflow	-54	82	169	285	404
Total other items (net)	211	103	-3	32	37
Changes in net reserves	87	-86	-16	90	167
Memo:					
Reserves excluding gold (mill. US$)	214	93	149	150	222
Reserves including gold (mill. US$)	419	345	295	295	404
Official exchange rate (local/US$)	0.6	1.6	2.5	3.4	5.1

Current account balance to GDP ratio (%)

EXTERNAL DEBT

	1980	1985	1990	1991	1992
Export ratios					
Long-term debt/exports	40.2	142.6	129.8	137.8	147.1
IMF credit/exports	0.0	20.4	0.3	0.0	0.0
Short-term debt/exports	5.2	23.8	28.9	26.9	37.4
Total debt service/exports	3.8	32.7	23.1	27.2	28.1
GDP ratios					
Long-term debt/GDP	12.9	40.7	39.7	45.4	51.8
IMF credit/GDP	0.0	5.8	0.1	0.0	0.0
Short-term debt/GDP	1.7	6.8	8.8	8.9	13.1
Long-term debt ratios					
Private nonguaranteed/long-term	0.0	3.5	7.0	9.2	5.0
Public and publicly guaranteed					
Private creditors/long-term	85.5	58.7	36.1	33.8	24.3
Official creditors/long-term	14.5	37.8	56.9	57.0	70.8

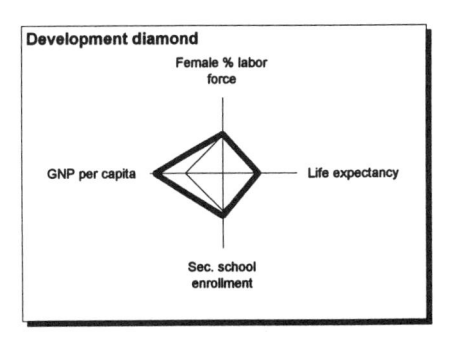

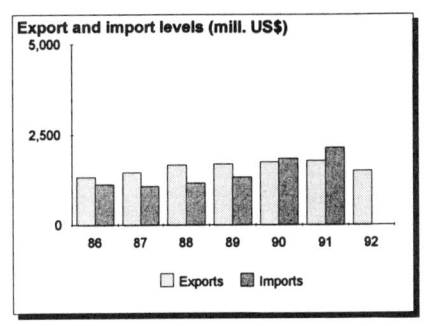

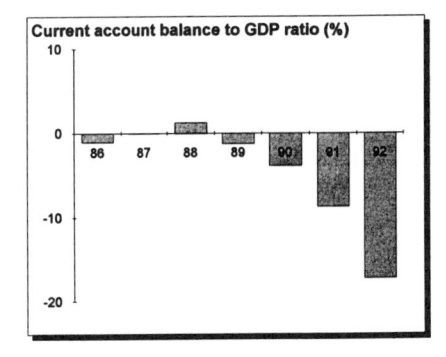

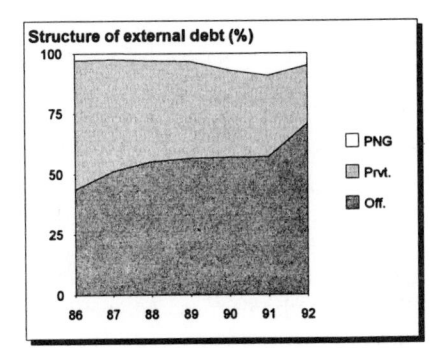

Structure of external debt (%) — PNG, Prvt., Off.

Technical Notes

The tables and graphs that follow each country text provide a uniform statistical framework for analyzing country economic performance. Most data are consistent with other World Bank publications such as *World Tables*, *World Debt Tables* and the *World Development Report*. Some data are the recent estimates from national publications data that may not conform to international concepts and definitions, but are considered to be useful in placing country policy decisions in context. These differences are generally not considered analytically significant for a particular country.

Population

Population numbers for mid-1991 are World Bank estimates. These are usually projections from the most recent population censuses or surveys; most are from 1980–91, and, for a few countries, from the 1960s or 1970s. Note that refugees not permanently settled in the country of asylum are generally considered to be part of the population of their country of origin.

Gross National Product (*GNP*)

GNP measures the total domestic and foreign value added claimed by residents. It comprises GDP (defined below) plus net factor income from abroad, which is the income residents receive from abroad for factor services (labor and capital) less similar payments made to nonresidents who contributed to the domestic economy. *GNP per capita* figures in U.S. dollars are calculated according to the *World Bank Atlas* method of conversion. The Atlas conversion factor for any year is the average of a country's exchange rate for that year and for the two preceding years, adjusted for differences in relative inflation between the country and the United States. This three-year average smooths fluctuations in prices and exchange rates for each country. To derive GNP per capita, the resulting GNP in U.S. dollars is divided by the midyear population for the latest of the three years.

For *income group and indebtedness level* definitions see the two classification tables at the back of the book.

Key Ratios

Key ratios are calculated as percentage shares of GDP or exports at current prices. The numerator of each ratio is defined below. The denominators (GDP and exports) are defined in the sections on production and balance of payments.

Gross domestic investment consists of outlays on additions to the fixed assets of the economy plus net changes in the level of inventories.

Exports (imports) of goods and nonfactor services represent the value of all goods and nonfactor services provided to (from) the rest of the world; they include merchandise, freight, insurance, travel, and other nonfactor services. The value of factor services, such as investment income, interest, and labor income, is excluded. Current transfers are also excluded.

Gross domestic savings are calculated by deducting total consumption from GDP.

Gross national savings equals gross domestic savings plus net factor income and net current transfers from abroad.

Current account balance after official transfers is the difference between (a) exports of goods and services (factor and nonfactor) as well as inflows of unrequited transfers (private and official) and (b) imports of goods and services as well as all unrequited transfers to the rest of the world. *Current account balance before official transfers* is the current account balance that treats net official unrequited transfers as akin to official capital movements. The difference between the two balance of payments measures is essentially foreign aid in the form of grants, technical assistance, and food aid, which, for most developing countries, tends to make current account deficits smaller than the financing requirement. The key ratio presented here is the current account balance before official transfers.

Interest payments (on long-term debt) are the actual amounts of interest paid in foreign currency, goods, or services by the borrower during the year. The exports in the denominator include goods and all services, including workers' remittances.

Total debt includes total outstanding external debt (long- and short-term debt and the use of IMF credit).

GDP: Production

In the sections on production and expenditure, ratios of GDP are calculated from data in current prices, and growth rates are calculated from data in constant prices.

Agriculture covers forestry, hunting, and fishing, as well as agriculture. In developing countries with high levels of subsistence farming, much agricultural production is either not exchanged or not exchanged for money. This increases the difficulty of measuring the contribution of agriculture to GDP and reduces the reliability and comparability of such numbers.

Industry comprises value added mining and quarrying; manufacturing (also reported as a separate subgroup); construction; and electricity, gas, and water.

Services comprises value added in all other branches of economic activity, including imputed bank service charges, import duties, and any statistical discrepancies noted by national compilers.

GDP measures the total output of goods and services for final use produced by residents and nonresidents, regardless of the allocation to domestic and foreign claims. It is calculated without making deductions for depreciation of fabricated assets or depletion and degradation of natural resources. The estimate of GDP used for ratio calculations in GDP: Production and GDP: Expenditure are on the same basis as the components—at purchaser values or at factor cost.

GDP: Expenditure

Private consumption is the market value of all goods and services, including durable products (such as cars, washing machines, and home computers) purchased or received as income in kind by households and nonprofit institutions. It excludes purchases of dwellings but includes the imputed rent for owner-occupied dwellings.

General government consumption includes all current expenditure for purchases of goods and services by all levels of government. Capital expenditure on national defense and security is regarded as consumption expenditure.

Gross domestic investment - See *Key Ratios*.

Exports/Imports of goods and nonfactor services - See *Key Ratios*.

GNP - See above.

GNY, or gross national income, in constant prices is derived as the sum of GNP and the terms of trade adjustment. The latter is equal to capacity to import (value of exports of goods and nonfactor services deflated by the import price index) less actual exports of goods and services in constant prices.

Prices and Government Finance

Consumer prices comprise the price index of goods and services used for private consumption of households.

Wholesale prices (or producer prices for some countries) monitor changes in prices of items at the first important commercial transaction. Preference is given to producer prices because the concept, weighting pattern, and coverage are more consistent with accounting and industrial production statistics. The price index covers a mixture of prices of agricultural and industrial goods at various stages of production and distribution.

Implicit GDP deflator is an overall measure of price performance in the economy. Derived by dividing current price estimates of GDP at market prices by constant prices.

Current budget balance is the excess of current revenue over current expenditure.

Overall surplus/deficit is total revenue and all grants received, less the sum of total expenditure and government lending minus repayment.

Poverty and Social

Population - See above.

Labor force comprises so-called "economically active" persons, including armed forces and unemployed but excluding homemakers and other unpaid caregivers and students.

Headcount index of poverty is estimated as the proportion of population under the poverty line. The poverty lines are country-specific and are not comparable across countries. These estimates are based on special surveys that, in most cases, are now over 10 years old.

Energy consumption per capita is the annual consumption of commercial primary energy (coal, lignite, petroleum, natural gas, and hydro, nuclear and geothermal electricity) in kilograms of oil equivalent per capita.

Infant mortality rate is the number of deaths of infants under one year of age per 1,000 live births in a given year. The data are a combination of observed values and interpolated and projected estimates.

Access to safe water is the percentage of population with reasonable access to safe water supply (includes treated surface waters or untreated but uncontaminated water such as that from springs, sanitary wells, and protected boreholes). In an urban area this may be a public fountain or standpost not more than 200 meters away. In rural areas it implies that members of the household do not have to spend a disproportionate part of the day fetching water. The definition of *safe* has changed over time.

Child malnutrition (under 5) is the percentage of children under five years with a deficiency or an excess of nutrients that interferes with health and genetic potential for growth. Methods of assessment vary, but the most commonly used are: less than 80 percent of the standard weight for age; less than minus two standard deviations from the 50th percentile of the weight-for-age reference population; or the Gomez scale of malnutrition.

Illiteracy (% of population age 15+) is the proportion of the population 15 years of age and older who cannot, with understanding, both read and write a short simple statement on everyday life. This is only one of the three widely accepted definitions and its application is subject to significant qualifiers in a number of countries. The data for the most recent estimates are from the illiteracy estimates and projections prepared in 1989 by UNESCO. More recent information and a modified model have been used, therefore the data for 1990 are not strictly consistent with those published in previous years.

Secondary enrollment (% school-age population) is the gross enrollment of students of all ages at the secondary level as a percentage of school-age children as defined by each country and reported to UNESCO. Although many countries consider secondary school age to be 12 to 17 years, others use different age groups. For some countries with universal secondary education, the gross enrollment ratios may exceed 100 percent because some pupils are younger or older than the country's standard secondary school age.

The *Development diamond* portrays relationships among four socio-economic indicators for a given country and compares them with the average of the country's income group. Female share of labor force, life expectancy, secondary school enrollment, and GNP per capita are presented, one on each axis, and then connected (with a bold line) to form a polygon—the "diamond." The shape of the diamond can thus easily be compared among countries. To broaden the comparison, the averages for each income group are indexed (equaled to 1), and the reference diamond (a square) represented by a fine line. Any point outside the reference diamond represents a value better than the group average, and any point inside the reference diamond represents a value below the group average. Since the indexes are of different values in different income groups, the comparison should be limited to the same income group.

Female % labor force is the female labor force as a percentage of total labor force.

Life expectancy at birth is the number of years a newborn infant would live if prevailing patterns of mortality at the time of its birth were to stay the same throughout its life. As in infant mortality rate, the data are a combination of observed values and projected estimates.

GNP per capita - See above.

Trade

The section includes information on export and import values and prices, with additional value data on the two main export commodities and major categories of imports. The categorization of exports and imports follows the Standard International Trade Classification (SITC), Series M, No. 34, Revision 1. Note that in some cases, (for example, fuel), the export subcategory may be listed more than once. These represent different forms of the commodity and are therefore shown separately.

Total exports (f.o.b.)/imports (c.i.f.)—merchandise exports and imports, cover, with some exceptions, international movements of goods across customs borders. Exports are valued f.o.b. (free on board) and imports c.i.f. (cost, insurance and freight) unless otherwise specified in the foregoing sources.

Food are the commodities in SITC Sections 0, 1, and 4 and Division 22 (food and live animals, beverages and tobacco, animal and vegetable oils and fats, oilseeds, oil nuts and oil kernels).

Manufactures comprises commodities in SITC Sections 5 through 9 (chemicals and related products, basic manufactures, machinery and transport equipment, other manufactured articles and goods not elsewhere classified) excluding Division 68 (nonferrous metals).

Fuel and energy comprises commodities in SITC Section 3 (mineral fuels and lubricants and related materials).

Capital goods comprise commodities in SITC Section 7 (machinery and transport equipment).

Export/import price index are price indexes for measuring changes in the aggregate price level of a country's merchandise exports and imports over time.

Terms of trade is the relative level of export prices compared with import prices, calculated as the ratio of a country's index of average export price to the average import price index.

Openness of economy is estimated as the sum of merchandise exports and imports as a share of GDP.

Balance of Payments

Exports/imports of goods and nonfactor services - See *Key Ratios*.

Resource balance is exports of goods and nonfactor services minus imports of goods and nonfactor services.

Net factor income is the income received from abroad for factor services (labor and capital) less similar payments made to nonresidents who contributed to the domestic economy.

Net current transfers are private net transfer payments—between private persons and nonofficial organizations of the reporting country and the rest of the world—that carry no provisions for repayment. Included are workers' remittances; transfers by migrants; gifts, dowries, and inheritances; and alimony and other support remittances. Net current transfers are equal to the unrequited transfers of income from nonresidents to residents minus the unrequited transfers from residents to nonresidents.

Current account balance - See *Key Ratios*.

Long-term capital inflow, comprises changes, apart from valuation adjustments, in residents' long-term foreign liabilities less their long-term assets, excluding any long-term items classified as reserves.

Total other items (net) comprise the sum of short-term capital, net errors and omissions, and capital transactions not included elsewhere.

Changes in net reserves comprise the net change in a country's holdings of international reserves resulting from transactions on the current and capital accounts. These include changes in holdings of monetary gold, SDRs, reserve position in the International Monetary Fund, foreign exchange assets, and other claims on nonresidents that are available to the central authority. The measure is net of liabilities constituting foreign authorities' reserves, and counterpart items for valuation of monetary gold and SDRs, which are reported separately in IMF sources.

Reserves excluding gold comprise a country's monetary authorities' (central bank, currency boards, exchange stabilization funds, and treasuries) holdings of SDR, reserve position in the International Monetary Fund, and foreign exchange.

Reserves including gold comprise international reserves excluding gold and official holdings of gold valued at year-end London market price.

Official exchange rate (local currency units/US$) is the official exchange rate as reported in the *International Financial Statistics* (line rf/wf - period average), expressed in units of national currency per U.S. dollar.

External Debt

Debt indicators presented in this section are ratios used to assess the external situation of developing countries. They are compiled on a consistent basis as reported to the World Bank's Debtor Reporting System by member countries. The ratios offer various measures of the cost of, or capacity for, servicing debt in terms of the foreign exchange or output foregone. External debt indicators are shown for the end of the year specified. The exports reported in this section include goods and all services, and workers' remittances.

Long-term debt is defined as debt that has an original or extended maturity of more than one year and that is owed to nonresidents and repayable in foreign currency, goods, or services. Long-term external debt has three components:

Public debt is an external obligation of a public debtor, including the national government, a political subdivision (or an agency of either), and autonomous public bodies.

Publicly guaranteed debt is an external obligation of a private debtor that is guaranteed for repayment by a public entity.

Private creditors includes bonds that are either publicly issued or privately placed; loans from private banks and other private commercial institutions; credits from manufactures, exports, for example; and bank credits covered by a guarantee of an export credit agency.

Official creditors includes loans from international organizations (multilateral loans); loans from governments and their agencies, loans from autonomous bodies; and direct loans from official export credit agencies.

Private nonguaranteed debt is an external obligation of a private debtor that is not guaranteed for repayment by a public entity.

IMF credit denotes repurchase obligations to the IMF with respect to all uses of IMF resources, excluding those resulting from drawings in the reserve tranche. It comprises purchases outstanding under the credit tranches, including enlarged access resources and all the special facilities (the buffer stock, compensatory financing, extended fund, and oil facilities), Trust Fund loans, and operations under the Structural Adjustment and Enhanced Structural Adjustment facilities.

Short-term debt is defined as debt that has an original maturity of one year or less. Available data permit no distinction between public and private nonguaranteed short-term debt.

Total debt service is the debt service payments (principal repayments and interest payments) on total long-term debt, use of IMF credit, and interest on short-term debt only.

Symbols and abbreviations

..	Data not available, or nonexistent
%	Percentage
0.0	Zero or less than half the unit shown
GATT	General Agreement on Tariffs and Trade
c.i.f.	cost, insurance, and freight
f.o.b.	free on board
GDP	gross domestic product
GNP	gross national product
MERCOSUR	Agreement between Argentina, Brazil, Paraguay, and Uruguay to form a common market
nfs	Nonfactor services
OECD	Organization for Economic Cooperation and Development
OECS	Organization of East Caribbean States
SDR	special drawing right

Table 1 Classification of economies by income and region, 1993

Income group	Subgroup	Sub-Saharan Africa[a] East & Southern Africa	West Africa	Asia East Asia and Pacific	South Asia	Europe and Central Asia Eastern Europe and Central Asia	Rest of Europe	Middle East and North Africa Middle East	North Africa	Americas
Low-income		Burundi Comoros Ethiopia Kenya Lesotho Madagascar Malawi Mozambique Rwanda Somalia Sudan Tanzania Uganda Zaire Zambia Zimbabwe	Benin Burkina Faso Central African Rep. Chad Equatorial Guinea Gambia, The Ghana Guinea Guinea-Bissau Liberia Mali Mauritania Niger Nigeria São Tomé and Principe Sierra Leone Togo	Cambodia China Indonesia Lao PDR Myanmar Solomon Islands Viet Nam	Afghanistan Bangladesh Bhutan India Maldives Nepal Pakistan Sri Lanka			Yemen, Rep.	Egypt, Arab Rep.	Guyana Haiti Honduras Nicaragua
Middle-income	Lower	Angola Djibouti Mauritius Namibia Swaziland	Cameroon Cape Verde Congo Côte d'Ivoire Senegal	Fiji Kiribati Korea, Dem. Rep. Malaysia Marshall Islands Micronesia, Fed. Sts. Mongolia Papua New Guinea Philippines Thailand Tonga Vanuatu Western Samoa		Albania Armenia Azerbaijan Bulgaria Czecho-slovakia[b] Georgia Kazakhstan Kyrgyzstan Moldova Poland Romania Tajikistan Turkmenistan Ukraine Uzbekistan	Turkey	Iran, Islamic Rep. Iraq Jordan Lebanon Syrian Arab Rep.	Algeria Morocco Tunisia	Belize Bolivia Chile Colombia Costa Rica Cuba Dominica Dominican Rep. Ecuador El Salvador Grenada Guatemala Jamaica Panama Paraguay Peru St. Lucia St. Vincent
	Upper	Botswana Mayotte Reunion Seychelles South Africa[a]	Gabon	American Samoa Guam Korea, Rep. Macao New Caledonia		Belarus Estonia Hungary Latvia Lithuania Russian Federation Yugoslavia[c]	Gibraltar Greece Isle of Man Malta Portugal	Bahrain Oman Saudi Arabia	Libya	Antigua and Barbuda Argentina Aruba Barbados Brazil French Guiana Guadeloupe Martinique Mexico Netherlands Antilles Puerto Rico St. Kitts and Nevis Suriname Trinidad and Tobago Uruguay Venezuela
No. of low- & middle-income economies: 162		26	23	25	8	22	6	9	5	38

Table 1 (*continued*)

Income group	Subgroup	Sub-Saharan Africa[a] East & Southern Africa	West Africa	Asia East Asia and Pacific	South Asia	Europe and Central Asia Eastern Europe and Central Asia	Rest of Europe	Middle East and North Africa Middle East	North Africa	Americas
High-income	OECD countries			Australia Japan New Zealand			Andorra Austria Belgium Denmark Finland France Germany Iceland Ireland Italy Luxembourg Netherlands Norway San Marino Spain Sweden Switzerland United Kingdom			Canada United States
	Non-OECD countries			Brunei French Polynesia Hong Kong Singapore OAE[d]			Channel Islands Cyprus Faeroe Islands Greenland	Israel Kuwait Qatar United Arab Emirates		Bahamas Bermuda Virgin Islands (US)
Total no. of economies: 201		26	23	33	8	22	28	13	5	43

a. For some analysis, South Africa is not included in Sub-Saharan Africa.
b. Refers to the former Czechoslovakia; disaggregated data are not yet available.
c. Refers to the former Socialist Federal Republic of Yugoslavia; disaggregated data are not yet available.
d. Other Asian economies—Taiwan, China.

Definitions of groups

These tables classify all World Bank member economies, plus all other economies with populations of more than 30,000.

Income group: Economies are divided according to 1991 GNP per capita, calculated using the *World Bank Atlas* method. The groups are: low-income, $635 or less; lower-middle-income, $636–2,555; upper-middle-income, $2,556–$7,910; and high-income, $7,911 or more.

The estimates for the republics of the former Soviet Union should be regarded as very preliminary; their classification will be kept under review.

Table 2 Classification of economies by major export category and indebtedness, 1993

| | Low- and middle-income ||||||| High-income ||
| | Low-income ||| Middle-income |||| |||
Group	Severely indebted	Moderately indebted	Less indebted	Severely indebted	Moderately indebted	Less indebted	Not classified by indebtedness	OECD	non-OECD
Exporters of manufactures			China	Bulgaria Poland	Hungary	Czechoslovakia[a] Korea, Dem. Rep. Korea, Rep. Lebanon Macao Romania	Armenia Belarus Estonia Georgia Kyrgyzstan Latvia Lithuania Moldova Russian Federation Ukraine Uzbekistan	Belgium Canada Finland Germany Ireland Italy Japan Luxembourg Sweden Switzerland	Hong Kong Israel Singapore OAE[b]
Exporters of nonfuel primary products	Afghanistan Burundi Equatorial Guinea Ethiopia Ghana Guinea-Bissau Guyana Honduras Liberia Madagascar Mauritania Myanmar Nicaragua Niger São Tomé and Principe Somalia Tanzania Uganda Viet Nam Zaire Zambia	Guinea Malawi Rwanda Togo	Chad Solomon Islands Zimbabwe	Albania Argentina Bolivia Côte d'Ivoire Cuba Mongolia Peru	Chile Costa Rica Guatemala Papua New Guinea	Botswana French Guiana Guadeloupe Namibia Paraguay Reunion St. Vincent Suriname Swaziland	American Samoa	Iceland New Zealand	Faeroe Islands Greenland
Exporters of fuels (mainly oil)	Nigeria			Algeria Angola Congo Iraq	Gabon Venezuela	Iran, Islamic Rep. Libya Oman Saudi Arabia Trinidad and Tobago	Turkmenistan		Brunei Qatar United Arab Emirates
Exporters of services	Cambodia Egypt, Arab Rep. Sudan	Benin Gambia, The Haiti Maldives Nepal Yemen, Rep.	Bhutan Burkina Faso Lesotho	Jamaica Jordan Panama	Dominican Rep. Greece	Antigua and Barbuda Barbados Cape Verde Djibouti El Salvador Fiji Grenada Kiribati Malta Martinique Netherlands Antilles Seychelles St. Kitts and Nevis St. Lucia Tonga Vanuatu Western Samoa	Aruba	United Kingdom	Bahamas Bermuda Cyprus French Polynesia
Diversified exporters	Kenya Lao PDR Mali Mozambique Sierra Leone	Bangladesh Central African Rep. Comoros India Indonesia Pakistan Sri Lanka		Brazil Ecuador Mexico Morocco Syrian Arab Rep.	Cameroon Colombia Philippines Senegal Tunisia Turkey Uruguay	Bahrain Belize Dominica Malaysia Mauritius Portugal South Africa Thailand Yugoslavia[c]	Azerbaijan Kazakhstan Tajikistan	Australia Austria Denmark France Netherlands Norway Spain United States	Kuwait

Table 2 (continued)

| | Low- and middle-income | | | | | | | High-income | |
| | Low-income | | | Middle-income | | | | | |
Group	Severely indebted	Moderately indebted	Less indebted	Severely indebted	Moderately indebted	Less indebted	Not classified by indebtedness	OECD	non-OECD
Not classified by export category							Gibraltar Guam Isle of Man Marshall Islands Mayotte Micronesia, Fed. Sts. New Caledonia Puerto Rico		Andorra Channel Islands San Marino Virgin Islands (US)
No. of economies 201	30	17	7	21	16	47	24	21	18

a. Refers to the former Czechoslovakia; disaggregated data are not yet available.
b. Other Asian economies—Taiwan, China.
c. Refers to the former Socialist Federal Republic of Yugoslavia; disaggregated data are not yet available.

Definitions of groups

These tables classify all World Bank member economies, plus all other economies with populations of more than 30,000.

Major export category: Major exports are those that account for 50 percent or more of total exports of goods and services from one category, in the period 1987–89. The categories are: nonfuel primary (SITC 0,1,2, 4, plus 68), fuels (SITC 3), manufactures (SITC 5 to 9, less 68), and services (factor and nonfactor service receipts plus workers' remittances). If no single category accounts for 50 percent or more of total exports, the economy is classified as *diversified*.

Indebtedness: Standard World Bank definitions of severe and moderate indebtedness, averaged over three years (1989–91) are used to classify economies in this table. Severely indebted means either of the two key ratios is above critical levels: present value of debt service to GNP (80 percent) and present value of debt service to exports (220 percent). Moderately indebted means either of the two key ratios exceeds 60 percent of, but does not reach, the critical levels. For economies that do not report detailed debt statistics to the World Bank Debtor Reporting System, present-value calculation is not possible. Instead the following methodology is used to classify the non-DRS economies. Severely indebted means three of four key ratios (averaged over 1988–90) are above critical levels: debt to GNP (50 percent); debt to exports (275 percent), debt service to exports (30 percent); and interest to exports (20 percent). Moderately indebted means three of four key ratios exceed 60 percent of, but do not reach, the critical levels. All other low- and middle-income economies are classified as less-indebted.

Not classified by indebtedness are the republics of the Former Soviet Union and some small economies for which detailed debt data are not available.

Distributors of World Bank Publications

ARGENTINA
Carlos Hirsch, SRL
Galeria Guemes
Florida 165, 4th Floor-Ofc. 453/465
1333 Buenos Aires

AUSTRALIA, PAPUA NEW GUINEA, FIJI, SOLOMON ISLANDS, VANUATU, AND WESTERN SAMOA
D.A. Information Services
648 Whitehorse Road
Mitcham 3132
Victoria

AUSTRIA
Gerold and Co.
Graben 31
A-1011 Wien

BANGLADESH
Micro Industries Development
Assistance Society (MIDAS)
House 5, Road 16
Dhanmondi R/Area
Dhaka 1209

Branch offices:
Pine View, 1st Floor
100 Agrabad Commercial Area
Chittagong 4100

76, K.D.A. Avenue
Kulna 9100

BELGIUM
Jean De Lannoy
Av. du Roi 202
1060 Brussels

CANADA
Le Diffuseur
C.P. 85, 1501B rue Ampère
Boucherville, Québec
J4B 5E6

CHILE
Invertec IGT S.A.
Americo Vespucio Norte 1165
Santiago

CHINA
China Financial & Economic
Publishing House
8, Da Fo Si Dong Jie
Beijing

COLOMBIA
Infoenlace Ltda.
Apartado Aereo 34270
Bogota D.E.

COTE D'IVOIRE
Centre d'Edition et de Diffusion
Africaines (CEDA)
04 B.P. 541
Abidjan 04 Plateau

CYPRUS
Center of Applied Research
Cyprus College
6, Diogenes Street, Engomi
P.O. Box 2006
Nicosia

DENMARK
SamfundsLitteratur
Rosenoerns Allé 11
DK-1970 Frederiksberg C

DOMINICAN REPUBLIC
Editora Taller, C. por A.
Restauración e Isabel la Católica 309
Apartado de Correos 2190 Z-1
Santo Domingo

EGYPT, ARAB REPUBLIC OF
Al Ahram
Al Galaa Street
Cairo

The Middle East Observer
41, Sherif Street
Cairo

FINLAND
Akateeminen Kirjakauppa
P.O. Box 128
SF-00101 Helsinki 10

FRANCE
World Bank Publications
66, avenue d'Iéna
75116 Paris

GERMANY
UNO-Verlag
Poppelsdorfer Allee 55
D-5300 Bonn 1

HONG KONG, MACAO
Asia 2000 Ltd.
46-48 Wyndham Street
Winning Centre
2nd Floor
Central Hong Kong

INDIA
Allied Publishers Private Ltd.
751 Mount Road
Madras - 600 002

Branch offices:
15 J.N. Heredia Marg
Ballard Estate
Bombay - 400 038

13/14 Asaf Ali Road
New Delhi - 110 002

17 Chittaranjan Avenue
Calcutta - 700 072

Jayadeva Hostel Building
5th Main Road, Gandhinagar
Bangalore - 560 009

3-5-1129 Kachiguda
Cross Road
Hyderabad - 500 027

Prarthana Flats, 2nd Floor
Near Thakore Baug, Navrangpura
Ahmedabad - 380 009

Patiala House
16-A Ashok Marg
Lucknow - 226 001

Central Bazaar Road
60 Bajaj Nagar
Nagpur 440 010

INDONESIA
Pt. Indira Limited
Jalan Borobudur 20
P.O. Box 181
Jakarta 10320

IRELAND
Government Supplies Agency
4-5 Harcourt Road
Dublin 2

ISRAEL
Yozmot Literature Ltd.
P.O. Box 56055
Tel Aviv 61560

ITALY
Licosa Commissionaria Sansoni SPA
Via Duca Di Calabria, 1/1
Casella Postale 552
50125 Firenze

JAPAN
Eastern Book Service
Hongo 3-Chome, Bunkyo-ku 113
Tokyo

KENYA
Africa Book Service (E.A.) Ltd.
Quaran House, Mfangano Street
P.O. Box 45245
Nairobi

KOREA, REPUBLIC OF
Pan Korea Book Corporation
P.O. Box 101, Kwangwhamun
Seoul

MALAYSIA
University of Malaya Cooperative
Bookshop, Limited
P.O. Box 1127, Jalan Pantai Baru
59700 Kuala Lumpur

MEXICO
INFOTEC
Apartado Postal 22-860
14060 Tlalpan, Mexico D.F.

NETHERLANDS
De Lindeboom/InOr-Publikaties
P.O. Box 202
7480 AE Haaksbergen

NEW ZEALAND
EBSCO NZ Ltd.
Private Mail Bag 99914
New Market
Auckland

NIGERIA
University Press Limited
Three Crowns Building Jericho
Private Mail Bag 5095
Ibadan

NORWAY
Narvesen Information Center
Book Department
P.O. Box 6125 Etterstad
N-0602 Oslo 6

PAKISTAN
Mirza Book Agency
65, Shahrah-e-Quaid-e-Azam
P.O. Box No. 729
Lahore 54000

PERU
Editorial Desarrollo SA
Apartado 3824
Lima 1

PHILIPPINES
International Book Center
Suite 1703, Cityland 10
Condominium Tower 1
Ayala Avenue, H.V. dela
Costa Extension
Makati, Metro Manila

POLAND
International Publishing Service
Ul. Piekna 31/37
00-677 Warzawa

For subscription orders:
IPS Journals
Ul. Okrezna 3
02-916 Warszawa

PORTUGAL
Livraria Portugal
Rua Do Carmo 70-74
1200 Lisbon

SAUDI ARABIA, QATAR
Jarir Book Store
P.O. Box 3196
Riyadh 11471

SINGAPORE, TAIWAN, MYANMAR, BRUNEI
Information Publications
Private, Ltd.
Golden Wheel Building
41, Kallang Pudding, #04-03
Singapore 1334

SOUTH AFRICA, BOTSWANA
For single titles:
Oxford University Press
Southern Africa
P.O. Box 1141
Cape Town 8000

For subscription orders:
International Subscription Service
P.O. Box 41095
Craighall
Johannesburg 2024

SPAIN
Mundi-Prensa Libros, S.A.
Castello 37
28001 Madrid

Librería Internacional AEDOS
Consell de Cent, 391
08009 Barcelona

SRI LANKA AND THE MALDIVES
Lake House Bookshop
P.O. Box 244
100, Sir Chittampalam A.
Gardiner Mawatha
Colombo 2

SWEDEN
For single titles:
Fritzes Fackboksforetaget
Regeringsgatan 12, Box 16356
S-103 27 Stockholm

For subscription orders:
Wennergren-Williams AB
P.O. Box 1305
S-171 25 Solna

SWITZERLAND
For single titles:
Librairie Payot
Case postale 3212
CH 1002 Lausanne

For subscription orders:
Librairie Payot
Service des Abonnements
Case postale 3312
CH 1002 Lausanne

THAILAND
Central Department Store
306 Silom Road
Bangkok

TRINIDAD & TOBAGO, ANTIGUA BARBUDA, BARBADOS, DOMINICA, GRENADA, GUYANA, JAMAICA, MONTSERRAT, ST. KITTS & NEVIS, ST. LUCIA, ST. VINCENT & GRENADINES
Systematics Studies Unit
#9 Watts Street
Curepe
Trinidad, West Indies

TURKEY
Infotel
Narlabahçe Sok. No. 15
Cagaloglu
Istanbul

UNITED KINGDOM
Microinfo Ltd.
P.O. Box 3
Alton, Hampshire GU34 2PG
England

VENEZUELA
Libreria del Este
Aptdo. 60.337
Caracas 1060-A